EU Strategies on Governance Reform

This book discusses the European Union's approach to governance reform in its development assistance relationships with various groups of developing countries. A group of expert authors outline the general features of the position on governance taken by the EU, which is currently the major multilateral donor of development assistance, and discuss the implementation of EU policies in a set of cases: the group of African, Caribbean and Pacific (ACP) states, the New Partnership for Africa's Development (NEPAD), Southeastern Europe, Central Asia, the Euro-Mediterranean, Latin America and fragile states.

The contributions to the book argue that the EU's position on governance reform, particularly since the adoption of the European Consensus on Development in 2005, has had distinctly neoliberal overtones. The EU's governance-related strategies have been instrumental to deepening market-based reform in aid-receiving countries. Policies on state-building adopted by the EU reflect mainly the interests of and ideas embraced by the EU and its member states. To an important extent, the rhetoric accompanying EU policies does not match with the political and social dynamics inherent in governance structures on the ground in many of its aid-recipient partner countries.

This book was published as a special issue of *Third World Quarterly*.

Wil Hout is Professor of Governance and International Political Economy at the International Institute of Social Studies, Erasmus University Rotterdam.

Thirdworlds
Edited by Shahid Qadir, *University of London*

THIRDWORLDS will focus on the political economy, development and cultures of those parts of the world that have experienced the most political, social, and economic upheaval, and which have faced the greatest challenges of the postcolonial world under globalisation: poverty, displacement and diaspora, environmental degradation, human and civil rights abuses, war, hunger, and disease.

THIRDWORLDS serves as a signifier of oppositional emerging economies and cultures ranging from Africa, Asia, Latin America, Middle East, and even those 'Souths' within a larger perceived North, such as the U.S. South and Mediterranean Europe. The study of these otherwise disparate and discontinuous areas, known collectively as the Global South, demonstrates that as globalisation pervades the planet, the south, as a synonym for subalterity, also transcends geographical and ideological frontiers.

Terrorism and the Politics of Naming
Edited by Michael Bhatia

Reconstructing Post-Saddam Iraq
Edited by Sultan Barakat

From Nation-Building to State-Building
Edited by Mark T. Berger

Connecting Cultures
Edited by Emma Bainbridge

The Politics of Rights
Dilemmas for feminist praxis
Edited by Andrea Cornwall and Maxine Molyneux

The Long War – Insurgency, Counter-insurgency and Collapsing States
Edited by Mark T. Berger and Douglas A. Borer

Market-led Agrarian Reform
Edited by Saturnino M. Borras, Jr.

After the Third World?
Edited by Mark T. Berger

Developmental and Cultural Nationalisms
Edited by Radhika Desai

Globalisation and Migration
New issues, new politics
Edited by Ronaldo Munck

Domestic and International Perspectives on Kyrgyzstan's 'Tulip Revolution'
Motives, mobilizations and meanings
Edited by Sarah Cummings

War and Revolution in the Caucasus
Georgia Ablaze
Edited by Stephen F. Jones

War, Peace and Progress in the 21st Century
Development, Violence and Insecurities
Edited by Mark T. Berger and Heloise Weber

Renewing International Labour Studies
Edited by Marcus Taylor

Youth in the Former Soviet South
Everyday Lives between Experimentation and Regulation
Edited by Stefan B. Kirmse

Political Civility in the Middle East
Edited by Frédéric Volpi

The Transformation of Tajikistan
Sources of Statehood
Edited by John Heathershaw

Movement, Power and Place in Central Asia and Beyond
Contested Trajectories
Edited by Madeleine Reeves

People Power in an Era of Global Crisis
Rebellion, Resistance and Liberation
Edited by Barry K. Gills and Kevin Gray

EU Strategies on Governance Reform
Between Development and State-building
Edited by Wil Hout

EU Strategies on Governance Reform
Between Development and State-building

Edited by
Wil Hout

LONDON AND NEW YORK

First published 2013
by Routledge

2 Park Square, Milton Park, Abingdon, Oxon OX14 4RN
711 Third Avenue, New York, NY 10017, USA

Routledge is an imprint of the Taylor & Francis Group, an informa business

First issued in paperback 2016

Copyright © 2013 Taylor & Francis.

This book is a reproduction of *Third World Quarterly*, vol. 31, issue 1. The Publisher requests to those authors who may be citing this book to state, also, the bibliographical details of the special issue on which the book was based.

All rights reserved. No part of this book may be reprinted or reproduced or utilised in any form or by any electronic, mechanical, or other means, now known or hereafter invented, including photocopying and recording, or in any information storage or retrieval system, without permission in writing from the publishers.

Notice:
Product or corporate names may be trademarks or registered trademarks, and are used only for identification and explanation without intent to infringe.

British Library Cataloguing in Publication Data
A catalogue record for this book is available from the British Library

ISBN 978-0-415-62203-5 (hbk)
ISBN 978-1-138-69127-8 (pbk)

Typeset in Times New Roman
by Taylor & Francis Books

Publisher's Note
The publisher would like to make readers aware that the chapters in this book may be referred to as articles as they are identical to the articles published in the special issue. The publisher accepts responsibility for any inconsistencies that may have arisen in the course of preparing this volume for print.

Contents

Notes on Contributors ix

1. Governance and Development: changing EU policies
   Wil Hout 1

2. The European Union, Good Governance and Aid Co-ordination
   Maurizio Carbone 13

3. Is the EU's Governance 'Good'? An assessment of EU governance in its partnership with ACP states
   Nikki Slocum-Bradley & Andrew Bradley 31

4. Governance and Relations between the European Union and Africa: the case of NEPAD
   Ian Taylor 51

5. The EU and Southeastern Europe: the rise of post-liberal governance
   David Chandler 69

6. The EU in Central Asia: successful good governance promotion?
   Katharina Hoffmann 87

7. Investigating the Two Faces of Governance: the case of the Euro-Mediterranean Development Bank
   Karim Knio 105

8. Global Europe, Guilty! Contesting EU neoliberal governance for Latin America and the Caribbean
   Rosalba Icaza 121

9. Between Development and Security: the European Union, governance and fragile states
   Wil Hout 139

10. Understanding EU Development Policy: history, global context and self-interest?
    Stephen R Hurt 157

Index 167

Notes on Contributors

Andrew Bradley is a Director at the International Institute for Democracy and Electoral Assistance (IDEA) in Stockholm, Sweden. Previously he was the Assistant Secretary-General for Political Affairs and Human Development of the African, Caribbean and Pacific (ACP) Group of States, and a career diplomat serving in South African Embassies and Missions in Canada, Switzerland and Belgium. At the ACP Group, he was responsible for the maintenance of ACP-EU relations, bi- and multi-lateral negotiations, migration, human and social development, conflict prevention and resolution, and the promotion of democracy, human rights, governance and the rule of law. As a diplomat, he was involved in the discussions/negotiations that brought about democratic change in South Africa, participated in the negotiations for South Africa's accession to the ACP Group and the Lomé Convention (now Cotonou Agreement), and acted as member of the South African Negotiating Team for the South Africa-EU Trade, Development and Cooperation Agreement (TDCA).

Maurizio Carbone is Professor of International Development and Jean Monnet Professor of EU External Relations in the Department of Politics at the University of Glasgow. His research focuses on EU external relations and the politics of international development. He has published in various journals, including *Journal of International Development*, *Journal of European Integration*, *Global Governance*, and *West European Politics*. His latest books include: *The European Union and International Development: The Politics of Foreign Aid* (Routledge, 2007); *New Pathways in International Development: Gender and Civil Society in EU Development Policy* (editor with M. Lister, Ashgate, 2006); and *Policy Coherence and EU Development Policy* (editor, Routledge, 2009). At the moment he is working on an edited book on the relations between the European Union and Africa (forthcoming with Manchester University Press) and a research book on the evolution of EU development policy (forthcoming with Oxford University Press).

David Chandler is Professor of International Relations at the University of Westminster, London. He is the founding Editor of the *Journal of Intervention and Statebuilding*. His recent books include: *International Statebuilding: The Rise of Post-Liberal Governance* (Routledge, 2010); *Hollow Hegemony: Rethinking Global Politics, Power and Resistance* (Pluto, 2009); *Empire in Denial: The Politics of State-Building* (Pluto, 2006); *Constructing Global Civil Society: Morality and Power in International*

NOTES ON CONTRIBUTORS

Relations (Palgrave, 2004) and *From Kosovo to Kabul: Human Rights and International Intervention* (Pluto, 2002).

Katharina Hoffmann is a PhD Student at the Centre for Russian and East European Studies at the University of Birmingham. She received her first Degree in East European Studies from the Free University in Berlin. Her current research focus is on regional organisations in the post-Soviet space and on political regimes in the Commonwealth of Independent States. She published 'Regionale Integration im postsowjetischen Raum? Kooperationsverhalten der Neuen Unabhängigen Staaten' [Regional Integration in the Post-Soviet Space? Cooperative Behaviour of the Newly Independent States] in: *Arbeitspapiere*, 85 (Forschungsstelle Osteuropa, Bremen, 2007) and 'Azerbaijan's Regional Policy: The Eurasian and European Dimensions' in *ADA Biweekly* 4(14), 2011.

Wil Hout is Professor of Governance and International Political Economy at the International Institute of Social Studies, Erasmus University Rotterdam. His research focuses on the political economy of North-South relations, governance strategies and development assistance policies. He has published in such journals as the *European Journal of International Relations, Development and Change, Journal of Development Studies, Third World Quarterly, Critical Asian Studies,* and *Acta Politica: International Journal of Political Science*. He is the author of *Capitalism and the Third World* (Edward Elgar, 1993) and co-editor of *Regionalism across the North-South Divide* (with Jean Grugel; Routledge, 1999). His latest book publications are *The Politics of Aid Selectivity* (Routledge, 2007), *EU Development Policy and Poverty Reduction* (editor, Ashgate, 2007) and *Governance and the Depoliticisation of Development* (co-editor with Richard Robison; Routledge, 2009). He is co-editor, with Henry Kifordu and Pedro Goulart, of a special issue of *The Open Areas Studies Journal* on 'Governance, Conflict and Dispute Resolution' (vol. 4, 2011).

Stephen R Hurt is Senior Lecturer in International Relations at Oxford Brookes University. His main research interests are in international political economy and development, with a special interest in South Africa and European Union development policy. He has published articles in *International Relations, Third World Quarterly* and the *Journal of Contemporary African Studies*. He has chapters in I. Taylor and P. Williams (eds) *Africa in International Relations* (Routledge, 2004), M.Carbone and M. Lister (eds) *New Pathways in International Development: Gender and Civil Society in EU Policy* (Ashgate, 2006) and D. Lee, I. Taylor & P. Williams (eds) *The New Multilateralism in South African Diplomacy* (Palgrave, 2006). In 2009 he was co-editor of a special issue of *The Round Table* on 'New Directions in International Relations and Africa'. His most recent work entitled 'The EU-SADC Economic Partnership Agreement Negotiations: "Locking-In" the Neoliberal Development Model in Southern Africa?' was published in *Third World Quarterly* in 2012.

Rosalba Icaza is Senior Lecturer in International Political Economy and Governance at the International Institute of Social Studies, Erasmus University Rotterdam. Her research focuses on the political economy of transborder civic resistance to open/neo-liberal regionalism in Latin America. She writes and teaches about paths of civic engagement on regionalisms across the world and their contributions to global epistemic justice. She is also interested in Third World and de-colonial feminist theories on social resistance to global and regional governance. Recent publications include '(Re)Thinking the "New" North America through Women's Citizenship Struggles in Mexico', in J. Ayres and L. MacDonald (eds), *North America in Question: Regional Integration in an Era of Economic Turbulence* (University of Toronto, 2011). She has published in such journals as *Globalizations, Feminist Economics,* the *Nordic Journal of Latin American and Caribbean Studies,* and *Pensamiento Propio.* Her book *Civil Society in the Making of Regionalisms: Power and Resistance across Borders* is forthcoming at Routledge in 2012.

Karim Knio is Senior Lecturer in Politics at the International Institute of Social Studies, Erasmus University Rotterdam. His research focuses on the political economy of governance, regionalism and trade with a focus on the Euro-Mediterranean region. He also has interests in industrial relations, EU democracy promotion programmes and Lebanese politics. Recent publications include chapters in M. Salih (ed.), *Interpreting Islamic Political Parties* (Palgrave Macmillan, 2009) and W. Hout and R. Robison (eds), *Governance and the Depoliticisation of Development* (Routledge, 2009) and a co-authored article in *The Roundtable* with Stephen Hurt and Magnus Ryner. His book *The EU Mediterranean Policy: Model or Muddle?* will be published by Palgrave Macmillan in 2012.

Nikki Slocum-Bradley is Program and Research Advisor at the Life & Peace Institute in Uppsala, Sweden, and Associate Research Fellow at the United Nations University Centre for Comparative Regional Integration Studies (UNU-CRIS) in Bruges, Belgium. Her research encompasses a broad range of issues at the nexus between psychology, sociology, politics and international relations. Examples include the social, psychological and cultural aspects of regional integration, globalisation and migration; the social and political consequences of different constructions/interpretations of reality; social norms, identities and inter-group relations; social-psychological approaches to conflict prevention; and qualitative methodology. She has published in a variety of journals across disciplines, including the *Journal of European Integration, Geopolitics, Identity, Journal for the Theory of Social Behaviour, Common Knowledge* and *Third World Quarterly.* She most recently edited and co-authored a book entitled *Promoting Conflict or Peace through Identity* (Ashgate, 2008). She has authored a variety of background papers for policy forums, including the ACP-EU Joint Parliamentary Assembly, the ACP Ministers of Migration meeting, and the ACP Ministers of Culture meeting. Her theoretical and methodological work has developed and advocated approaches to social science that are more adept at addressing contemporary social issues. In this vein, she has also published a *Participatory Methods Toolkit* (2003, 2006, King Baudouin Foundation, Flemish Institute for Science and Technology Assessment).

Ian Taylor is Professor of International Relations at the University of St Andrews and at the University of Stellenbosch, South Africa. He is the author of *The Forum on China-Africa Cooperation* (Routledge, 2011); *The International Relations of Sub-Saharan Africa* (Continuum, 2010); *China's New Role in Africa* (Lynne Rienner, 2009); *The United Nations Conference on Trade and Development* (Routledge, 2007); *China and Africa: Engagement and Compromise* (Routledge, 2006); *NEPAD: Towards Africa's Development or Another False Start?* (Lynne Rienner, 2005); and *Stuck in Middle GEAR: South Africa's Post-Apartheid Foreign Relations* (Praeger,

2001). He has also co-edited, among others, *Afro-Regions: The Dynamics of Cross-border Micro-Regionalism in Africa* (Nordic Africa Institute, 2008); *The New Multilateralism in South Africa's Diplomacy* (Palgrave Macmillan, 2006); and *The Potentiality of 'Developmental States' in Africa: Botswana and Uganda Compared* (Codesria, 2005).

Governance and Development: changing EU policies

WIL HOUT

ABSTRACT *This introductory article to the special issue on European Union, development policies and governance discusses how notions of ('good') governance have come to dominate development discourses and policies since the mid-1990s. The article argues that governance was part of the so-called Post-Washington Consensus, which understands governance reform as part of the creation of market societies. Although academics have commonly emphasised the fact that governance concerns the rules that regulate the public sphere, the dominant understanding of (good) governance in policy circles revolves around technical and managerial connotations. The second part of the article introduces some important features of EU development policy, and argues that this is essentially neoliberal in nature and favours a technocratic approach to governance reform. The EU's main instrument in relations with developing countries is the Country Strategy Paper, which includes a set of governance indicators for the assessment of the political situation in partner countries. In addition, the European Union has developed a 'governance profile', which consists of nine components.*

Since the mid-1990s conceptions of governance have occupied a central place in development discourses and policies. Academically the rise of the governance concept can be attributed, to an important extent, to the institutionalist wave that has swept across the social sciences.[1] For the policy world the emphasis on institutions and governance in the so-called new institutional economics, and the embrace of the latter by the World Bank, was highly relevant. Governance came to the rescue of neoliberal approaches to development, which were experiencing a crisis as a result of the failure of 'market-fundamentalist' structural adjustment policies.[2]

The adoption of governance into the vocabulary of development has, in the words of some observers, been interpreted as a change from the market-based 'Washington Consensus' to an institution-oriented 'Post-Washington Consensus'. As famously argued by former World Bank chief economist Joseph Stiglitz:

> the policies advanced by the Washington Consensus are not complete, and they are sometimes misguided. Making markets work requires more than just low

inflation; it requires sound financial regulation, competition policy, and policies to facilitate the transfer of technology and to encourage transparency, to cite some fundamental issues neglected by the Washington Consensus.[3]

The argument adopted by Stiglitz and others was that attention tor governance and institutions had proven to be a necessary complement to the building or deepening of markets. Thus, it was argued, specific institutional frameworks were necessary counterweights to 'market failure'.

The reasoning that the focus on governance represented a change away from market fundamentalism has been challenged by various scholars.[4] They argue that the Post-Washington Consensus is essentially neoliberal in character, as it continues to see the market as the pre-eminent, fundamentally benign force of development, and the state as subject to the interest of rent-seeking actors.

One of the main implications of the adoption of the governance concept into the neoliberal development framework, which perceived governance *as a function of* the building of markets, is that it came to be understood in predominantly technocratic terms. As the World Bank has put it, 'the ability of the state to provide institutions that make markets more efficient is sometimes referred to as good governance'.[5] Thus, 'good governance' seeks to ensure efficiency in public administration and public finance management, rule of law, decentralisation and regulation of corporate life, including competition laws and anti-corruption watchdogs, arms-length procurement processes and the outsourcing of public services and supply. Conceived as a form of authority outside politics and the traditional realm of administration, it is a means to claim autonomy for technocratic authority from what are seen as distributional coalitions.

The 'good governance' approaches of development agencies tend to take one of two forms. The first of these approaches has been taken by those agencies that interpret governance quality as a prerequisite for the effectiveness of development and associated aid instruments. This use of governance has its origins in the analyses of Burnside and Dollar on aid effectiveness. According to these two World Bank analysts, development assistance would be effective only in countries that have adopted good governance and good policies.[6] Various development agencies have applied this logic since the late 1990s with the adoption of selectivity principles in aid allocation. For example, the World Bank implemented performance-based allocation of loans and grants given by its International Development Agency (IDA), while the USA adopted the Millennium Challenge Account.[7] The European Union has moved in this direction to a certain extent with the adoption into the African, Caribbean and Pacific (ACP) framework of a 'governance incentive tranche', which should lead to allocations of aid funds on the basis of the governance situation and reform commitments in recipient countries.[8]

The second approach to 'good governance' has been applied by agencies that take the improvement of governance and the strengthening of institutions as the prime target of assistance policies. This position is located more squarely within dominant development policies, which see the building of (state) institutions as a major objective of foreign aid. As was the case with the first approach to governance discussed above, these policies find support in the strategy advocated by the World Bank, namely that 'effective aid supports institutional development and policy reforms that are at the heart of successful development'.[9] The EU's orientation to this approach can be found, among others, in the recent identification of issue areas where European Community aid was felt to have clear value added, and which mentioned 'institutional capacity building' as the sixth target.[10]

The dominant understanding of (good) governance in policy circles fails to recognise the essentially political character of governance issues, which relate to existing power relations in society and concern 'the formation and stewardship of the formal and informal rules that regulate the public realm, the arena in which state as well as economic and societal actors interact to make decisions'.[11] Problems such as the access of marginalised groups to political decision making or the attempts of powerful groups to manipulate governance reform to their advantage have generally received much less attention from the development agencies than have public sector reform, public finance management and decentralisation, to mention but three popular issues.[12]

Europe as a development actor

This special issue of *Third World Quarterly* takes stock of the ways in which one of today's most important development actors, the European Union,[13] has implemented policies related to governance in its external development relations. The thrust of the argument presented in the following contributions is that EU development policies are essentially neoliberal in character and that their governance-related strategies in effect display a technocratic orientation and are instrumental to deepening market-based reform in aid-receiving countries.

EU development assistance

In recent years the European Union has become one of the major multilateral agencies in the field of development assistance. Not counting the aid flows originating from the EU member states, European development assistance increased to $11.6 billion in 2007, which amounted to over one-and-a-half times the aid provided by the World Bank through its IDA window in the same year.[14] The three main objectives of EU development assistance, according to article 177 of the Treaty Establishing the European Community, are:

- the sustainable economic and social development of the developing countries;
- the smooth and gradual integration of these countries into the world economy; and
- the campaign against poverty.

EU development assistance policies are seen as 'complementary' to those of the member states.

The main target of EU development policies has traditionally been the group of member states' former colonies in Africa, the Caribbean and the Pacific (commonly referred to as ACP countries). After an initial period in which contacts with the former African colonies were regulated by the 'Regime of Association' (1957) and two Yaoundé Conventions (1963–75), European relations with the ACP have been governed by four Lomé Conventions (1976–2000) and by the Cotonou Agreement (since 2000), which included aid and trade instruments. Institutionally support for the ACP countries has been financed through the European Development Fund (EDF), which is replenished periodically by the EU member states.

Aid to the ACP countries has continued to account for a sizeable proportion of total EU development assistance. Since the coming into force of the Cotonou Agreement, aid to the ACP has increased from slightly under €2 billion in 2001 to €4.8 billion in 2008. ACP's relative share in EU external assistance has remained more or less stable, at 35.4% in 2001 and 37.8% in 2008. In 2005 member states pledged €22.7 billion to the European Development Fund, to be allocated to the ACP countries between 2007 and 2013.[15]

Apart from its agreements with the ACP, the European Union has maintained relations with most other regions in the developing world. Assistance to non-ACP countries is not financed out of the EDF, but is included in the regular EU budget for development aid, usually referred to as the Development Cooperation Instrument (DCI). Particularly important is the EU's European Neighbourhood Policy, which covers such diverse regions as the Middle East, North Africa and six former Soviet republics in Eastern Europe and the Caucasus. Table 1 shows that the EU's external assistance has retained its focus on these countries: aid to countries in the Middle East increased from 5.3% to 6.1% between 2004 and 2008, while Eastern European countries saw their share grow from 13.2% to 17.4%. The share of North African countries decreased in relative terms (from 6.4% in 2004 to 4.5% in 2008), although the absolute amount of aid to this region grew by roughly 14%. Aid to Asian countries (excluding the Middle East) fell in relative terms from 12.8% of total European aid in 2004 to 10.1% in 2008. Although the EU has developed ideas on a partnership with Latin America, the share of EU aid flowing to countries in this part of the world has dropped from 8.1% in 2004 to 5.3% in 2008.

In terms of policy formulation, the European Council and European Commission have exhibited much activity in the area of development cooperation since the turn of the century, as evidenced by a joint statement on development policy issues in November 2000. This declaration focused on poverty reduction as the 'principal aim' of the EU's development policy and highlighted the need to 'refocus' its activities to a limited number of sectoral priorities in order to enhance impact. EU development

TABLE 1. Regional distribution of aid commitments to developing countries (ODA), 2004 and 2008

	2004		2008	
	Allocation (€ million)	% of total allocation	Allocation (€ million)	% of total allocation
Europe	996	13.2	2093	17.4
Africa				
North of Sahara	480	6.4	546	4.5
South of Sahara	2428	32.2	4726	39.3
Regional	2	0.0	–	–
America				
North and Central	317	4.2	329	2.7
South	230	3.1	312	2.6
Regional	63	0.8	2	0.0
Asia				
Middle East	398	5.3	735	6.1
South and Central	517	6.9	886	7.4
Far East	391	5.2	233	1.9
Regional	52	0.7	91	0.8
Oceania	52	0.7	19	0.2
Bilateral unallocated	1172	15.5	1677	14.0
Multilateral	441	5.9	366	3.0
Total	7538	100.0	12014	100.0

Source: European Commission, *Annual Report 2009 on the European Community's Development and External Assistance Policies and their Implementation in 2008*, SEC(2009)831 final, 30 June 2009, p 200.

assistance was argued to provide value added in the following six issue areas:

- the link between trade and development;
- regional integration and cooperation;
- support for macroeconomic policies and the promotion of equitable access to social services;
- transport;
- food security and sustainable rural development; and
- institutional capacity building.[16]

Several years later, in December 2005, the European Council, Commission and Parliament agreed on another joint statement, labelled the 'European Consensus on Development' in a clear attempt to juxtapose it to the Washington Consensus dominated by the World Bank and the US government. The European Consensus was an attempt to formulate 'for the first time, a common vision that guides the action of the EU, both at its Member States and Community levels, in development cooperation'.[17] According to the Consensus, 'the primary and overarching objective of EU development cooperation is the eradication of poverty in the context of sustainable development, including pursuit of the Millennium Development Goals (MDGs)'.[18] Several 'common principles' of European development co-operation were laid down; most notably these were: ownership and partnership; the need for engaging in political dialogue with developing countries; the participation of civil society, including economic and social partners; the promotion of gender equality and women's rights; and attention to state fragility.[19] Aid effectiveness would be enhanced, according to Council, Commission and Parliament, by concentrating development assistance on a limited number of activities where the EU possessed a 'comparative advantage'. The activities singled out were the following:

- trade and regional integration;
- the environment and the sustainable management of natural resources;
- infrastructure, communications and transport;
- water and energy;
- rural development, territorial planning, agriculture and food security;
- governance, democracy, human rights and support for economic and institutional reforms;
- conflict prevention and fragile states;
- human development; and
- social cohesion and employment.[20]

EU development assistance and governance

The main tool in the relationship between the European Community and partner developing countries is the Country Strategy Paper (CSP). In line with the practice of many international development agencies, the European Community formulates a medium-term strategy for the provision of development assistance on the basis of a country's official national policy priorities. Developing countries have usually laid down their priorities in Poverty Reduction Strategy Papers (PRSPs), which are required for getting support from the World Bank and IMF. According to the European Commission, the establishment of a common framework for the formulation of CSPs makes 'a significant contribution to achieving the goal of multiannual programming and to increasing the effectiveness and quality of the EU's external aid'.[21]

As part of the 'country diagnosis', a CSP is required to contain an analysis of the political—along with the economic, social and environmental—situation in the partner country. An important set of governance indicators is included among the assessment of the political situation, such as:

- the main obstacles at the national level for the protection of and respect for human rights;
- the observance of democratic principles, as related to elections and change of government;
- the organisation of the government and decision-making procedures, including the division of power over different levels of government, transparency and accountability of key political institutions, measures countering corruption and other forms of economic criminality, and the rule of law and the independence of the judiciary; and

- evidence pointing at state fragility, such as the incapacity to perform basic government functions (security, social services and human rights).[22]

In addition to applying these indicators, the European Commission has argued that in fragile states, post-conflict countries and specific cases of countries that have yet to achieve 'structural stability' or are showing signs of increasing instability, greater attention should be paid to analysing measures taken to ensure security and stability. Such measures would include conflict prevention and management, post-conflict intervention strategies (demobilisation, disarmament, reintegration—in particular of women and child soldiers—rebuilding, humanitarian mine clearance, and support for action against illegal arms trafficking and dissemination of small arms and light weapons, etc), and the introduction of the rule of law and democracy (including broader participation of civil society and a more equitable distribution of power).[23]

Accompanying the Communication on 'Governance in the European Consensus', the European Commission published a methodology for assessing developing countries' governance quality. In the first instance the so-called 'governance profile' was developed for ACP countries, but later releases of the profile have dropped the reference specifically to the ACP group. The profile was set up as a 'programming tool', the main objectives of which are 'to help identifying specific areas of cooperation (weaknesses) and agreeing on benchmarks and targets for reform (Government commitments), or on sectoral performance indicators, if governance is a focal area'.[24] The governance profile was meant for application by the European Commission, and would not necessarily reflect a common understanding of governance quality in the recipient country: 'The governance profile is not meant to be done necessarily jointly with the partner country but its content should be shared (*but not negotiated and agreed*) with the partner country during the programming dialogue'.[25]

The governance profile developed by the European Commission consists of nine components, which are subdivided into a variety of specific issues. The profile is summarised in Table 2. The governance profile as used by the European Commission draws heavily on the work done by staff at the World Bank Institute, resulting in the *Worldwide Governance Indicators* dataset.[26] The first six components are based on the six elements of the *Worldwide Governance Indicators*. The final three indicators (on social governance, international and regional context, and quality of partnership) have been developed by staff at the Commission. Of the nine components, two (political/democratic governance and internal and external security) seem to address political issues of governance most directly, while two (internal and external security, and international and regional context) appear to be most directly related to the problems faced by fragile states. Two components (political governance/rule of law and control of corruption) primarily assess the presence of legal instruments, while two (government effectiveness and economic governance) are essentially meant to scrutinise the management of economic policies and policy making. The component on social governance relates to the implementation of a variety of social policies. The final

TABLE 2. The European Commission's governance profile

Components	Items
1. Political/democratic governance (WBI's voice and accountability)	a. Human rights b. Fundamental freedoms c. Electoral process d. Principles of constitutional democracy
2. Political governance/rule of law: Judicial and law enforcement system	
3. Control of corruption	
4. Government effectiveness	a. Institutional capacity b. Public finance management
5. Economic governance (WBI's regulatory quality)	a. Private sector/market-friendly policies b. Management of natural resources
6. Internal and external security (WBI's political stability and absence of violence)	a. Internal stability/conflict b. External threats and global security
7. Social governance	
8. International and regional context	a. Regional integration b. Involvement in regional initiatives on governance and peer-review mechanisms (such as APRM) c. Migration
9. Quality of partnership	a. Political dialogue b. Programming dialogue c. Non-state actors

Note: WBI refers to the World Bank Institute's *Governance Matters* indicators.
Source: European Commission, *Staff Working Document Accompanying the Communication 'Governance in the European Consensus on Development: Towards a Harmonized Approach within the European Union'*, SEC(2006)1020, 30 August 2006, pp 13–29.

component is geared to assessing the implementation of EU development projects and programmes. In addition, the inclusion of an item on migration in the eighth component appears to be informed mainly by concerns in the European Union about possible immigration.[27]

Outline of this special issue

The contributions to this special issue contest recent EU approaches to governance and development. As highlighted above, the articles are informed by the general understanding that the EU's approach to development and governance is essentially neoliberal in character and reflects a technocratic, instrumental orientation premised on the need to deepen market-based reforms in the countries of the South.

The first article, by Maurizio Carbone, discusses the EU's take on governance in the context of the development policies that have been implemented since the turn of the century. In particular, Carbone focuses on the attempt of the European Commission to harmonise the approach to governance, revolving around the idea of 'democratic governance'. The article argues that the EU's initiative seems to have been in line with the principles of aid effectiveness stemming from the Paris Declaration, but that implementation of the policy is lacking. Such 'policy evaporation' seems to be caused, to a significant extent, by the difficulty of achieving intra-EU co-ordination. A direct consequence of this appears to be a reduction in the leverage of developing countries in relation to the European Union.

Nikki Slocum-Bradley and Andrew Bradley focus in their article on the relationship with ACP countries since the adoption of the Cotonou Agreement in 2000. Discussing various instruments that have been applied in EU–ACP relations, the authors assess the extent to which these relations conform to the EU-endorsed principles of 'good governance', and whether they contribute to sustainable development and poverty reduction in the ACP countries. Slocum-Bradley and Bradley conclude that the governance rhetoric adopted by the European Union is contradicted, in a good number of cases, by the actual implementation of the policies, and that EU instruments are not necessarily conducive to the development of ACP partners.

In the third article Ian Taylor discusses relations between the European Union and Africa, particularly the EU position on the New Partnership for Africa's Development (NEPAD) and its governance aspirations. According to Taylor, Western support of NEPAD's neoliberal, technocratic agenda took insufficient account of the nature of the regimes in Africa and, more importantly, the political economy of rule in many countries of the continent. Thus, Western countries ended up supporting the personalised power structures of rulers who showed little or no commitment to the principles of good governance preached by the donors. Finally, the increased importance of China as a partner of African governments may make the EU's emphasis on governance largely irrelevant, although Taylor points out that, in the longer run, China may be motivated by similar concerns about the governance of African countries as the European Union.

In his article on the EU and southeastern Europe David Chandler focuses on the impact the EU is having on the candidate member states in the region. Chandler argues that the EU is exercising considerable regulatory power over the countries of southeastern Europe, based on essentially depoliticised and technocratic conceptions of management. The EU's approach to the region, he argues, is based on a 'post-liberal' discourse of governance, which focuses on technical and administrative capacity rather than legitimacy. The EU, while couching its methods of rule in terms of partnership and ownership, is dominating the region by, *inter alia*, Europeanising the candidate states' governance institutions and attempting to create a policy-advocating civil society. The state institutions in the regions have consequently been bereft of possibilities for engaging with and representing social interests.

In her article on EU relations with the former Soviet republics of Central Asia Katharina Hoffmann focuses on the claim that the recent EU partnership strategy for the region is aimed at the promotion of good governance. Building on the literature on external democracy promotion, in particular in relation to post-communist countries, Hoffmann argues that the regimes of the Central Asian countries have essentially remained authoritarian after the disappearance of the USSR. She indicates that the regimes have invariably have neopatrimonial features, such as personalised power and the monopolisation of resources by the regime. In such an environment the promotion of good governance is not likely to be successful. Hoffmann explains the continued engagement of the European Union, despite the absence of progress in the area of governance and democratisation, with reference to the EU's security and economic interests, which revolve around access to sources of energy (in particular, natural gas) and concerns about terrorism, drug trafficking and organised crime.

In the following article Karim Knio discusses the EU's strategy for the Mediterranean, and focuses on the discussion surrounding the creation of a Euro-Mediterranean Development Bank (EMDB) for the countries in the region. The article revolves around the polarity in the literature on governance and institutions. According to Knio, there is a stark contrast between the 'techno-managerial' position in the institutionalist literature, which can be considered to be 'power insular', and certain 'power sensitive' approaches, which focus on interests and power dynamics underlying certain governance arrangements. The two 'faces' of governance are represented, Knio argues, in the debate about the EMDB. The first approach to the Bank emphasises its limited mandate and subordinate role to its parent institution, the European Investment Bank, allowing little influence by the Mediterranean countries. The second approach emphasises the independence of the EMDB, and grants the countries of the region a say in its governance structure. Knio concludes that the technocratic approach of the European Union has prevailed, thus leading to the maintenance of an institution that will primarily assist small and medium-sized enterprises in the region.

Rosalba Icaza's article addresses the neoliberal nature of the European Union's approach to Latin America and the Caribbean, as well as resistance to the regional project within the region's civil society. Icaza argues that the strategic partnership for the region on the EU's part was driven primarily by the desire to liberalise trade and investment. In her view, market actors, most notably multinational companies, are seen as the key drivers of regionalism and development. This approach to regionalism is contrasted with approaches that emphasise resistance to neoliberal regionalism and claims for 'cognitive justice'. The latter approaches question the claims made for neoliberal modes of governance and aim to increase the political visibility of forms of knowledge that would normally be ignored. Icaza's article analyses the activities of the so-called Permanent People's Tribunals against European Multinationals and Neo-liberalism as attempts to question the violations of rights of Latin American people by European MNCs or their local subsidiaries.

The last research article in this special issue, by Wil Hout, focuses on the European Union's approach to governance in failed states. Arguing that the EU's fragile state agenda was spurred, in the first place, by the desire to address security issues in developing countries, the article emphasises that the EU, like most Western development agencies, has approached state fragility primarily in terms of a governance deficit. Hout analyses the governance-oriented measures that were adopted in the CSPs that the European Commission formulated in consultation with the governments of five so-called fragile states. He concludes that there is a substantial difference between the political analyses made in the CSPs and the policies adopted by the EU for reconstructing governance in fragile states, which consist mainly of technocratic measures. Issues of state capture, human rights and inequalities are generally left unaddressed in the EU' approach.

Stephen Hurt's review article discusses five recent books on EU development policy. Hurt focuses on four main themes in the books under review: the historical legacies, the global context, the increasing uniformity of the EU's approach to different parts of the developing world, and the role of self-interest. Hurt emphasises the EU's strategy of attempting to lock-in liberal capitalism to regional projects across the developing world. He also argues that, apart from ideological motives related to the emphasis on the MDGs, self-interest has started to occupy a more important role in EU development policies in recent times. The difficulty in reconciling principles of policy coherence with the EU's approach to development and external relations, according to Hurt, is witness to this tension.

Notes

The articles in this special issue have greatly benefited from the support received from the working group on North–South Development Issues that was part of the EU-supported Network of Excellence on Global Governance, Regionalisation and Regulation (Garnet). The articles were discussed at two workshops held at the International Institute of Social Studies (ISS) in July and November 2008, as well as at the fourth Garnet Annual Conference in Madrid in November 2009.

1. For instance, see SN Sangmpam, 'Politics rules: the false primacy of institutions in developing countries', *Political Studies*, 55(1), 2007, pp 201–224.
2. Among others, see D Craig & D Porter, *Development beyond Neoliberalism? Governance, Poverty Reduction and Political Economy*, London: Routledge, 2006.
3. JE Stiglitz, *More Instruments and Broader Goals: Moving toward the Post-Washington Consensus*, WIDER Annual Lectures 2, Helsinki: UNU World Institute for Development Economics Research, 1989, p 1.
4. See, for instance, Craig & Porter, *Development beyond Neoliberalism?*, p 93; and Z Öniş & F Şenses, 'Rethinking the emerging Post-Washington Consensus', *Development and Change*, 36(2), 2005, p 285.
5. World Bank, *Building Institutions for Markets: World Development Report 2002*, New York: Oxford University Press, 2002, p 99.
6. C Burnside & D Dollar, *Aid, Policies and Growth*, World Bank Policy Research Working Paper 1777, Washington, DC: World Bank, 1997; and Burnside & Dollar, *Aid, Policies, and Growth: Revisiting the Evidence*, World Bank Policy Research Working Paper 3251, Washington, DC: World Bank, 2004.
7. See, for example, W Hout, *The Politics of Aid Selectivity: Good Governance Criteria in US, World Bank and Dutch Foreign Assistance*, London: Routledge, 2007.
8. European Commission, *Governance in the European Consensus on Development: Towards a Harmonised Approach within the European Union*, Communication from the Commission to the Council, the European Parliament, the European Economic and Social Committee and the Committee of the Regions, COM(2006)421 final, 30 August 2006, p 12.
9. World Bank, *Assessing Aid: What Works, What Doesn't and Why*, New York: Oxford University Press, 1998, p ix.
10. European Community, *Development Policy of the European Community—Statement by the Council and the Commission*, 2000, pp 3–6, at http://ec.europa.eu/development/icenter/repository/council 20001110_en.pdf, accessed 28 August 2009.
11. G Hyden, J Court & K Mease, *Making Sense of Governance: Empirical Evidence from 16 Developing Countries*, Boulder, CO: Lynne Rienner, 2004, p 16.
12. Cf R Robison, 'Strange bedfellows: political alliances in the making of neo-liberal governance', in W Hout & R Robison (eds), *Governance and the Depoliticisation of Development*, London: Routledge, 2009, pp 17–20.
13. In this issue the term 'European Union development policies' will refer to the policies implemented at the level of the Union. Formally speaking, on the basis of the Treaty of Maastricht of 1992,

development policy is part of the first 'pillar' of the European Union. This pillar is also referred to as the European Community, and is regulated by articles 177–181 of the Treaty Establishing the European Community. The common development policies of the EU are implemented by the European Commission. Where analyses refer to the assistance policies of the member states in addition to Community policies, this will be mentioned explicitly.

14 Organisation for Economic Co-operation and Development, *OECD.Stats*, Table 2A: ODA disbursements, at http://stats.oecd.org/Index.aspx?DatasetCode=TABLE2A, accessed 28 August 2009.
15 European Commission, *Highlights—Annual Report 2006 on the European Community's Development Policy and the Implementation of External Assistance in 2005*, Luxembourg: Office for Official Publications of the European Communities, 2006, p 12; European Commission, *Annual Report 2006 on the European Community's Development Policy and the Implementation of External Assistance in 2005*, Luxembourg: Office for Official Publications of the European Communities, 2006, p 9; and European Commission, *Annual Report 2009 on the European Community's Development and External Assistance Policies and their Implementation in 2008*, SEC(2009)831 final, 30 June 2009, p 196.
16 European Community, *Development Policy of the European Community*, pp 3–6.
17 European Union, 'The European Consensus on Development', Joint Statement by the Council and the Representatives of the Governments of the Member States Meeting within the Council, the European Parliament and the Commission, *Official Journal of the European Union*, 24 February 2006, C46/01, pp 1–19.
18 *Ibid*, p 2.
19 *Ibid*, pp 3–5.
20 *Ibid*, pp 11–15.
21 European Commission, *Increasing the Impact of EU Aid: A Common Framework for Drafting Country Strategy Papers and Joint Multiannual Programming*, Communication from the Commission to the Council and the European Parliament, COM(2006)88 final, 2 March 2006, p 5.
22 *Ibid*, pp 12–14.
23 *Ibid*, p 14.
24 European Commission, *Staff Working Document Accompanying the Communication 'Governance in the European Consensus on Development: Towards a Harmonized Approach within the European Union'*, SEC(2006)1020, 30 August 2006, p 11.
25 *Ibid*, emphasis added.
26 D Kaufmann, A Kraay &P Zoido-Lobatón, *Governance Matters*, Policy Research Working Paper 2196, Washington, DC: World Bank, 1999. The dataset is available at http://info.worldbank.org/governance/wgi/index.asp, accessed 8 December 2009.
27 The Communication on 'Governance in the European Consensus' announced the introduction of an incentive reserve related to countries' governance plans, amounting to €2.7 billion out of the €22.6 billion allocated to the 10th EDF. The incentive reserve would be distributed with the use of the governance profile on the basis of 'the assessment of the [governance] situation and the reform commitments given in the dialogue'. European Commission, *Governance in the European Consensus on Development*, p 12. A recent paper by Molenaers and Nijs indicates that the governance incentive has, so far, amounted to little more than a formal exercise. See N Molenaers & L Nijs, 'The bumpy road from rhetoric to reality: the EC on the slippery slope—does the governance incentive tranche strengthen or weaken aid effectiveness under the umbrella of the Paris Declaration?', paper presented at the 12th EADI General Conference, Geneva, 24–28 June 2008.

The European Union, Good Governance and Aid Co-ordination

MAURIZIO CARBONE

ABSTRACT *This article reviews the EU's distinctive approach to good governance, based on policy dialogue and incentives, in light of the significant transformations that have occurred in EU development policy since the early 2000s. The argument made here is that only when the EU decided to act as a single actor was it possible to agree on a harmonised approach to good governance. By doing so, the EU sought to promote aid effectiveness and at the same time raise its profile in international politics, thus challenging the leadership of the World Bank and of the USA. It is concluded that not only has the gap between the EU's lofty ambitions and the implementation record remained wide, but also that the search for better co-ordination between European donors has resulted in decreased policy space for developing countries.*

It is often said that, when the efforts of the European Community (EC) and the 27 member states are combined, the European Union is the most generous donor in international development, providing more than half of the world's total foreign aid. The amount of resources administered at the EC level has gradually increased but the largest chunk (83% of the total in 2008) is still managed autonomously by the member states, which have consistently refused to transfer more of their sovereignty to the supranational level.[1] This poor record in co-ordination and complementarity has not only compromised the EU's efforts towards better and faster aid delivery, but has also reduced its impact in the international arena. Since the beginning of the new century, however, some significant changes have become evident. The European Consensus on Development—signed by the European Commission, Parliament and Council in December 2005—for the first time ever committed the member states and the EC to a shared vision on international development. The European Consensus was allegedly the most significant of various examples of the EU's ambition to become not only a single but also a distinctive actor in international development, as an alternative to the Washington Consensus (including its revised form). In fact, while the Lomé Convention was initially celebrated as a model of North–South co-operation, the EU was accused of following trends set by international organisations, particularly the Bretton Woods institutions, since the mid-1980s. The adoption of an ambitious agenda on aid effectiveness in 2006–07, which complemented the pledges made by the member states to collectively increase their volume of aid, has further qualified the EU's ambitions to voice its message in the fight against world poverty.

The case of 'good governance' is a good example of the EU's lofty aspirations. In particular, the communication on *Governance in the European Consensus on Development*, issued by the European Commission in August 2006 and endorsed by the Council in October 2006, advanced the idea of a harmonised, as well as innovative, approach to good governance. With this initiative the EU's aim was to reach two different goals and two different targets. On the one hand, the initiative was a way to promote aid effectiveness while attempting to strengthen the profile of the EU in international politics. On the other hand, it targeted developing countries— which were meant to benefit from more co-ordinated and efficient aid—and the World Bank and the USA, although the latter two were not mentioned in official papers.[2] The World Bank had introduced the concept of good governance in the late 1980s and had, since then, influenced the development policy of various international donors, including some EU countries. With the launch of the Millennium Challenge Account in 2002 the USA had taken the principle of selectivity to the extreme, although more recently some funds have been allocated to countries which did not meet the required threshold.

While acknowledging that good governance can be treated as both a goal of and a condition for development co-operation, this article concentrates mainly on the latter. For this purpose the article is divided into two broad parts. The next section sets the context. It introduces the concept of good governance and its trajectory in international development, before sketching the global agenda on aid effectiveness. The third section focuses on the European Union. It first discusses the evolution of the EU as a single development actor. Then it traces the itinerary of good governance within the EU, including the proposals made by the European Commission, the discussions within the Council and the views of civil society organisations. Finally, it investigates the links between the EU's agendas on good governance and aid co-ordination, particularly the initial implementation of joint programming and division of labour. The argument advanced here is that the EU may only in theory have offered an alternative, allegedly more progressive, approach compared with the prevailing development paradigm (propagated by the World Bank and the USA), in an attempt to raise its profile in the international arena. The gap between the EU's high ambitions and its practice has not only remained wide, but the search for greater co-ordination between European donors has also resulted in a further decrease of the policy space for developing countries.

Good governance and international development

The concept of good governance emerged in the circle of donor agencies between the end of the 1980s and the beginning of the 1990s and has since become one of the most used (and misused) terms in academic and policy debates.[3] The World Bank was the driving force behind this new agenda, so much so that within a few years it became the main, if not the sole, reference point for donors.[4] Other international organisations have tried to challenge the Bank's leadership, but without much success. Despite its extensive usage and application, the concept of good governance remains controversial for various reasons. First, there is no accepted definition. This is not a semantic issue, but has significant policy implications: by emphasising different aspects of the good governance concept, donors have pursued goals that arguably do not belong to this agenda. Second, good governance may be seen as a goal of or a condition for development co-operation. On the one hand, considering it as a goal implies a focus on building institutions in recipient countries, at the level both of the state and of civil society. On the other hand, its use as a criterion to allocate aid means the imposition of new forms of political conditionality, in parallel to economic conditionalities that have been applied since the 1980s.[5] Finally, donors may consider different strategies to assist good governance in recipient countries:

- persuasion: they engage in dialogue with recipients;
- capacity-building support: they channel funds to governance projects;
- conditionality: they attach conditions, more or less strictly, to aid packages to induce political and administrative reforms in recipient countries; and
- selectivity: they reward countries with a proven record of good governance.[6]

Conditionality and selectivity

Following the decade of economic conditionality, which coerced developing countries to adopt structural adjustments into their macroeconomic frameworks, the end of the Cold War, when democracy spread in many parts of the world, was a favourable time for the Bretton Woods institutions to launch the good governance agenda.[7] This was also the period in which renewed emphasis was placed on the state, in response to the previous decade, when the myth of the market had prevailed and the private sector had been considered more conducive to economic development. Corruption and the lack of transparency were identified as two central obstacles to better performance of the state—interestingly, despite its proclaimed apolitical nature, the World Bank had identified Africa's development problem as a 'crisis of governance' in a 1989 report. A debate started on what good governance was about and on what donors could do to promote it. Recipient governments were urged to reform the public sector in order to achieve the objective of reducing poverty.[8] The World Bank initially tried to steer away from politics and emphasised only the technocratic aspects of good governance, linked to the state's capacity to use foreign aid effectively, such as public-sector management, accountability, the legal framework for development, and transparency. It was only towards the end of the 1990s that the World Bank's concept of governance broadened to more political issues, including citizen participation. Yet it could still be concluded that the World Bank had a pivotal role in depoliticising the issue of good governance.[9]

This debate received a crucial stimulus when the World Bank published its seminal report on *Assessing Aid* in 1998. Based on a series of econometric studies conducted by a small group of economists, the report showed that aid would boost economic growth and alleviate poverty in those countries that adopted sound economic policies, but would not have measurable effects in countries with poor policies. By sound policies, the Bank meant open trade regimes, fiscal discipline and low inflation rates. As to good governance, the report took a narrow view, referring to respect for the rule of law, quality of the bureaucracy and control of corruption. A reallocation of aid to 'good policy–high poverty' countries, the argument ran, would lead to a significant reduction of poverty.[10] Thus, the World Bank and various donors, including in the EU, shifted from supporting projects aimed at promoting good governance into requiring good governance as a condition for receiving aid— in other words, from conditionality to selectivity. This meant acknowledging that conditionality had not produced the expected results, but it also allowed donors to get away from the monitoring of the implementation of reforms. Moreover, the Country Policy and Institutional Assessment (CPIA), which covers macroeconomic and development policy, economic and public sector management, and institutional capacity and competence, started to be used widely by various donors.[11]

A number of governments in developing countries were unwilling to carry out the stipulated reforms because conditions were felt to be inappropriate for their society. In addition they lamented that World Bank representatives dictated the content of lending without their direct involvement. Taylor, for example, interpreted this practice as a 'hegemonic discourse pursued by the North in an attempt to define the South in its own image'.[12] Some attempts were made to correct this situation. The launch of the Comprehensive Development Framework (CDF) and the Poverty Reduction Strategies Papers (PRSPs) sought to promote a holistic approach to development, placing new emphasis on ownership of the reform process by the recipient country's government and on partnership between governments, development co-operation agencies, civil society, and the private sector. The reforms continued to be criticised because of the level of commitment required from recipient governments before they would receive aid. Many governments simply did not have the capacity to conduct reforms or lacked legitimacy among their citizens. Grindle, for example, advanced the idea of 'good enough governance' to indicate 'a condition of minimally acceptable government performance and civil society engagement that does not significantly hinder economic and political development and that permits poverty reduction initiatives to go forward'.[13]

Enhancing the quality of foreign aid

While the good governance agenda has been driven by the Bretton Woods institutions, the OECD's Development Assistance Committee (DAC) is generally seen as pushing the issue of aid co-ordination more than any other international actor. Already in the early 1990s the DAC had managed to bring bilateral agencies together to build a common approach to participatory development and good governance. The 1993 High-Level meeting established an *ad-hoc* working group with the aim of shifting aid relationships towards local initiatives and partnership between various actors (governments, civil society, NGOs, donors). Moreover, being the 'donors' club', and thus reflecting the views of bilateral agencies, the DAC did have some comparative advantage over other players. Considering that donors had started to integrate good governance principles with their development co-operation programmes, one of the aims of the DAC was to learn 'lessons from experience' and 'best practices of operational relevance'. The *ad-hoc* group, however, reached an impasse because of the difference of opinion among donors about the notion of good governance; the positions of development ministries and agencies diverged also on how to implement the good governance agenda.[14]

Nevertheless the DAC was instrumental in putting the issues of aid co-ordination and harmonisation on the global agenda. The issue of aid effectiveness became even more urgent when in the early 2000s international donors, with the EU in a leading position, decided to reverse the declining trends in the volume of aid. While during the 1990s it looked as if foreign aid was withering away, after less than a decade DAC members had more than doubled the resources going to developing countries, increasing their combined budgets from US$52 billion in 2000 to almost $120 billion in 2008.[15] The number of actors—both public and private donors—providing foreign assistance had increased significantly. For instance, it was calculated that, in 2006, there were about 225 bilateral donor agencies and 242 multilateral agencies working in development co-operation; to this we should add the so-called 'emerging donors' and the growing number of private donors, such as foundations and business corporations. The proliferation of donors produced a system that often lacks coherence, in which "the combined effort adds up to less that the sum of its parts".[16]

Aid effectiveness was addressed at a first summit held in Rome in 2003, although it was not until the second meeting in Paris in 2005 that aid co-ordination and harmonisation received global attention. The ensuing Paris Declaration on Aid Effectiveness, adopted on 2 March 2005 by the representatives of about 100 developed and developing countries, laid down a practical, action-oriented roadmap to improve the quality of aid and its impact on development. The Declaration comprised 56 commitments organised around five principles:

- ownership: developing countries would exercise leadership over their development policies and strategies and co-ordinate development efforts;
- alignment: donors would align their overall support with the partner country's national development strategies, institutions and procedures;
- harmonisation: donors would reduce the administrative burden of the recipient countries;
- managing for results: donors and recipient countries would work towards improving decision-making processes on aid; and
- mutual accountability: donors and recipient countries would hold each other mutually accountable for development results.

The Paris Declaration (with commitments reiterated at a third summit in Accra in 2008) broke new ground for achieving greater aid effectiveness on the basis of shared principles and measurable indicators. It soon became the main reference point for donor agencies and for finance ministries in developing countries, a tool which would allow actors to project their claims on the politics of aid relationships and at the same time enter into debates about technical issues. Four years later, however, limited progress has been made on most of the 56 commitments, leading some commentators to talk about 'aid effectiveness fatigue'.[17]

The European Union and democratic governance

The European Union has come relatively late to the debate on governance and development, failing to achieve a co-ordinated approach not only on this but also on most other development issues. Some member states followed the lead of the World Bank; others continued to base their aid allocation process on different criteria. The European Commission itself was criticised for having sacrificed its progressive development programme on the altar of economic and political conditionality. More generally, as a consequence of the failure to co-ordinate and effectively divide tasks, the EU has largely punched below its weight. This section looks first at the efforts towards a co-ordinated EU development policy before analysing the efforts towards a harmonised approach to good governance.

Towards a coordinated development policy

The aspiration of the EU to become a single development actor dates back to the origins of the EU itself. The decision to create the European Development Fund (EDF) in the late 1950s was, for some, the first step in a process of communitisation of aid. For more than 30 years the amount of resources transferred to the supranational level kept increasing, but full integration of aid was never considered seriously. After a long break the debate somehow re-started with the Treaty of Maastricht (1991–93). Some proposals were made for a 'common development policy', but they were rejected in the Council. The three new principles for EU development policy—complementarity, co-ordination, and coherence—seemed to show that attitudes were changing and that European donors were more willing to co-ordinate their policies. The European Commission issued a number of communications, which were generally followed by resolutions of the Council, and set up various pilot projects. The results of all these initiatives were meagre: co-ordination and complementarity worked poorly, mainly because of the resistance of (a large majority of) member states. Moreover, an overstretched and fragmented development programme, partly resulting from the EU's changing membership, generated significant criticism of the European Commission. The consequence was that a number of member states started questioning the value added of a development policy conducted at the supranational level.[18]

In the light of such criticisms, the European Commission started an extensive reform process, which involved both the bilateral and multilateral dimensions of EU development policy. Poverty eradication became the primary goal of EC development policy and areas of intervention were reduced to those in which the EC was deemed to have a comparative advantage. Aid was committed and then disbursed following the adoption of a Country Strategy Paper (CSP), while new political issues (the fight against terrorism, migration, and good governance) and participatory development entered the aid discourse.[19]

The reform season also involved the EU as a multilateral donor. In particular, in the context of the Financing for Development conference held in Monterrey in March 2002, the member states for the first time pledged collectively to increase their volume of aid from 0.33% to 0.39% of their gross national income. In May 2005, they committed to a more ambitious target: reaching 0.56% by 2010 and 0.7% by 2015.[20] These commitments on aid quantities were complemented by the new agenda on aid effectiveness, proposed by the European Commission in March 2006 and endorsed by the Council in October 2006. Of particular interest for this article is the idea of a Joint Programming Framework (JPF), which includes two stages: 1) joint Commission and member state analyses; and 2) joint response strategies, including the identification of co-operation objectives and focal areas, and the division of tasks among European donors.[21] The ultimate aim of the JPF was to increase the synchronisation of the programming processes of the member states and the European Commission and to facilitate the gradual alignment of donor policies with the development plans of the recipient countries.[22]

The European Consensus on Development, signed in December 2005, provided a policy platform setting out common objectives and principles. The novelty of the Consensus was that it committed the member states not only as participants in the common development policy but also as bilateral donors. This new 'European vision of development' reaffirmed that the primary objective of development policy is poverty eradication. It reiterated the commitments made by all member states to delivering more and better aid, and to promoting policy coherence for development. It established that the EU would promote a number of values, such as respect for human dignity, freedom, democracy, equality, the rule of law, and human rights;

that it would encourage gender equality, participation of non-state actors, political dialogue and ownership; and that it would promote multilateralism and, within the framework of the United Nations, contribute to a system of rules, institutions and international instruments set up and implemented by the international community.[23] The European Consensus not only identified 'good governance, democracy and respect for human rights as integral to the process of sustainable development and as a major objective of EU development policy', but also established that the allocation of aid given by European donors should be based on transparent and objective criteria.[24]

The operationalisation of the European Consensus, and a central component of the EU's aid effectiveness agenda, is the Code of Conduct on Complementarity and Division of Labour, adopted by the Council in May 2007 following a proposal made by the European Commission in February 2007. The Code of Conduct was presented as a voluntary, 'self-policing' document, open to non-EU donors. One of its most important components is the idea that member states should concentrate their activities in a limited number of priority countries, making sure, through dialogue with their EU peers, that adequate funding is allocated to those countries that are generally overlooked ('aid orphans') and to those countries that represent a threat to regional stability and international security ('fragile states').[25] The exercise of responsibility towards these forgotten states, together with the search for enhanced complementarity of efforts in 'aid darlings' to prevent waste of resources, is a manifestation of the fact that the EU cares about all developing countries, regardless of their colonial past or strategic importance. In this sense, the agreement on a harmonised approach to good governance, analysed in the next sub-section, can be seen as a way to implement the idea of a common EU identity in the international arena, as suggested by the European Consensus on Development, and at the same time as a way to enhance aid effectiveness.

Towards a harmonised approach to democratic governance

'Good governance' made its first appearance in an official EU document in November 1991, when a resolution of the Council established that the EU would 'support efforts of developing countries to advance good governance'. The concept of good governance was borrowed from the World Bank. The three largest member states—France, UK, and Germany—as well as Belgium and the Netherlands, had already integrated issues of human rights, democracy and good governance into their development policies between 1989 and 1991. The Nordic countries had an established tradition in this field. Only the member states in southern Europe lagged behind. It is against this background that the EU's Development Council had adopted a number of resolutions in the early 1990s that elevated democracy promotion as an overarching objective of both EC and member states' development policies, and that the Treaty of Maastricht included democracy and the rule of law as objectives of all the EU's external policies, including foreign affairs.[26]

The Lomé Convention (1975–2000), which for many years had been one of the most important expressions of the EU's identity in international affairs, made neutrality in political affairs one of its most celebrated features, at least until the mid-1980s. Following some confrontational discussions during the negotiation of Lomé III (1985) and Lomé IV (1990), it was under Lomé IV-bis (1995) that the African Caribbean and Pacific (ACP) countries accepted the inclusion of a human rights clause as an 'essential element' of the co-operation agreement, violation of which would lead to the possible suspension of aid. In the context of negotiations on the Cotonou Agreement (which was meant for the 2000–20 period), the EU member states and the European Commission pushed for the inclusion of good governance (considered by the ACP countries as too vague a concept, which could open the door to interference in their domestic affairs) as an 'essential element', but after extensive discussions it was included only as a 'fundamental element': this meant that only serious cases of corruption and mismanagement of resources would constitute grounds for the suspension of aid. The Cotonou Agreement introduced also the most comprehensive framework for the involvement of non-state actors in the development process and strengthened the political dimension, which included issues that had previously fallen outside the field of development co-operation (peace and security, arms trade, migration, drugs and corruption).[27]

In October 2003 the European Commission adopted a communication offering what was defined as a 'pragmatic' approach to (good) governance, based on dialogue and capacity building.[28] The starting point was a critique of the prevailing 'one-size-fits-all' approach, to be replaced with a sort of 'à la carte' approach, tailored to specific situations. The EU (including its member states) could decide to allocate aid to good performers ('effective partnerships'), with the aim of increasing the returns of tax-payers money as much as possible. In this case the preferred aid modality would be budget support. But there are other situations that would need to be considered. In the case of 'difficult partnerships', the priority would be to find a solution to an existing crisis, by trying to engage with local authorities and by taking political initiatives both internationally and regionally. In this case humanitarian and food aid would be preferred modalities, as well as support for civil society. In 'post-conflict situations', the priority would be to prevent a return to war. This implies identifying the root causes of the conflict, getting a reconciliation process under way, establishing a link between emergency aid, rehabilitation and long-term development, and providing neutral humanitarian aid. While this communication was meant to cover only EC development policy, one of its interesting elements was a call for better co-ordination among all EU member states, which meant 'adopting common policy principles in this specific area'.

This last is the departure point of the new communication adopted by the European Commission in August 2006 on 'democratic governance'.[29] Given the scope of this article, three issues deserve particular attention: its comprehensive view, harmonisation between donors, and the incentive-based approach. First, the Commission emphasised an evolution in its thinking: from the understanding of good governance as a technocratic issue, focused mainly on the fight against corruption, to a holistic view, encompassing several dimensions—political, economic, social and cultural. Good governance, thus, would include access to health, education and justice, pluralism in the media, the functioning of parliament, and the management of public accounts and natural resources. It was confirmed that poverty eradication remains the central goal of EU development policy and that democratic governance is only a means towards that end. Moreover, it was reiterated that good governance cannot be imposed from the outside ('ownership over conditionality') and must not lead to new conditions ('dialogue over sanctions'). But the most relevant change was that the European Commission sought to harmonise EC and member states' approaches to good governance. This would presuppose joint analysis and dialogue with the partner countries as well as a common programming framework. Interestingly, Commissioner for Development Louis Michel argued, in a speech at the World Bank in April 2006, that 'if there is one area where harmonisation is needed, it is this. We may differ on some aspects of governance, but it seems to me these divergences are not sufficiently large to generate a system of additional and chaotic layers of successive and disparate conditionalities, even contradictory ones'. Furthermore, political dialogue, referred to as the primary instrument for the promotion of good governance, should actively involve both the EC and the member states.

An innovative component was believed to be the idea of an incentive-based approach to good governance, with the aim of rewarding recipient countries for their governance commitments. These extra funds (European Community Governance Incentive Tranche—ECGIT) would be allocated on the basis of a process that involves the elaboration of a Governance Profile by the European Commission and an Action Plan by the partner country.[30] However, questions were raised immediately on whether the Governance Initiative, initially set up only for ACP countries, was an answer to exogenous preoccupations and an exercise to capture aid, rather than a policy tool for reform.[31] The European Commission has stated on many occasions that the incentive tranche does not represent a new form of conditionality, but is a sort of encouragement to engage in reforms and consolidate democratic practices.[32] Nevertheless, it was established that the Governance Profile 'is not meant to be done necessarily jointly with the partner country but its content should be shared (but not negotiated and agreed) with partner country during the programming dialogue'.[33]

The discussion within the Council—in the Development Working Group and the Coreper in September–October 2006 and at the ministerial level at the General Affairs Council on 16 October 2006—confirmed that the member states were willing to pursue a unitary approach to good governance, which by itself was a radical change from previous practices. In the past, not only had member states resisted attempts of the European Commission to interfere with their development policies, but they had also taken (at least in majority) a different approach. The European Commission, using a longer term perspective, had pursued a 'positive conditionality' approach.

The Council, by contrast, had been more inclined towards a 'negative conditionality' approach, revolving around the adoption of visible measures that could be sold politically to their domestic constituencies.[34] In this case all member states accepted the incentive- and dialogue-based approach proposed by the European Commission. They also confirmed that the best way to implement the new consensual approach would be through shared analyses and common programming frameworks, 'with a view to providing coherent, complementary and harmonised support to in-country democratic processes'.

Some differences of opinion existed on co-ordination between the EU and other donors. Some member states (the UK and Denmark) emphasised that the EU should support existing co-ordination efforts, such as the PRSPs and Joint Assistance Strategy (JAS). Other member states (France, Italy and Spain) sought to downplay the link between EU-led and international co-ordination processes. The final version was, as often in EU negotiations, a compromise, which read as follows: 'whenever possible, be part of these existing processes, in order to avoid unnecessary parallel processes'.[35]

The line taken by the EU, and particularly the EC, was criticised by non-state actors. At one level they denounced the fact that they were not sufficiently involved throughout the decision-making process. This lack of consultation, it was argued, was linked to the European Commission's desire to have clear guidelines for the upcoming programming exercise for the 10th EDF (2008–13). A survey of about 50 NGOs in developing countries confirmed that consultation with Southern civil society was quick and superficial, at best, whereas parliaments were not involved at all. The conclusion is that the EU was using good governance not only as a way to push new conditionalities on developing countries, but was pursuing its own interest in a number of areas: economic governance was defined very narrowly, referring exclusively to the private sector and market-friendly environments, and to issues that were not identified as priorities by recipient governments. In the area of security reference was made to regional and intra-state conflicts, but high prominence was given to the fight against international terrorism and to the non-proliferation of weapons of mass destruction. Finally, it was not clear why the 'management of migration flows' figured in the list of issues to be included in the definition of democratic governance.[36]

The gap between intentions and reality

In spite of these criticisms, the intentions of the European Union in proposing a new agenda on democratic governance were good in theory. The primary message—harmonisation of donor practices while guaranteeing dialogue with partner countries—was in line with the principles of aid effectiveness agreed at the Paris summit in 2005. The secondary message was that of strengthening the EU's identity *vis-à-vis* other actors in international development. The two targets in this case were the USA and the World Bank. The European Commission was very keen on saying that its approach represented a significant change from traditional conditionality to a more 'collaborative approach', based on persuasion rather than coercion. While the World Bank uses indicators to rank countries, the EU governance profiles are qualitative rather than quantitative. Moreover, by emphasising dialogue, the EU sought to distance itself from the USA, which was using foreign aid strategically (in the case of resources managed through USAID) or was applying the principle of selectivity quite rigidly (in the case of resources channelled through the Millennium Challenge Account).[37]

As in other cases, the EU has suffered from policy evaporation: the existence of a gap between rhetoric and the implementation record. The assessment of the multi-annual programming exercise has shown mixed results, at best. In general, member states look favourably upon the common format for CSPs, but experience on the ground shows that this process is complex, because of the heterogeneous nature of donor programming and mechanisms, insufficient communication between headquarters and in-country staff, capacity constraints that prevent all EU donors from participating in discussions on a regular basis, not forgetting tensions with other donor-wide harmonisation processes. The provisional conclusion of the multi-programming approach, at least at the end of 2009, was that 'whilst it was developed to build a comprehensive and exhaustively coherent approach, it also tends to make the process more complex and demanding for the donors participating in the joint programming exercise'.[38]

The implementation of the Code of Conduct on Complementarity and Division of Labour has also presented various shortcomings. The causes of the lack of progress on the division of labour are consultation fatigue and loss of visibility on the donor side and (perceived) hesitations on the recipient side, which not only has limited capacities to lead the co-ordination process but also fears a potential loss of resources and the imposition of stricter conditionalities. This in a way seems to confirm more general trends about the global agenda on aid harmonisation. In fact, it has been argued that the limited development gains resulting from the reduction of transaction costs in the aid allocation process are outweighed by the asymmetrical conditions under which discussions about aid effectiveness take place, which exacerbate the imbalances of power between donors and recipients. Contrary to the stated objectives, the effect of aid co-ordination and harmonisation may have been a further circumscribing of national autonomy over development processes.[39]

Similarly disappointing results have been produced by the new governance initiative for ACP countries. First, the process of launching the ECGIT was rushed and poorly sequenced with recipient development processes. The commitment to reforms varies substantially across ACP countries; the EU assumed that all countries would engage in reforms in order to get the tranche, discounting the fact that even the efforts required for writing the Action Plans may have been too high *vis-à-vis* the limited resources that had been made available. Moreover, considering that the incentive tranche was funded from the EDF pot that had already been agreed for 2008–13, various ACP countries perceived it as simply making funds conditional on good governance. Second, while member states engaged in some useful discussions about partner countries' governance, and in a few cases some of them used EU-led governance profiles for their own development co-operation strategies, more generally, apart from information sharing and joint analysis, this governance exercise failed to produce enhanced donor co-ordination and joint actions. Third, the writing of the governance profiles and the action plans was a process mainly limited to the European Commission, member states, and recipient governments (in that precise order of importance). Participation of civil society was absent or largely superficial. Fourth, the actual disbursement of the tranches shows that the large majority of countries (around 70%) have received an equal amount of incentives. The logic of compromise between various member states, who wanted to 'protect' their close partners in Africa, is the explanation for this outcome. Politics, in other words, prevailed over the more technocratic allocation of funds on the basis of governance indicators.[40]

Nevertheless, some positive developments may be expected in the future. True, the implementation of the aid effectiveness agenda lags behind, although this should not be a surprise considering the significance of the transformations introduced. As for good governance, lessons can be learnt from the few cases where there was a joint effort of all EU donors, who contributed, in a sort of division of labour, on the basis of their experience and expertise in a specific sector of the governance field. In this sense, democratic governance was a prominent issue under the Czech presidency in the first half of 2009. An initial discussion of the subject took place at an informal meeting of development ministers in Prague in January 2009. It was subsequently partially sidelined because of the debate on the consequences of the global financial crisis for developing countries, but was eventually discussed at length at the General and External Relations Council (GAERC) of 18 and 19 May 2009. In its conclusions, the Council not only reaffirmed its support for the ECGIT, despite its initial shortcomings, but also emphasised the need to use political dialogue more systematically and urged the member states and the European Commission to strengthen their efforts to improve harmonisation of practices.[41]

Conclusion

Since the beginning of the 2000s EU development policy has undergone a number of substantial transformations. On the one hand, increases in the volume of aid have been accompanied by several initiatives to enhance the quality of aid. On the other hand, the adoption of the European Consensus on Development, and its follow-up measures, have sent the message that the EU aspires to project a single vision on international development.

The first conclusion of this article is that the case of good governance cannot be seen in isolation from this general context. After introducing the notion in the late 1980s, the World Bank became the incontestable leader in the field and good governance was placed at the heart of the development co-operation programmes of most international donors. The European Union was reactive and divided. Some member states endorsed the new agenda;

others and the European Commission challenged it. Only when the EU decided to act increasingly as a single actor did it prove possible to agree on a harmonised approach to good governance—something that would have been simply unthinkable at the end of the 1990s.

With the European Commission's communication and the Council's conclusions (August–October 2006), the EU has sought to go beyond the 'conditionality trap' by combining incentives with dialogue and promoting ownership of actions and targets, while enhancing the effectiveness and impact of its aid by better co-ordinating efforts in its relations with developing countries and by projecting a common vision on the subject. The intentions of the European Commission are clear: 'A concerted approach is the only way for the EU to make itself heard in the international debate on governance. The EU must make a stand on this key issue of international development.'[42] This takes us to an ongoing debate, which concerns the extent to which the EU is able to project a common identity in the international arena and whether the EU is a leader or a follower in international development. In the 1970s and (part of the) 1980s it was argued that the Lomé Convention represented the EU's progressive and distinctive approach to international development. Gradually that policy identity was compromised, if not completely lost.[43] The recent adoption into the EU's development discourse of concepts such as ownership, participation and capacity building, which are meant to be the 'European alternative' to dominant international practices, some have argued, in reality resonates with the language found in the publications of the Bretton Woods institutions.[44] Taking a slightly different approach, the EU at times may need to trade some policy autonomy for more effective collaboration with other global actors, but from the perspective of recipient states this is 'welcome and long overdue'.[45] This article has suggested, and this is the second conclusion, that since the beginning of the 2000s the European Union, by acting as a single actor, has been able to shape the pace of international development in a significant way. The increase of the volume of aid and the commitments to address aid fragmentation, as well as the new agenda on good governance, show that the EU may have imported ideas from somewhere else, but by making firm commitments and taking ambitious decisions it has also conditioned the behaviour of other international actors, which have had no other choice than to follow the EU's lead.

Finally, and this is the third conclusion of this article, the agreement on a harmonised approach on good governance may have implied more European and possibly better aid, but it has certainly meant decreasing ownership and possibly less development. The EU may like to be perceived as a normative power, but the need to accommodate various positions undermines its leadership aspirations in international development. In other words, there are often trade-offs between the EU's 'will to power' and its actual record as a progressive development actor that takes the needs of developing countries to heart. The rhetoric of policy statements frequently does not meet the practice on the ground. In fact, developing countries have found their policy space for negotiations with the EU progressively reduced. The initial experience with joint programming and division of labour and the implementation of the Governance Initiative shows that there are several gaps between the theory and the practice of development policy and that policy evaporation is still a major problem faced by the EU in its relations with the developing world. More importantly, in some cases the democratic governance exercise may 'distract' developing states from other important economic and social development tasks. This leads to a paradoxical situation in which the EU seems preoccupied with improving its development record and image, but at the same time fails to take into account the voice of the developing countries, including that of local civil society.

Notes

1 Development Assistance Committee, *Development Cooperation Report 2008*, Paris: OECD, 2009.
2 This article, in addition to an analysis of primary sources, is based on a number of interviews with aid officials in the European Commission, some member states and some African countries, conducted by the author in May 2006 and in May–June 2009.
3 For a general introduction to the governance–development link, see B Smith, *Good Governance and Development*, Basingstoke: Palgrave Macmillan, 2007. See also G Hyden, J Court & K Mease, *Making Sense of Governance: Empirical Evidence from Sixteen Developing Countries*, Boulder, CO: Lynne Rienner, 2004; and M Kjaer, *Governance*, Cambridge: Polity Press, 2004.
4 For example, in the summer of 1998 the Dutch Minister of Development Co-operation announced a substantial reduction of countries receiving aid. Other European countries, by contrast, have resisted this trend. See W Hout, *The Politics of Aid Selectivity: Good Governance Criteria in World Bank, US and Dutch Development Assistance*, London: Routledge, 2007.
5 P Hoebink, 'European donors and "good governance": condition or goal', *European Journal of Development Research*, 18(1), 2006, pp 131–161.
6 E Neumayer, *The Pattern of Aid Giving: The Impact of Good Governance on Development Assistance*, London: Routledge, 2003.
7 O Stokke (ed), *Aid and Political Conditionality*, London: Frank Cass, 1995; and M Doornbos, '"Good governance": the rise and decline of a policy metaphor?', *Journal of Development Studies*, 37(6), 2001, pp 93–108.
8 M Doornbos, 'Good governance: the pliability of a policy concept', *Trames*, 8(4), 2004, pp 372–387; and G Harrison, 'The World Bank, governance and theories of political action', *British Journal of Politics and International Relations*, 7(2), 2005, pp 240–260.
9 W Hout & R Robison (eds), *Governance and the Depoliticisation of Development*, London: Routledge, 2009.
10 These conclusions have been contested on a number of fronts, and the literature keeps increasing. For reviews, see H Hansen & F Tarp, 'Aid and growth regressions', *Journal of Development Economics*, 64, 2001, pp 547–560; and Tony Addison & George Mavrotas (eds), *Development Finance in the Global Economy: The Road Ahead*, Basingstoke: Palgrave Macmillan, 2008.
11 The IMF articulated its views on (good) governance only in 1997, when it published a document called *Good Governance: The IMF's Role*. The governance agenda in the IMF, according to Thirkell-White, has been driven by financial technocrats, who have narrowly focused on macroeconomic considerations in the formulation and implementation of the IMF's aid policy. Similarly, for Ian Taylor the concept of good governance has been used by the IMF as 'an ultimate attempt to reconfigure territories in order to make them most attractive to international capital'. See B Thirkell-White, 'The IMF, good governance and middle-income countries', *European Journal of Development Research*, 15(1), 2003, pp 99–125; and I Taylor, 'Hegemony, neoliberal "good governance" and the International Monetary Fund: a Gramscian perspective', in M Bøås & D McNeill (eds), *Global Institutions and Development: Framing the World?*, London: Routledge, 2004, p 124.
12 Taylor, 'Hegemony, neoliberal "good governance" and the International Monetary Fund', p 124.
13 M Grindle, 'Good enough governance: poverty reduction and reform in developing countries', *Governance*, 17, 2004, p 526.
14 K Masujima. 'Good governance and the Development Assistance Committee', in Bøås & McNeill, *Global Institutions and Development*; and Hoebink, 'European donors and "good governance"'.
15 DAC, *Development Cooperation Report 2008*.
16 *Ibid*, pp 29–30.

17 FRIDE, 'From Paris to Accra: building the global governance of aid', August 2008, at http://www.fride.org/download/DB_Paris_to_Accra_ENG_aug08.pdf, accessed 10 August 2009.
18 K Arts & AK Dickson (eds), *EU Development Cooperation: From Model to Symbol*, Manchester: Manchester University Press, 2004; and M Holland, *The European Union and the Third World*, New York: Palgrave, 2002. See also C Santiso, 'Reforming European foreign aid: development cooperation as an element of foreign policy', *European Foreign Affairs Review*, 8(1), 2003, pp 401–422.
19 For an analysis of the recent changes in EU development policy, see M Carbone (ed), *Perspectives on European Politics and Society*, 9(2), 2008, special issue. This issue includes articles by S Dearden on the reform process, J Mackie on the Cotonou Agreement, M Carbone on participation, and J Orbie and G Faber on trade and development.
20 M Carbone, *The European Union and International Development: The Politics of Foreign Aid*, London: Routledge, 2007.
21 Development Assistance Committee, *Peer Review of the European Community*, Paris: OECD, 2007.
22 European Commission, *Financing for Development and Aid Effectiveness—The Challenges of Scaling EU Aid 2006–2010*, COM(2006)85, 2 March 2006; European Commission, *EU Aid: Delivering More, Better and Faster*, COM(2006)87, 2 March 2006; and European Commission, *Increasing the Impact of EU Aid: A Common Framework for Drafting Country Strategy Papers and Joint Multiannual Programming*, COM(2006)88, 2 March 2006.
23 European Parliament, Council and Commission, 'The European Consensus on Development', *Official Journal of the European Union*, 24 February 2006, C 46, pp 1–19.
24 Ibid.
25 Another important commitment for member states (the EC had already implemented this) was to focus activities only on three sectors per developing country, particularly in those areas where they could add the most value, while taking into account what other donors were doing. See European Commission, *EU Code of Conduct on Division of Labour in Development Policy*, COM(2007)72, 28 February 2007; Council, 2800th Council Meeting, External Relations, 9471/1/07 REV 1 Press 103, Brussels, 14 May 2007.
26 Smith, *Good Governance and Development*, p 150; SC Carey, 'European aid: human rights versus bureaucratic inertia', *Journal of Peace Research*, 44(4), 2007, pp 447–464; KE Smith, *European Union Foreign Policy in a Changing World*, Cambridge: Polity, 2008; and SC Zanger, 'Good governance and European aid: the impact of political conditionality', *European Union Politics*, 1(3), 2000, pp 293–317.
27 K Arts, *Integrating Human Rights into Development Cooperation: The Case of the Lomé Convention*, The Hague: Kluwer Law International, 2000; P Hilpold, 'EU development cooperation at a crossroads: The Cotonou Agreement of 23 June 2000 and the principle of good governance', *European Foreign Affairs Review*, 7, 2002, pp 53–72; C Santiso, 'Sisyphus in the castle: improving European Union strategies for democracy promotion and governance conditionality', *European Journal of Development Research*, 15(1), 2003, pp 1–28; M Carbone, 'Theory and practice of participation: civil society and EU development policy', *Perspectives on European Politics and Society*, 9(2), 2008, pp 241–255; and O Babarinde & G Faber (eds), *The European Union and Developing Countries: The Cotonou Agreement*, Leiden: Brill, 2005.
28 European Commission, *Governance and Development*, COM(2003)615, 20 October 2003.
29 European Commission, *Governance in the European Consensus on Development: Towards a Harmonized Approach within the European Union*, COM(2006)421, 30 August 2006.
30 See also the introduction of this special issue on the details of the ECGIT methodology. A similar approach is used by the British Department for International Development (DFID). The central assumption of the Drivers of Change (DOC) approach is that reducing poverty is about 'intervening in historical processes and not simply rational planning'. Going beyond the dominant good governance agenda, this approach reflects the wider recognition of 'the inherently political nature of the implementation and efficacy of aid'. See V Chhotray & D Hulme, 'Contrasting visions of aid and governance in the 21st century: the White House Millennium Challenge Account and the DFID's Drivers of Change', *World Development*, 37(1), 2009, p 40.
31 'A new governance: the European Commission needs to go one notch further', at http://challengeforeurope.blogactiv.eu, 11 June 2009, accessed 10 October 2009.
32 Interviews by the author, June 2009; and DAC, *Peer Review of the European Community*, p 64.
33 European Commission, *Commission Staff Working Paper Accompanying the Communication 'Governance in the European Consensus on Development: Towards a Harmonized Approach within the European Union'*, SEC(2006)1020, 30 August 2006.
34 M Fouwels, 'The European Union's Common Foreign and Security Policy and human rights', *Netherlands Quarterly of Human Rights*, 3, 1997, pp 291–324; and Hilpold, 'EU development cooperation at a crossroads'.
35 Council of the European Union, 2756th Council meeting, General Affairs and External Relations, Luxembourg, 16–17 October 2006, 13340/07 (Presse 265); and interviews by the author, May 2006.

36 Concord Cotonou Working Group, *Whose Governance?*, Brussels: Concord, June 2006; CIDSE, *Governance and Development Cooperation: Civil Society Perspectives on the European Union Approaches*, Brussels: CIDSE, nd.
37 Interviews by the author, May–June 2009.
38 European Commission, *An EU Aid Effectiveness Roadmap to Accra AND Beyond: From Rhetoric to Action, Hastening the Pace of Reforms*, SEC(2008)435; and European Commission, *Aid Effectiveness after Accra: Where Does the EU Stand and What More Do We Need to Do?*, SEC(2009)443, 8 April 2009.
39 Y Tandon, 'Southern discomfort', *Development + Cooperation*, 7–8, 2008, at http://www.inwent.org, accessed 10 October 2009; and R Bissio, *Paris Declaration on Aid Effectiveness*, Human Rights Council, Geneva, 7–15 January 2008. See also G Hyden, 'After the Paris Declaration: taking on the issue of power', *Development Policy Review*, 26(3), 2008, pp 259–274.
40 European Commission, *Supporting Democratic Governance through the Governance Initiative: A Review and the Way Forward*, Commission Staff Working Paper, SEC(2009)58, 19 January 2009; N Molenaers & L Nijs, *The Bumpy Road from Paris to Brussels: The European Commission Governance Initiative Tranche*, Discussion Paper 8, Antwerp: Institute for Development Policy and Management, 2008; Molenaers & Nijs, 'From the theory of aid effectiveness to the practice: the European Commission's Governance Incentive Tranche', *Development Policy Review*, 27(5), 2009, pp 561–580; and F Ceuppens, *EC Support to Governance is a 'Moving Target': Where do We Stand Regarding EU–Africa Relationships?*, ECDPM, September 2006.
41 S Meyer, *Governance Assessments and Domestic Accountability: Feeding Domestic Debate and Changing Aid Practices*, FRIDE Working Paper 86, June 2009. An interesting debate also occurred on the basis of a Dutch proposal for a more extensive use of budget support in the relations between the EU and the developing world. This proposal proved highly controversial and discussions were postponed as some member state governments found it difficult to justify it to their parliaments. Interviews by the author, June 2009.
42 European Commission, *Governance in the European Consensus*, p 20.
43 Arts & Dickson, *EU Development Cooperation*.
44 M Farrell, 'Internationalising EU development policy', *Perspectives on European Politics and Society*, 9(2), 2008, pp 225–240.
45 M Holland, 'The EU and the global development agenda', *Journal of European Integration*, 30(3), pp 343–362.

Is the EU's Governance 'Good'? An assessment of EU governance in its partnership with ACP states

NIKKI SLOCUM-BRADLEY & ANDREW BRADLEY

ABSTRACT *Distinguishing between '(good) governance' as a process and an outcome, this article examines both the processes and outcomes of governance in the context of the EU's relationship with ACP states since the adoption of the Cotonou Agreement. The article discusses and assesses a variety of governance mechanisms, including the European Commission's use of the governance concept, Economic Partnership Agreements, manifestations of partner preferences, the European Development Fund, the revision of the Cotonou Agreement, and Fisheries Partnership Agreements. Specific examples of the wielding of each mechanism are assessed based upon two criteria: the extent to which the wielding of the mechanism by the EU is a manifestation of 'good governance', and the extent to which the mechanisms have resulted, or are likely to result, in the sustainable development of and reduction of poverty in ACP countries. The examples are chosen to illustrate contradictions between rhetoric and practice and the consequential negative (actual and potential) impact upon development in ACP states. The article ends with some suggestions for improving the EU's governance processes and their outcomes for development.*

This article examines the forms of governance being promoted and exhibited by the EU[1] in its relationship with the African, Caribbean and Pacific (ACP) group of states within the framework of the Cotonou Agreement (2000–20). The article distinguishes between forms of governance promoted rhetorically versus those manifested in practice. The purpose of the comparison is a twofold evaluation. First, the article evaluates the extent to which the concept of 'good governance', as promoted by the EU, is applied by it within the context of its relationship with ACP states. Second, it assesses the extent to which governance strategies displayed by the EU promote sustainable development and the reduction of extreme poverty in ACP states. It is posited that, like most other donor agencies, the EU does not clearly articulate the objectives of its governance agenda, and acts in such a way that its processes of governance and their outcomes fail to fulfil the criteria for good governance that it sets for others.

The article first introduces the ACP group, and the EU bodies that are relevant to its relationship with ACP states. We then briefly discuss key concepts that structure the ACP–EU relationship, including governance, development, partnership and power. Next, various governance instruments employed by the EU in its relationship with the ACP states are identified. Examples of each instrument are discussed and assessed based upon two criteria: the extent to which the wielding of the mechanism by the EU is a manifestation of 'good governance', and the extent to which the EU's wielding of the mechanism has resulted, or is likely to result, in the sustainable development of and reduction of poverty in ACP countries. The final section summarises the assessment and offers recommendations for improving consistency between the governance that the EU applies in its relations with ACP states and the governance it alleges to promote through its development co-operation relations with them.

Actors and key concepts

The actors

The ACP group of states is constituted by 79 developing countries, all but one (Cuba) of which has signed the Cotonou Agreement, which officiates the relationship between the ACP group and the EU. The group's founding statute is the Georgetown Agreement (signed on 6 June 1975), and it has a permanent Secretariat, which is based in Brussels. The Summit of ACP Heads of State and Government is the supreme organ of the group, while the ACP Council of Ministers is the group's main decision-making body. The Council is assisted by a Brussels-based ACP Committee of Ambassadors in the execution of its tasks. The group is structured into six regions: the Caribbean, the Pacific, West Africa, Central Africa, East Africa and Southern Africa.[2]

The European Commission (EC) comprises a number of services that have a direct influence on ACP–EC relations, including 'DG [Directorate General] Development and Relations with African, Caribbean and Pacific States', responsible for development policy; 'DG External Cooperation Programmes' (EuropeAid), responsible for the implementation of development programmes and projects; 'DG Relex', responsible for external relations; 'DG Trade'; and 'ECHO', responsible for humanitarian aid. These services operate in a semi-autonomous fashion and have different interpretations of the objectives enshrined in the European Consensus on Development.[3] In addition, most of the 27 EU member states possess national development policies and instruments.

Governance

The word 'governance' derives from a Greek word that means 'to steer'. Academics from diverse disciplinary backgrounds have elaborated upon the 'steering' concept. Kooiman concurs with the work of Rosenau in defining governance as 'all those activities of social, political and administrative actors that can be seen as purposeful efforts to guide, steer, control or manage societies'.[4] Rosenau elaborates by saying that governance encompasses the activities of government as well as 'many other channels through which commands flow', and includes framing goals, issuing directives, pursuing policies and changing norms.[5] Smouts emphasises governance as a process that necessitates continual interaction and Finkelstein highlights the role of 'purposive actors' in this process.[6] Similarly, the definition of governance proposed by Mayntz as 'forms of collective regulation of social circumstances'[7] and that of Lange and Schimank as 'patterns of regulating interdependence'[8] highlight the mutual influence of all concerned actors in a holistic manner on each other in the direction of their affairs.

Within a policy context, in a Communication in 2003, the European Commission has described governance as 'the rules, processes, and behaviour by which interests are articulated, resources are managed, and power is exercised in society'. It further specifies that 'the way public functions are carried out, public resources are managed and public regulatory powers are exercised is the major issue to be addressed in that context', and that 'governance concerns the state's ability to serve the citizens'.[9]

The above definitions focus on governance as a process, leaving the goals and outcomes of these processes unspecified. In contrast, a definition of governance emanating from the World Bank directly incorporates development as a goal of governance and thereby stipulates not only what governance is as a process, but also what the *outcome* of the process should be. In defining governance as 'the manner in which power is exercised in the management of a country's economic and social resources for development', the World Bank explicitly makes a normative statement.[10] However, even when not made explicit, assertions about governance often carry a covert idea about what the ends of governance processes should be.

The 'good' in 'good governance'[11] has sometimes been employed as an adverb, to evaluate the process of governance; in other instances it is used as an adjective, to evaluate the outcomes of this process. For example, the United Nations Commission on Human Rights identifies the key attributes of 'good governance' as: transparency, responsibility, accountability, participation, and responsiveness (to the needs of the people). Thus, in this conception the normative evaluation 'good' addresses the *processes* of governance, not its outcomes. Orienting more toward the *outcomes* of governance, UN Resolution 2000/64 expressly links good governance to 'prompting growth and sustainable human development'.[12] Former UN Secretary-General Kofi Annan argued in 1997 that 'good governance and sustainable development are indivisible'.[13] Article 9.3 of the Cotonou Agreement defines good governance as:

> the transparent and accountable management of human, natural, economic and financial resources for the purpose of equitable and sustainable development. It entails clear decision-making procedures at the level of public authorities,

transparent and accountable institutions, the primacy of the rule of law in the management of resources and capacity building for elaborating and implementing measures aiming in particular at preventing and combating corruption.

Here, the evaluation 'good' captures both the process of governance ('management') and its (intended) outcome, which is specified as 'equitable and sustainable development'.

A lack of good governance might be called 'poor' or 'bad' governance. As with its counterpart, an unfavourable evaluation of governance can either describe the process or the outcomes of governance. Bad governance—or, more aptly, 'poorly governed'—can describe opaque (as opposed to transparent) management, a lack of clearly defined rules and procedures, or a failure to implement such rules and procedures (eg not being accountable to the defined rules and procedures). However, opacity and *ad hoc* decision making may or may not result in deprivation or lack of choice (outcomes).[14] On the other hand, 'bad' can evaluate the outcomes of governance and be understood as management of human, natural, economic and financial resources that contributes to or entrenches deprivation.

Development

The EU's theoretical understanding of the concept 'development' is captured in the European Consensus on Development that was adopted in 2006.[15] The Consensus is grounded on the principle of sustainable, equitable and participatory human and social development, and it emphasises the promotion of human rights, democracy, the rule of law and good governance. Similarly, the Cotonou Agreement underscores economic, social and cultural facets of development, which clearly concurs with a broad conception of human development that encompasses reducing 'deprivation' as well as broadening choice.[16]

As discussed in the introduction to this issue and in Carbone's contribution, governance is a concept that has come to play a very prominent role in discussions about sustainable development. Montagner discusses three ways in which the term governance has been used in the context of the EU's development politics. These include governance applied to the European space and to Community politics, (good) governance within partner countries of the EU, and governance at the heart of the 'organisational field' of civil society.[17] More recently some attention has been paid to 'aid governance', whereby donors have been under pressure to apply governance principles in the management of their aid to developing counties.[18] The present study is interested not only in the governance of aid, but in all aspects of governance within the context of the ACP–EU 'partnership'.

Partnership and power

According to Webster's unabridged encyclopaedic dictionary, a 'partnership' is 'the state or condition of being a partner; participation; association; joint interest'. The partnership principle has been introduced in the context of contemporary development co-operation to suggest an evolution from the traditional vertical relation between the donor and recipient to a relationship characterised by co-operation between equals. For example, in describing 'good governance', UN Resolution 2000/64 recognises 'the value of partnership approaches to development cooperation and the inappropriateness of prescriptive approaches'.[19]

On 23 June 2000, in Cotonou, the EU signed a Partnership Agreement with the ACP group of states. The so-called Cotonou Agreement was heralded as the 'most advanced and comprehensive development cooperation agreement between the North and the South' by the then EU Commissioner for Development and Humanitarian Aid, Mr Poul Nielson, who also specified that 'partnership goes hand-in-hand with ownership and mutual confidence'.[20] In addition, at the second EU–Africa Summit in 2007, an Africa–EU Strategic Partnership was endorsed to formalise a partnership based on the principles of equality, partnership and ownership to guide future co-operation.[21] As suggested in the definition, a partnership is generally not an end in itself, but a means to achieve common objectives. The objectives of the ACP–EU partnership, as stipulated in the Cotonou Agreement (Part I, Title I, Chapter I, Article 1), are:

> to promote and expedite the economic, cultural and social development of the ACP States, with a view to contributing to peace and security and to promoting a stable and democratic political environment. The partnership shall be centred on the objective of reducing and eventually eradicating poverty consistent with the objectives of sustainable development and the gradual integration of the ACP countries into the world economy.

In studying governance, Yanakopoulos argues the importance of studying the actors, their relationships and the quality of these relationships, emphasising the role of power asymmetries in relationships between actors. Yanakopoulos and other authors have particularly underscored the power asymmetries between the 'North' and 'South'. A BOND briefing paper argues that, although 'donors prefer to focus the governance lens more narrowly within the confines of recipient countries, this distorts understanding of the ways in which global power structures impact on national politics'.[22] The power differential between donor and developing countries in turn influences development, as noted by Birdsall, who writes that 'the powerful make and implement the rules, as the limited access of developing countries to certain rich-country markets suggest[s].'[23] As global power structures have an important impact on ACP national and regional politics, an understanding of governance processes and outcomes can only be gained by considering these power structures.

Power asymmetries infiltrate all aspects of the ACP–EU partnership, including provisions designed to govern the relationship. An examination of the use of one of the provisions for political dialogue between the ACP and the EU illuminates the actual—in contrast to the rhetorical—distribution of power. In its Communication on Governance and Development, the

European Commission has discussed the modalities in the Cotonou Agreement that provide for 'consultation procedures' within the context of 'policy dialogue', which is seen as a key element of good governance. The Communication refers to Article 9 of the Agreement, which specifies that respect for human rights, democratic principles and the rule of law constitute 'essential elements' of the partnership and that good governance is its 'fundamental element'.[24] Article 96, paragraph 27 of the Agreement:

> foresees that in cases of violation of one of [the] essential elements one party can invite the other party to hold consultations...Consultations under Article 96 aim at examining the situation with a view to finding a solution acceptable to both parties. If no solution is found, or in emergency cases, or if one party refuses the consultations, appropriate measures can be taken.

Although this provision is phrased to allow either party to invoke it, only the EU has ever done so, reflecting the division of power within the relationship. All 14 cases to date in which consultations were undertaken in accordance with Article 96 were subsequent to alleged violations by ACP states. The manner in which these consultations have been conducted, and the imposition of commitments on the country in question, have led ACP Heads of State and Government to include in ACP Summit Declarations an appeal to the EU to avoid recourse to unilateral measures.[25] Despite many apparent violations that could be framed under Articles 96 and 97 of the Cotonou Agreement, the ACP group has never called the EU for consultations. Examples include the violation of the human rights of ACP immigrants in EU member states,[26] the shipping of toxic waste on EU registered ships, and cases of fraud and corruption at EU institutions and in EU member states. It could be argued that the provision to allow either of the parties to the Cotonou Agreement to call for consultations is in fact misleading, since the ACP group does not have the means to impose 'appropriate measures' as defined in Article 96.

The imbalance of power between the partners trickles down to many other manifestations, including the extent to which joint 'fact finding missions' are deployed to political 'hot spots' by the ACP–EU Joint Parliamentary Assembly. The EU can use development aid, trade preferences and other 'carrots' to push its agenda and interests, and the (threat of) withdrawal of these as 'sticks'. The ability to distribute these resources affords the EU with a considerable degree of 'power', and the exercise of that power is governance, in accordance with the European Commission definition cited above.[27] While access to resources gives the possessor *potential* power, it can also be argued that aid-recipient countries grant the EU this power by allowing the resources that the EU has at its disposal to be used as leverage. If aid recipients were to decline the aid, either categorically or under specific circumstances, these elements of 'power' would dissipate. In other words, it is the recipients' desire for these resources, and willingness to be manipulated in order to access them, that turns the potential power into real power.

Governance mechanisms and governance assessments

Distinguishing governance as a purposive activity from governance as an explanatory tool (for example to explain development policy failures), Yanakopoulos has investigated the mechanisms through which governance as a purposive activity occurs.[28] In this section we examine governance mechanisms used by the EU in the context of its relationship with the ACP group. According to the Cotonou Agreement and other policy papers, in its relations with ACP states the EU employs, *inter alia*, the following instruments to promote good governance in development co-operation: conditionalities,[29] 'additional support' for results-oriented reforms, incentives, and 'appropriate measures' (sanctions) as specified in Articles 96 and 97 of the Cotonou Agreement. However, it can be argued that EU governance is manifested through additional practices, which include the determination of priority areas and recipients to benefit from financial assistance; negotiation strategies, such as stipulations for the configuration of negotiation partners and linking financial perspectives with certain policy orientations; the identification of interlocutors as development partners; trade and commercial practices within development co-operation, such as Economic Partnership Agreements (EPAs); Fisheries Partnership Agreements (FPAs) and subsidies; and the design of other policies that influence the ACP–EU relationship.[30]

This section examines a variety of EU instruments and practices that are in fact governance mechanisms. These mechanisms are assessed with regard to 1) whether the way in which they are wielded exemplifies 'good governance' as a process; and 2) whether these processes have resulted or are likely to result in 'good governance' as an outcome, in particular sustainable development and poverty reduction. The examples presented here are chosen for their capacity to illustrate contradictions and undesirable consequences. Thus we critically highlight examples of bad governance rather than offering a representative sample of governance mechanisms and their use.

Wielding the 'governance' concept

The first mechanism we examine is use of the concept of '(good) governance'. Adding adjectives such as 'bad' or 'good' to governance, and specifying a desired outcome of governance processes, such as sustainable development, makes more explicit the normative aspect inherent to the concept's use. However, whether or not certain outcomes of governance processes are included explicitly or only presumed implicitly when the concept is employed, it has been argued that the mere use of the concept has been an act of governance. For instance, Campbell argues that 'the notion of governance as proposed by the multilateral financial institutions entails a particular concept of the state, of its role, of its desirable evolution, of state–market relations, of the exercise of power and of a particular political project.'[31] Campbell accuses such institutions of lacking transparency in their use of the concept of governance because they obscure its 'political' dimension in portraying it as merely technical.

Various authors have argued that the EU has imposed its own models for governing and other priorities under the rubric of promoting 'good governance'.[32] This is evident in the EU's Governance Initiative for ACP states and the associated 'governance incentive tranche',[33] developed in 2007. Based upon the EU's assessment of countries' 'governance profiles' (see the introduction to this special issue for a discussion of this mechanism), countries are encouraged to provide 'relevant, ambitious and credible commitments to reform' in their 'Governance Action Plans' (GAPs).[34] The amount of the 'incentive tranche' is unilaterally determined by the European Commission, and this 'additional support' is utilised to effect the reforms stipulated in the GAP. Thus the 'governance incentive tranche', for which €2.7 billion was allocated under the 10th European Development Fund (EDF) (2008–13), and the procedure through which it is allocated manifest a kind of *ex-ante* rather than *ex-post* conditionality. BOND argues that:

> although not presented in this way, [governance criteria and] assessment mechanisms involve political processes driven by donor government interests. They lack transparency and fail to explicitly acknowledge the value-laden assumptions, and their selective application, regarding models of 'good governance'. In this regard, they mark a regressive shift away from the more explicit focus and at least policy level commitment to quality assurance of process and not product. The use of 'governance' assessments, either to justify or hold back development assistance is inherently 'anti-developmental' and undermines good governance.[35]

The EU's use of the good governance concept is exemplified in its failure to distinguish between 'good' and 'democratic' governance and by the elements subsumed under these rubrics. In various Commission documents the terms 'good' and 'democratic' governance are used interchangeably.[36] For example, its Communication on Governance states that '*good* governance, though a complementary objective, is basically a means towards the ends represented by poverty reduction and the other MDGs'. The document specifies that aspects of '*democratic* governance' include:

> the affirmation of the rights of citizens on the road to sustainable development and respect of human rights and fundamental freedoms (including freedom of expression, information and association); support for democratisation processes and the involvement of citizens in choosing and overseeing those who govern them; respect for the rule of law and access for all to an independent justice system; access to information; a government that governs transparently and is accountable to the relevant institutions and to the electorate; human security; management of migration flows; effective institutions, access to basic social services, sustainable management of natural and energy resources and of the environment, and the promotion of sustainable economic growth and social cohesion in a climate conducive to private investment.[37]

The failure to distinguish between 'good' and 'democratic' allows one issue to be guised in the rubric of another. For example, it can be argued that 'access to basic social services' and 'management of migration flows' have nothing to do with '*democratic* governance' but have a lot to do with '*good* governance'. Ironically, an earlier Commission Communication clearly makes this distinction by stating that 'governance concerns the state's ability to serve the citizens. Such a broad approach allows conceptually to disaggregate governance and other topics such as human rights, democracy or corruption.'[38]

By framing a laundry list of its own priorities as aspects of 'good governance', and designing mechanisms purportedly to evaluate countries' achievements at attaining this 'goodness', the EU attempts to establish a particular set of social norms and conventions to guide the decisions and actions of its developing partners. In concurrence, BOND points out that:

> some of the indicators in the 'governance profiles' have little to do with a government's ability to act in the interests of the country's citizens and of poverty eradication, and are more to do with EU interests—for example what the EU thinks the government should do to stem migration, or to create an 'investment-friendly' climate.[39]

Various NGOs have noted the divergence between the governance priorities outlined by the EU and the priorities expressed by NGOs in aid-recipient countries.[40] Concord cites an example of a case in which the EU imposed its priorities over those of an aid-recipient country under the auspices of promoting 'good governance':

> In Zambia, the government has chosen to prioritise Health and Education as priority sectors for EC Aid. But the EU has rejected these priorities while imposing unclear and dubious priorities such as governance and competitiveness. By doing so, Brussels clearly disrespects Zambia's sovereignty. It is particularly severe as it concerns a country, like others in the Southern Africa region, which is highly hit by HIV/AIDS, that is destroying its fragile basic social system.[41]

Ironically, CIDSE has also argued that even the Commission's process of defining and setting the criteria for 'governance' has failed to adhere to its own criteria for good governance. Although the issues paper released by the European Commission claims that its approach is process-oriented, broad, inclusive and in particular facilitates civil society participation, CIDSE sees 'grave contradictions between the Commission's definition and principles of governance and its own actions in this field'.[42]

Hidden under the guise of the rubrics 'good governance' and 'incentives', the EU continues to coerce development partners to follow EU positions and policies. Contrary to the criterion of good governance as a process, this practice lacks transparency and results in a lack of ownership among the countries targeted by the policies. Furthermore, the outcome of this governance may also be less than 'good', since priorities are set that are not necessarily in the best interest of the developing country, as exemplified in the case of Zambia.

Economic Partnership Agreements

The Cotonou Agreement stipulates that EPAs will be negotiated in order to better integrate the ACP states into the global economy, to promote sustainable development and to eradicate poverty in these countries.[43] Both the content of these agreements—which were still being negotiated when this article was penned—as well as the process of negotiations can be seen as mechanisms of governance.

The EPA negotiation process was to a great extent stipulated by the EU, by some accounts against the will—and interests—of the ACP states. First, the EU stipulated that EPAs were to be concluded not with the ACP group as a whole, but with six regions within the group. Furthermore, no country could negotiate within more than one region. Since some countries in Africa are members of more than one regional organisation, they were forced to choose between these groupings. The resulting negotiating groups coincide neither with the six regions of the ACP group, nor with the membership patterns of the regional organisations. In other words, new regional groupings were formed on the basis of countries' interests for the purpose of negotiating EPAs with the EU. The ACP group has expressed concern that pre-existing regional integration processes have been stalled as a result of the focus placed upon the new alignments for EPA negotiations—in spite of the fact that supporting *existing* regional integration efforts is allegedly the main goal of these agreements.[44] Bilal and Stevens have underscored the dangers to African regional integration efforts posed by the signing of 'interim' EPAs by some, but not all, members of the African negotiating groups, which precisely described the state of affairs when this article went to press. These authors describe one of the challenges that EPAs pose for African regional integration:

> A common perception, expressed by many countries, is that there is little coherence between the EPA agenda and the regional integration processes in Africa. One particular concern has been that countries in the same economic region might liberalise different baskets of products and so create new barriers to intra-regional trade in order to avoid trade deflection. This concern has been vindicated by the interim EPAs that have been agreed.[45]

Thus, the EU's stipulations for negotiations and the content of interim EPAs have affected the geopolitical structure of African regions of the ACP group and threatened existing regional integration processes.

By insisting on moving negotiations to the regional level, the EU finessed the possibility of more concerted action on behalf of the group as an entity.[46] The regional negotiating groups are smaller and thus have less power to negotiate an agreement that favours the interest of the developing countries. Because of the EU's relative power and ability to assert its will, the developmental consequences of the still incomplete results of the regional negotiations have been a matter of great concern. In its 2009 Resolution the ACP Council of Ministers underscored 'the absence of a comprehensive development oriented EPA'.[47] We now turn to examine the potential of the

EPAs for promoting sustainable development and reducing poverty in ACP countries.

The nature of EPAs, whereby the EU and ACP regions are supposed to open their markets to each other in a reciprocal fashion, has been underscored as problematic by various development-oriented committees and organisations.[48] NGOs and the European Parliament's development committee have emphasised the need for additional funds to assist developing countries to adjust to the competition induced through market openness. Even European Commissioner for Trade, Peter Mandelson, has stated that 'trade will not promote development without parallel investment in the supply side'.[49] Mandelson's acknowledgement is sustained and elaborated by scholars who argue that market openness can contribute to within-country inequality, so 'integration with the global economy is not a substitute for an anti-poverty strategy'.[50] Prerequisites for countries to benefit from globalisation-induced growth are internal patterns of growth, and specialisation and forms of integration. Without these factors in place, 'many low-income countries could be locked in an international poverty trap through integration'.[51]

In spite of the widespread recognition that developing countries must first make various adjustments before they have the potential to benefit from opening their markets, in the content of the interim EPAs, 'no clear pattern can be identified that the poorer countries have longer to adjust than the richer ones or of the EPAs being tailored to development needs (however defined)'.[52] In their assessment of the interim agreements, Bilal and Stevens conclude that:

> the picture that emerges is entirely consistent with the hypothesis that countries have a deal that reflects their negotiating skills and the EU's interest: that countries able to negotiate hard, knowing their interests (which were not incompatible with those of the European Commission) have obtained a better deal than those lacking these characteristics.[53]

Furthermore, the Commission has refused requests for additional funding for adjustment programmes that would allow the developing countries to take advantage of opportunities created through EPAs. For example, a letter signed by the Commission's Deputy Director for Trade, Karl Falkenberg, and the Director General for Development and Relations with African, Caribbean and Pacific States, Stefano Manservisi, rejected the Pacific region's proposal that certain concessions on market access on their part be compensated by the EU with additional funding for adjustment costs.[54] Even though the Commission has repeatedly argued that adjustment funding would be provided through the EDF rather than the EPAs, the 10th EDF has not allocated any additional funds for EPA-related adjustment costs. Bilal and Stevens have argued that, 'in terms of predictable levels available for the years to come, one thing is clear: the EDF cannot be the only source of AFT [Aid for Trade]'.[55] Oxfam International has concluded that, 'without funding for adjustment, an EPA cannot hope to provide a developmentally supportive framework in countries with limited capacities and resources'.[56] Thus, as matters currently stand, EPAs are more likely to entrench rather than reduce poverty.

Partner preferences

While the EU is attempting to consolidate itself as a unified actor on the global stage (see Carbone's contribution in this issue), some of its actions have contributed to the fragmentation and deconstruction of the ACP Group.[57] In its dealings with the ACP countries the Commission has in recent years shown various signs of withdrawing from the group as an interlocutor. It has designed separate strategy papers for its relations with the Caribbean, the Pacific, South Africa and 'Africa', and it later elaborated a 'joint strategy' with the latter.[58] Seemingly in contradiction of the Commission's rationale for the latter strategy—that is, to have one common strategy for Africa—the Commission has separate strategies for South Africa and for several northern African countries, which are addressed in the European Neighbourhood Policy (ENP).[59] In a further manifestation of disfavour for the ACP group, the former European Commissioner for Development and Humanitarian Aid, Louis Michel, publicly expressed a preference for working with the regions. The Commission has granted high levels of support, financial and otherwise, to the African Union, often with only the reluctant and *post hoc* approval of the ACP group. These actions undermine the ACP group and empower the actors favoured by the Commission. This form of EU governance has a direct impact on the kinds of actors that are empowered to act on behalf of ACP interests and on development. One possibility is that this process will result in dissolution of the ACP group as such. If this is the case, the full weight of the group will be lost and developing countries will need to defend their interests in negotiations with the EU using smaller groupings. This could result in less advantageous outcomes for sustainable development and poverty reduction in developing countries.[60]

The European Development Fund

The EDF is the main instrument for providing EU aid for development in ACP states, to be distributed as stipulated in country and regional strategies.[61] In accordance with the Cotonou Agreement, 'ACP States and Regions shall determine the development strategies for their economies and societies in all sovereignty'.[62] In practice, negotiations over the setting of development priorities in ACP countries and regions take place in an environment of 'trade-offs' between the aid recipients and the EU. The result of these negotiations is that the EU's external priorities and commitments are pursued, while the ACP group plays a minor role in the programming of EU financial resources. The EU's ability to impose its agenda on ACP states and regions reflects the inequality of the partnership and the imbalance of power; the fact that it does so contradicts the Cotonou Agreement stipulation that development strategies shall be determined 'in all sovereignty' by the regions and countries concerned. This contradiction reflects not only a lack of transparency in the agenda-setting process but also means that the EU is left entirely unaccountable for the consequences thereof. Both transparency and accountability are key aspects of good governance, as characterised by the EU itself. Furthermore, contrary to the ownership criterion of good governance, Bilal and Stevens conclude that 'EU donors' procedures and practices are not conducive to full ownership'.[63]

Revision of the Cotonou Agreement

The EU's imposition of its agenda, and the inequality and power imbalance in the ACP–EU partnership, were also made glaringly evident during the negotiations on the 2005 revision of the Cotonou Agreement. The negotiations reached an impasse with the EU's insistence on including an article on 'cooperation in countering the proliferation of weapons of mass destruction', and its reluctance to provide details on the next multi-annual financial framework for the period 2008–13.[64] To unblock the impasse, the EU negotiators offered the ACP Council of Ministers a so-called 'package deal', whereby a multi-annual financial framework would be provided on condition that the ACP group accept the inclusion of the proposed article. Thanks to the consequent inclusion of the article, ACP countries are now further burdened with border-control responsibilities, in order to prevent weapons trafficking, but they have been allocated no additional resources to cover the high cost of these imposed duties. Consequently, in order to cover the costs of this EU priority, funds must be diverted from other 'development' priorities. Neither the negotiation process, nor the foreseeable outcomes for sustainable development bear the marks of good governance.

Fisheries Partnership Agreements

The report of a fact-finding mission undertaken by a delegation of the ACP–EU Joint Parliamentary Assembly to the Seychelles during April 2008 states that, during the mission, certain issues were raised in relation to the FPA between the Seychelles and the EU.[65] Non-state actors complained of little EU involvement in the implementation of this Agreement. In particular, they claimed that Seychellois seamen serving on EU registered vessels did not receive the full wage they were entitled to under the FPA, and they pointed out that the EU had been paying the same licensing fee for tuna for some 30 years, despite much higher market prices in recent years. They also claimed that EU sanitary and phyto-sanitary rules were inconsistent or applied in an arbitrary manner.[66] Furthermore, there is evidence that EU fishing vessels have vastly underreported, and thus not fully paid for, their catches. The EU's failure to implement consistent standards and rules, as well as its dictation of how remuneration is to be spent, are characteristic of poor governance processes. Its failure to pay fair wages to citizens of developing countries, to pay fair licensing fees, and to enforce honest reporting and payments by its vessels starkly detract from the good governance goal of poverty reduction. Finally, contrary to the principle of ownership, Seychellois authorities have argued that the FPA dictates how their government is to utilise the remuneration the EU pays under the Agreement.[67] These practices are likely to have a detrimental impact on sustainable development.

ACP–EU relations on fishing are currently governed by 'bilateral' agreements between the Commission and individual ACP states. According to the report of the Joint Parliamentary Assembly, the Seychelles and surrounding countries requested the Commission to consider a regional fisheries agreement, but this was turned down.[68] The Commission also rejected repeated requests from the Pacific for a regional fisheries agreement. According to Oxfam International, 'the EU's pursuit of bilateral fisheries agreements is inconsistent with their state [sic] aim of promoting regional cooperation in the Pacific and tends to divide the Pacific over the benefits from one of the region's key resources'.[69]

The regional contention resulting from the bilateral agreements poses a threat not only to co-operation, integration and political stability in the region but also to long-term, sustainable economic development. Failure to solidify a regional approach to manage such important finite resources could easily lead to every country grabbing—or selling the rights to grab—as much as they can while the supply lasts. This would quickly result in a complete depletion of the fish population, which would have a devastating effect on the Pacific economy, way of life, and the health of its people. Already, as a result of the FPAs, the strong presence of EU fishing boats has rendered local fishing companies unable to compete. Labourers from ACP countries have lost their jobs in the local fishing industries and have thus been forced to migrate—often without legal documentation—to look for other work.

Concluding discussion

The EU has considerable resources at its disposal that reflect the significant power differential between it and the ACP group. It wields a variety of mechanisms to govern these resources in its relationship with ACP states. By illuminating a few of these mechanisms this article has endeavoured to shed some light on these governance processes and their outcomes. There is considerable evidence that some policies pursued by the EU are not conducive to the promotion of sustainable development, the alleviation of poverty, and the gradual integration of ACP states into the world economy. The EU has abused its power advantage to impose its political will and economic agenda. The processes which the EU, and especially the Commission, has used to steer the members of the ACP group towards compliance with its own interests and agendas are far from transparent. The opaque nature of these processes, and the fact that they leave the EU entirely unaccountable for their consequences, are trademarks of processes of bad governance.

The EU is not managing its relations with the ACP group in accordance with its vows to respect ACP sovereignty and promote ownership of adopted policies and practices. A genuine partnership between the EU and the ACP group must be based on a jointly developed, structured co-operation framework that sets out the responsibilities of both sides, includes regular and transparent dialogue, and allows the developing countries to take the lead in the formulation of their own development strategies. All provisions of the Cotonou Agreement should be regarded as subordinate to the key objectives of the Agreement, including 'appropriate measures', conditionalities, and—perhaps more importantly—how these are determined.

As a result of some of the current realities of political and social power dynamics in some African countries, which Taylor (in this issue) has illuminated, one cannot advocate simply writing a blank check to developing country governments. On the other hand, the EU's 'paternalistic' claims (see Carbone, this issue) that it should stipulate how aid is used because it knows what is best for the aid recipients must be grounded in evidence. Evidence provided in this paper demonstrates that the governance outcomes do not justify the governance means employed by the EU. While the EU governance processes discussed have been marked by coercion, the outcomes bode ill for sustainable development in ACP countries. Policies that support sustainable development include paying fair wages and fees for services rendered, applying standards fairly, and resisting the temptation to exploit resources that sustain ACP economies and ways of life. By contrast, on various accounts the EU has promoted policies and engaged in practices that have contributed to further deprivation in ACP states and regions.

Interference in ACP development agendas is only justified when it can be shown that their implementation would not serve the ACP peoples. When this is the case, or if ACP countries fall short of expectations, rather than imposing duties upon the ACP group that it is ill-suited to fulfil, the EU should first provide the group with the means for capacity building and institutional support that will allow for the development of a capable, credible and respected partner.

What else can be done to promote the gradual integration of ACP states into the global economy? According to Nissanke and Thorbecke, 'whether global market forces establish a virtuous circle or a vicious circle depends on the initial conditions at the time of exposure and the effective design and implementation of policies to manage the integration process'.[70] Consequently these authors advocate the constitution of global governance structures that promote development. Birdsall also claims that 'the global economy needs the civilising hand of appropriate intervention', which she argues must include more transfers from rich to poor countries, more active management of global problems such as money laundering, tax evasion, sovereign bankruptcy, capital flight, global health and environmental issues, and a 'global social contract'.[71] In order to support the integration of ACP countries into the global economy in a way that promotes sustainable development and poverty reduction, the EU should first ensure that global governance structures are in place that can competently manage the integration process. To support the creation of, and provide resources for, competent, transparent and accountable global structures would be acts of good governance.

To a certain extent, the ACP group elevates the Commission to its relatively powerful position by failing to act in a collective fashion in order to condense and wield potential power of its own. The group does have potential carrots and sticks at its disposal. For example, collectively ACP states have attractive natural resources and vast markets, access to which is desired not only by the EU but also others (such as China and the USA). Furthermore, the collective voice of 79 developing countries, plus the support of development-friendly NGOs and other benefactors, could exert a considerable amount of normative pressure. They might begin with a critique of the Commission's wielding of governance mechanisms.

Since the Commission's power leverage largely derives from its command of the EDF, changes in how this fund is governed could make the system less prone to the abuse of power. While the EDF is funded by voluntary contributions from EU member states, it is managed by the Commission. Notwithstanding the at least rhetorical stipulation that funding decisions be made in consultation with the ACP group, the Commission currently has sole decision-making powers over the disbursement of the EDF. As it is a separate instrument from the EU general budget, the European Parliament has no oversight over the Commission's management of the EDF. EU member states and the Parliament generally act as checks and balances to the Commission, and they have frequently critiqued the Commission's actions in relations with developing countries. Thus, a system of development aid and co-operation that has these checks and balances in place might prove more adept at engaging in well governed and development-conducive partnerships. A partner that manifests the criteria of good governance in its relationships, especially in those with weaker counterparts, will also be better positioned to advocate good governance.

Notes

The views expressed in this paper are those of the authors. They do not necessarily reflect the views of the UN, UNU, UNU–CRIS or the ACP group of states.

1 Unless otherwise stated, the acronym EU will be used throughout the remainder of the paper, also when referring to the earlier European Economic Community (EEC) and the present European Community (EC).
2 A Bradley, 'The role and relevance of traditional organizations/groups in the international environment are being challenged by the emergence of new groupings and alliances: a study of the African, Caribbean and Pacific Group of States (ACP group)', unpublished dissertation, Free University, Brussels, 2004.
3 ECDPM & ActionAid, *Whither EC Aid?*, Discussion note, 2007, at http://weca.files.wordpress.com/2008/01/weca-initial-discussion-note-22jan07.pdf, accessed 12 November 2009.
4 J Kooiman, *Modern Governance*, London: Sage, 1993, p 2. Cf J Rosenau, *Governance without Government: Order and Change in World Politics*, Cambridge: Cambridge University Press, 1992.
5 J Rosenau, 'Governance in the twenty-first century', *Global Governance*, 1(1), 1995, p 14.
6 MC Smouts, 'The proper use of governance in international relations', *International Social Science Journal*, 50(155), 1998; and LS Finkelstein, 'What is global governance?', *Global Governance*, 1(1), 1995, p 368.

7 As quoted in A Draude, *Wer regiert wie? Für eine äquivalenzfunktionalistische Beobachtung von Governance in Räumen begrenzter Staatlichkeit*, SFB-Governance Working Paper, No 2, January 2007, p 4, at http://www.sfb-governance.de/publikationen/sfbgov_wp/wp2/sfbgov_wp2.pdf, accessed 12 November 2009 (authors' translation from German). In original: 'aller nebeneinander bestehenden Formen der kollektiven Regelung gesellschaftlicher Sachverhalte'.
8 As quoted in A Draude, *Wer regiert wie?*, p 6 (authors' translation from German). In original: 'Muster der Interdependenzbewältigung'.
9 European Commission, *Governance and Development*, Communication from the Commission to the Council, the European Parliament and the European Economic and Social Committee, COM(2003)615, 20 October 2003, para 4.
10 World Bank, *Governance and Development*, Washington, DC: World Bank, 1992, p 1.
11 See Carbone's article in this issue for a more extensive history of the term's use in development co-operation.
12 UNHCHR, *Good Governance—Human Rights in Development*, at http://www2.ohchr.org/english/issues/development/governance/, accessed 12 November 2009.
13 K Annan, *Inaugural Address*, International Conference on Governance for Sustainable Growth and Equity, New York: United Nations, 28–30 July 1997, at http://mirror.undp.org/magnet/icg97/ANNAN.HTM, accessed 12 November 2009.
14 See AK Sen, *Development as Freedom*, New York: Knopf, 1999; EW Nafziger, 'From Seers to Sen: the meaning of economic development', UNU-WIDER Research Paper No. 2006/20, February 2006, available at http://website1.wider.unu.edu/publications/rps/rps2006/rp2006-20.pdf; and E Thorbecke, 'The evolution of the development doctrine, 1950–2005', in G Mavrotas & Shorrocks (eds), *Advancing Development: Core Themes in Global Economics*, New York: Palgrave Macmillan, 2007, pp 50–62, 3–36.
15 European Commission, *Governance in the European Consensus on Development: Towards a Harmonised Approach within the European Union*, Communication from the Commission to the Council, the European Parliament, the European Economic and Social Committee and the Committee of the Regions, COM(2006) 421 final, 30 August 2006. In his contribution to this issue, Carbone discusses this document and the history of the EC's use of the development concept.
16 Ibid.
17 M Montagner, *De l'usage du concept de gouvernance dans les politiques de développement: note de synthèse du dossier*, at http://www.institut-gouvernance.org/en/analyse/fiche-analyse-253.html, accessed 12 November 2009.
18 F Ceuppens, *EC Support to Governance is a 'Moving Target': Where do We Stand Regarding EU–Africa relationships?*, at http://europafrica.net/2006/10/14/ec-support-to-governance-is-a-%E2%80%9Cmoving-target%E2%80%9D-where-do-we-stand-regarding-eu-africa-relationships, accessed 12 November 2009.
19 UNHCHR, *Good Governance—Human Rights in Development*.
20 Quoted in theTrumpet.com, at http://www.thetrumpet.com/index.php?q=1263.0.35.0, accessed 12 November 2009.
21 African Union, *The Africa–EU Strategic Partnership: A Joint Africa–EU Strategy*, Adopted by the Lisbon Summit, 9 December 2007; and African Union, *First Action Plan (2008–2010) for the Implementation of the Africa–EU Strategic Partnership*, Final, as endorsed by the Africa–EU Ministerial Troika, Accra, 31 October 2007.
22 H Yanakopoulos, 'The rise of trans-national coalitions of NGOs', *Global Society*, 19(3), 2005, p 2.
23 N Birdsall, 'Stormy days on an open field: asymmetries in the global economy', in Mavrotas & Shorrocks, *Advancing Development*, p 242.
24 European Commission, *Governance and Development*. See also Carbone, this issue.
25 At the third, fourth and fifth summits of ACP Heads of State and Government, held in 2002, 2004 and 2006.
26 For a critical report on EU treatment of ACP migrants, see ACP–EU JPA Bureau, *Draft Report on the Joint Mission of the JPA to Malta and the Canary Islands (Spain) 29 October to 3 November 2006*, Brussels, 15 February 2007.
27 European Commission, *Governance and Development*.
28 Yanacopulos, 'The rise of trans-national coalitions of NGOs'.
29 While the Cotonou Agreement refers to 'conditionalities', later policy documents declare an attempt to move away from their use.
30 For example, policy changes outlined in the Lisbon Treaty are likely to significantly influence the EU's relationship with the ACP group.
31 B Campbell, 'Aid governance and transparency: essential preconditions or new conditionality? And on whose development agenda?' paper presented to the 821st Wilton Park Conference on 'Scaling Up and Absorbing Resources: Challenges for Poverty Eradication', 25–28 October 2006, at http://www.er.uqam.ca/nobel/ieim/IMG/pdf/BCampbell_CEMLP_Aid_Governance_and_Transparency_2006_1028.pdf, accessed 12 November 2009.

32 Montagner, *De l'usage du concept de gouvernance dans les politiques de développement*.
33 The tranche is allocated and disbursed as 'additional resources' to the initial country allocation. See European Commission, *Supporting Democratic Governance through the Governance Initiative: A Review and the Way Forward*, Commission Staff Working Paper SEC(2009)58 final, Brussels, 2009. Assessments of the use of the tranche are given in N Molenaers & L Nijs, 'From the theory of aid effectiveness to the practice: the European Commission's Governance Incentive Tranche', *Development Policy Review*, 27(5), pp 561–580; and in Carbone's contribution to this issue.
34 European Commission, *Supporting Democratic Governance*, p 6.
35 BOND, *Governance: Who Sets the Agenda? The European Commission Communication on Governance in the European Consensus on Development*, Briefing Paper, October 2006, available at www.bond.org.
36 European Commission, *Supporting Democratic Governance*, pp 3–4; and EC, *Governance in the European Consensus on Development*.
37 European Commission, *Governance in the European Consensus on Development*, section 1.1.
38 European Commission, *Governance and Development*, section 1.4.
39 BOND, *Governance*.
40 CIDSE, *Governance and Development Cooperation: Civil Society Perspectives on the European Union Approach*, CIDSE Background Paper, August 2006, available at www.cidse.org.
41 Concord, *Governance*, Concord Cotonou Working Group Briefing Paper, ACP–EU Joint Parliamentary Assembly, Kigali (Rwanda), 17–22 November 2007.
42 CIDSE, *Governance and Development Cooperation*, p 3. See also Carbone, this issue, for a discussion of CIDSE's critique.
43 The Cotonou Agreement stipulates that the parties would conclude new World Trade Organization (WTO)-compatible trading arrangements by 2008. EPAs were meant to be free trade agreements that would end the non-reciprocal and preferential trading arrangements between the EU and ACP states, which are incompatible with WTO rules.
44 ACP Secretariat, *Resolution on Economic Partnership Agreements (EPAs) of the 89th Session of the ACP Council of Ministers, held in Brussels, Belgium from 25–27 May 2009*, Ref ACP/25/008/09 (final version), Brussels, 2009.
45 S Bilal & C Stevens (eds), *The Interim Economic Partnership Agreements between the EU and African States: Contents, Challenges and Prospects*, ECDPM Policy Management Report 17, Maastricht: ECDPM, 2009, p 4, at http://www.ecdpm.org/Web_ECDPM/Web/Content/Download.nsf/0/B6CB574AC6DA08AAC125760400322BDE/$FILE/pmr17-def.pdf, accessed 12 November 2009.
46 N Slocum-Bradley, 'Constructing and de-constructing the ACP group: actors, strategies and consequences for development', *Geopolitics*, 12(4), 2007, pp 635–655.
47 ACP Secretariat, *Resolution on Economic Partnership Agreements*, pp 1, 2, 4.
48 For example Oxfam International, *Slamming the Door on Development: Analysis of the EU's Response to the Pacific's EPA Negotiating Proposals*, Oxfam Background Paper, December 2006.
49 P Mandelson, *Trade at the Service of Development*, Lecture at the London School of Economics, 4 February 2005, p 10, at http://www2.lse.ac.uk/PublicEvents/pdf/20050204-Mandelson.pdf, accessed 12 November 2009.
50 M Nissanke & E Thorbecke, 'A quest for pro-poor globalization', in Mavrotas & Shorrocks, *Advancing Development*, p 258. Cf Birdsall, 'Stormy days on an open field'.
51 UNCTAD, *The Least Developed Countries Report 2002: Escaping the Poverty Trap*, Geneva: UNCTAD, 2002, p 265.
52 Bilal & Stevens, *The Interim Economic Partnership Agreements between the EU and African Sates*, p 3.
53 Ibid, p 4.
54 Oxfam International, *Slamming the Door on Development*.
55 Bilal & Stevens, *The Interim Economic Partnership Agreements between the EU and African States*, p 225.
56 Oxfam International, *Slamming the Door on Development*, p 5.
57 Slocum-Bradley, 'Constructing and de-constructing the ACP group'.
58 European Commission, *EU–Caribbean Partnership for Growth, Stability and Development*, Communication from the Commission to the Council, the European Parliament and the Economic and Social Committee, 2 March 2006, COM(2006)86 final; EC, *EU Relations with the Pacific Islands: A Strategy for a Strengthened Partnership*, Communication from the Commission to the Council, the European Parliament and the European Economic and Social Committee, 29 May 2006, COM(2006)248; EC, *Towards an EU–South Africa Strategic Partnership*, Communication from the Commission to the Council and the European Parliament, 28 June 2006, COM(2006)347; EC, *EU Strategy for Africa: Towards a Euro-African Pact to Accelerate Africa's Development*, Communication from the Commission to the Council, the European Parliament and the European Economic and Social Committee, 12 October 2005, COM(2005)489 final; and EC, *The EU–Africa Strategic Partnership*, 27 June 2007, COM(2007)357.

59 According to the EC website, 'the European Neighbourhood Policy applies to the EU's immediate neighbours by land or sea—Algeria, Armenia, Azerbaijan, Belarus, Egypt, Georgia, Israel, Jordan, Lebanon, Libya, Moldova, Morocco, Occupied Palestinian Territory, Syria, Tunisia and Ukraine'. See http://ec.europa.eu/world/enp/policy_en.htm, accessed 12 November 2009.
60 See Slocum-Bradley, 'Constructing and de-constructing the ACP group', for a more extensive discussion of the de-construction of the ACP group.
61 The 10th EDF, to be disbursed during the period 2008–13, amounts to €22 682 million This fund is divided between national and regional indicative programmes, intra-ACP programmes and projects, investment facilities, EU Overseas Countries and Territories and the European Commission itself (to cover expenditures for programming and implementation, such as its offices and staff in developing countries).
62 Part 1, General provisions, Title 1, Chapter 1, Article 2.
63 Bilal & Stevens, *The Interim Economic Partnership Agreements between the EU and African States*, p 230.
64 Part 1, Title II, Article 11b. See also the 10th EDF, Annex 1b.
65 ACP–EU Joint Parliamentary Assembly, *Report of the ACP–EU JPA Delegation—Fact-Finding Mission to Seychelles: 25–27 April 2008*, Ref APP/100.290/BURv01-00 & CR\717175EN.doc, Brussels, 2008.
66 *Ibid*, p 5. For example, different maximum levels of cadmium were set for EU Overseas Countries and Territories, such as Reunion, and the Seychelles. Furthermore, all Seychelles vessels are required to have non-wooden decks, while the majority of EC vessels still use wooden decks
67 *Ibid*, p 5.
68 *Ibid*, p 7.
69 Oxfam International, *Slamming the Door on Development*, p 5.
70 Nissanke & Thorbecke, 'A quest for pro-poor globalization', p 265.
71 Birdsall, 'Stormy days on an open field', p 243.

Governance and Relations between the European Union and Africa: the case of NEPAD

IAN TAYLOR

ABSTRACT *The New Partnership for Africa's Development (NEPAD) was launched in 2001 as the pre-eminent vehicle to promote Africa's recovery. Initially it was enthusiastically promoted by a select number of countries in Africa, as well as by key members within the G-8. The European Union was active in its support, particularly* vis-à-vis *governance issues, stating that the EU 'finds that Africa's development efforts are best served by a greatly sharpened focus on NEPAD as the basis for partnership between Africa and the international community'. However, there have been significant problems facing NEPAD. These revolve around the actual extant political economy and dominant political cultures across Africa, which the technocratic neoliberal agenda of 'good governance' cannot deal with. Furthermore, the rise of Chinese engagement with Africa adds a major difficulty to Brussels' claim to be a key engine in supporting NEPAD's goals regarding governance and development. Indeed, the emergence of Chinese actors in Africa threatens to make much of the EU's policies on governance largely irrelevant, although it is acknowledged that, in the long term, Beijing's policy interests are not served by chaotically ruled states.*

The New Partnership for Africa's Development (NEPAD) was launched in Abuja, Nigeria, in October 2001.[1] Its emergence arose from the mandate granted to five African heads of state (Algeria, Egypt, Nigeria, Senegal, South Africa) by the then Organisation of African Unity (OAU) to work out a development programme to spearhead Africa's renewal. At its launch NEPAD was excitedly promoted by a select number of countries in Africa, as well as by the G-8, as a means to stimulate what was termed the 'African Renaissance', a pet project of South Africa's then president, Thabo Mbeki.[2] The European Union was initially very supportive of NEPAD and has, rhetorically at least, remained committed in its support.

The governance aspect of NEPAD was what particularly attracted the support of the EU elites and sat alongside other EU frameworks for promoting 'good governance' in Africa, notably the Cotonou Agreement, the

(African Union) AU–EU Strategic Partnership and its related Plan of Action. From the EU's standpoint, there are three regimes of co-operation with Africa, namely sub-Saharan co-operation, which is synchronised by the Trade and Cooperation Agreement with South Africa, and by the Cotonou Partnership Agreement; the Mediterranean model applied by the EU in its relations with the Mediterranean littoral states of Africa in agreement with the Barcelona Process of 1995; and the Euro-Africa summit, initially held in 2000. For the EU, NEPAD was an additional mechanism for such 'partnerships'.

In its promotion of 'good governance' one commentary averred that 'the EU tends to export to third countries the EU model of political and economic development based upon economic liberalization and the rules of [the] free market, democratic norms and practices, and human rights protection'.[3] Commitments to promote democratic principles, the rule of law and human rights are explicitly set out in the EU Treaty (Articles 6 and 11). What is remarkable about this venture is that it is based on the European experience and on particular liberal readings of that experience, which is then extrapolated and exported as *universal*, as if the EU project is both unproblematic and uncontested.

In August 2006 the European Commission launched a new communiqué on *Governance in the European Consensus on Development: Towards a Harmonised Approach within the European Union*. Paragraph 13 of the document reaffirmed that 'development is a central goal by itself, and that sustainable development includes good governance, human rights and political, economic, social and environmental aspects'.[4] Among the common values avowed by the declaration was the following: 'EU partnership and dialogue with third countries will promote common values of: respect for human rights, fundamental freedoms, peace, democracy, good governance, gender equality, the rule of law, solidarity and justice'.

Previously the heads of state of NEPAD's five African sponsor nations had visited Brussels in October 2001 to present their project. This resulted in a common statement articulating strong EU support for NEPAD and establishing a follow-up mechanism, to focus particularly on capacity building. In 2002 at the United Nations General Assembly, Ole Moesby, Deputy Permanent Representative of Denmark to the UN, stated on behalf of the EU that:

> The European Union fully supports NEPAD as an overarching and integrated policy framework for African efforts that will no doubt contribute towards the realisation of the United Nations Millennium Declaration and the internationally agreed development goals...[T]here are...encouraging signs of development. The commitment to good governance by African leaders as embodied in NEPAD and also in the Constitutive Act of the African Union, the promising GDP growth rates of 5% a year or more in some 15 African countries, and the recent positive prospects of ending some of Africa's protracted conflicts in Angola, the Democratic Republic of Congo (DRC), Ethiopia/Eritrea and Sierra Leone...the European Union finds that Africa's development efforts are best served by a greatly sharpened focus

on NEPAD as the basis for partnership between Africa and the international community.⁵

The European Union Delegation to the African Union further underlined this, stating that 'the support that the EU has brought to NEPAD since its conception is largely based on...commitment to core values, especially democracy, human rights, good governance and the rule of law'.⁶ Indeed, 'The EU strongly supports the political values at the heart of NEPAD, because they correspond with the "essential elements" of the EU's external cooperation policy regulated by the Maastricht Treaty and completed by the Lomé/Cotonou principles, the Mediterranean process and the Agreement with South Africa. These are good governance, strengthening democratic practices, respect for human rights and the rule of law.'⁷

NEPAD was grounded on the premise that 'good governance' is a prerequisite for Africa's renewal. Under this rubric the continent's leaders were supposed to actively introduce and support such initiatives that would improve the quality of governance in Africa (as defined by orthodox, Western prescriptions).⁸ In return, Africa's 'development partners', including the EU, pledged to support NEPAD. It should be noted that Brussels did not see NEPAD as a channel for financial resources or new co-operation instruments. There was, however, concurrence that the EU would contribute to selected areas, key among them promoting peace and security; strengthening institutions and governance; and fostering trade, investment, economic growth and sustainable development.

The problems facing the EU in this endeavour, both in terms of the actual extant political economy and dominant political cultures across Africa and of the rise of Chinese (and others') engagement with Africa are addressed in this paper. But in a nutshell, what the EU's engagement with NEPAD demonstrated in part was the clash between divergent notions or practices of what constitutes governance.

NEPAD's prescriptions

According to official NEPAD sources (the website, but also numerous other NEPAD -related documents), the project was based on the following principles:

- good governance as a basic requirement for peace, security and sustainable political and socioeconomic development;
- anchoring the development of Africa on its resources and resourcefulness of its people;
- partnership between and among African peoples;
- acceleration of regional and continental integration;
- forging a new international partnership that changes the unequal relationship between Africa and the developed world; and
- ensuring that all partnerships with NEPAD are linked to the Millennium Development Goals and other agreed development goals and targets.⁹

NEPAD had a great deal to say on democracy and governance and in some ways was a Democratic Charter for Africa. Paragraph 43 asserted that 'democracy and state legitimacy have been redefined to include accountable government, a culture of human rights and popular participation as central elements', while paragraph 45 stated that 'across the continent, democracy is spreading, backed by the African Union (AU), which has shown a new resolve to deal with conflicts and censure deviation from the norm', the norm being 'accountable government, a culture of human rights and popular participation as central elements'. As a result, said paragraph 49, 'African leaders will take joint responsibility for...promoting and protecting democracy and human rights in their respective countries and regions, by developing clear standards of accountability, transparency and participatory governance at the national and sub-national levels'. This was particularly imperative because 'African leaders have learnt from their own experiences that peace, security, democracy, good governance, human rights and sound economic management are conditions for sustainable development' (paragraph 71). Indeed:

> development is impossible in the absence of true democracy, respect for human rights, peace and good governance. With the New Partnership for Africa's Development, Africa undertakes to respect the global standards of democracy, which core components include political pluralism, allowing for the existence of several political parties and workers' unions, fair, open, free and democratic elections periodically organized to enable the populace to choose their leaders freely. (paragraph 79)

Thus, 'the New Partnership for Africa's Development [had], as one of its foundations, the expansion of democratic frontiers and the deepening of the culture of human rights. A democratic Africa [would] become one of the pillars of world democracy, human rights and tolerance' (paragraph 183).

Overall, through examining the various priorities and initiatives, it is clear that NEPAD fitted with the 'Post-Washington consensus', which asserted that what was required for African regeneration was a competent—if not developmental—state that had the ability and political will to confront graft and, in doing so, to set free the potential human resources and capabilities of Africa. Indeed, the EU itself noted that 'The support that the EU has brought to NEPAD since its conception is largely based on the fact that it found in NEPAD principles that it values much itself'.[10] At the same time, as we have noted, NEPAD openly linked development with orthodox notions of what constituted both 'good governance' and 'democracy'. The banal way NEPAD digested standard Western-derived ingredients for development suggested that the claims of the Executive Secretary of the UN's Economic Commission for Africa that NEPAD was 'the most important advance in development thinking for Africa in the past forty years' were somewhat overblown.[11]

The idea of partnership with the developed world was, as its name suggested, central to NEPAD. Indeed, a renegotiated relationship with the global community through a new 'partnership' with the West was repeatedly cast as being necessary, particularly if the continent was to access the resources that NEPAD argued were needed to kick start and then sustain the continent's recovery. Yet the idea of a 'partnership' between the West and Africa over NEPAD was, from the start, flawed; the power differentials were simply too immense. In fact, as commentators have noted, the use of the supposedly equalising and levelling word 'partnership' to portray and describe 'development relationships' was actually an endeavour to disavow and obscure European paternalism, with its roots firmly embedded in the colonial experience.[12]

Yet, clearly, the discourse of 'partnerships' does not—and is not supposed to—alter any existing unequal power relations that may exist between donors and recipients. Rather, the discourse is a rhetorical device to camouflage material processes of exploitation and unequal exchange. As one commentary noted, 'NEPAD's...shortcoming was that it was framed within the old belligerent and patronising relationships of "us" against "them", and therefore talk of "new" partnerships between "developed" G-8 countries and "underdeveloped" African nations was a poor smokescreen. It failed to demonstrate the reality of the touted partnerships and the exit plan out of the "donor–beggar" relationship'.[13] The global context undermined any such exit, given that 'not only has the international leverage of African leaders been drastically diminished in the globalizing post-Cold War world, they now sail in the largely uncharted waters of eroding norms of sovereignty, dwindling Western concern with Africa's poverty, a vacuum of ideological visions and the growing power of external non-state actors such as multinational corporations, non-governmental organizations, crime syndicates and CNN'.[14] How a 'partnership of equals' can be constructed in such a milieu is, obviously, deeply problematic.

One of the most eye-catching aspects of NEPAD was its stated position that, if Africa was to begin to emerge from poverty, the continent required a GDP growth rate of 7% per annum and that, given Africa's present low saving and investment ratio, the continent would need $64 billion of resource inflows *every* year. As paragraph 147 asserted, 'Africa needs to fill an annual resource gap of 12 per cent of its GDP, or $64 billion. This will require increased domestic savings, as well as improvements in the public revenue collection systems. However, *the bulk of the needed resources will have to be obtained from outside the continent*' (emphasis added).

NEPAD was, basically, a deal between elites: African leaders would somehow hold each other accountable and would practice neoliberal 'good governance' and, in return, Western elites would commit themselves to aiding Africa's 'renaissance'. As the *East African* newspaper noted, 'in its expression, NEPAD exemplified an elitist approach to African issues that sought to integrate Africa into the Western hemisphere's economic and political scheme of things'.[15] Problematically, this in fact granted outsiders the role of 'rescuing' the continent from its perceived malaise, with internal African actors (very much restricted to local elites) playing a supporting role at best. NEPAD in this sense might be seen as an elaborate attempt to guarantee the continuation of resource flows to Africa in order to maintain the personal rule of various autocrats on the continent, rather than any genuine project to reconfigure Africa's place in the world.[16] If such analysis was correct, then the rhetorical commitment of the EU to supporting 'good governance' was further undermined. That EU representatives presumably sat straight-faced as Olusegun Obasanjo or Hosni Mubarak (or Thabo Mbeki for that matter) proclaimed their commitment to 'good governance' supports such an assertion and demonstrated the elitism of the whole endeavour.

A key problem facing the African continent and the notion of EU–NEPAD 'partnerships' on 'governance' was the ability or otherwise of such initiatives to successfully operate in the context of neo-patrimonialism and Big Men politics, with its alternative notions of governance. Any assessment of the political situation on the continent undermined the potency of the renewal project as a means towards better governance as defined by the EU and by NEPAD documents. Why this is so is what we turn to next.

Dancing with the Big Men: the problematic partners

Obviously, Africa's regeneration was not—and never has been—simply a question of advancing 'good leadership' or 'good government'; the structural impediments to African trade are equally important and here, the European Union is *highly* culpable. Certainly, a voluntarist approach to Africa's development or the neglect of the nature of the continent's historic relationships within the international system are central to any evaluation. But, using NEPAD's own declared statements, its ambitious economic plans and political pronouncements were profoundly compromised from the start. Indeed, the failure to act in any meaningful way regarding malgovernance (according to NEPAD) and human rights as situations presented themselves indicated fairly quickly that NEPAD had a rather muted, if not minimal, impact on the African milieux.

According to the Nigerian political scientist Claude Ake, 'we are never going to understand the current crisis in Africa...as long as we continue to think of it as an economic crisis'.[17] Indeed, one of the fundamental problems in large parts of post-colonial Africa is that the ruling classes lack hegemony. The early years of post-colonial rule rapidly collapsed into autocracy and fiasco. Accordingly, the ethico-political feature, which in a hegemonic project functions to support constructing economic constitution but also provides a mitigating and legitimising aspect, is absent across many parts of Africa and was definitely lacking at the time of the birth of NEPAD, despite Mbeki's (increasingly desperate) assertions about an ongoing 'renaissance'. As a result, the ruling classes' domination and their systems of governance are articulated through both the menace and tangible exercise of violence *and* the distribution of material benefits to cliques in neopatrimonial regimes.[18] Without these two modalities—both unfavourable to long-term development and stability—the African ruling elites cannot reign. *This* is the sort of governance that actually exists in Africa and, for those inside the patronage loops, it works.

The non-hegemonic nature of much of Africa's ruling elites means that the relative autonomy of the state, which would make possible the types of reforms demanded by NEPAD (and the EU), would make autocracy superfluous and would produce the soil in which the accepted liberal democratic model might be nurtured, is not in attendance. Indeed, the modern state that the EU assumes and demands is dependent upon the fundamentally bourgeois liberal difference between the public and the private, which then allows space for politics to take on characteristics that are seen as different from economics. Yet the very core of politics in large parts of Africa is the negation of any division between the public and the private. While this is at the core of actually-existing governance in much of Africa, it must be said that this is exercised with no apparent concern over its effect on those upon whom this supremacy is visited.

Fatton has argued that 'the absence of a hegemonic bourgeoisie, grounded in a solid and independent economic base and successfully engaged in a private accumulation of capital, has transformed politics into material struggle'.[19] As a result, the bourgeoisie in Africa is generally weak and nascent, translating into economic irrationality from the vantage point of broad-based and inclusive development (although connected elites prosper). Instead of a stable hegemonic project that binds different levels of society together, an intrinsically *unstable* personalised system of domination exists. Absolutism holds sway and power is upheld through patrimonialism by means of the commandeering of state resources. Corruption, not hegemonic rule, is the governance glue that binds the system together and links the patron and his predatory and parasitic ruling class together. It *is* a form of governance, but not as we know it, if using liberal Western tools of analysis.

Because the EU's own conception of 'good governance' is technocratic and apolitical (see the Introduction to this special issue) the personalisation of political power—either at the low or high social levels—which stakes out well defined roles within most African polities, is barely understood by the EU's own officers, even in the field.[20] When and where the EU speaks regarding 'governance' this is in a technical sense and misses the *political* dimensions and problems. Indeed, the EU's own prescriptions for designing 'good governance' structures draws upon the international financial institutions' 'broadly agreed best international practices of economic management'.[21] What is interesting is that the EU's own definition of governance could be satisfied—however perversely—by neo-patrimonialism:

> Governance concerns the state's ability to serve the citizens. It refers to the rules, processes, and behaviours by which interests are articulated, resources are managed, and power is exercised in society. The way public functions are carried out, public resources are managed and public regulatory powers are exercised is the major issue to be addressed in this context. In spite of its open and broad character, governance is a meaningful and practical concept relating to the very basic aspects of the functioning of any society and political and social systems. It can be described as a basic measure of stability and performance of a society.[22]

Neo-patrimonial systems certainly serve *some* citizens and these systems do operate along well understood lines of processes and behaviours, through which various interests are articulated, resources are distributed, and power is exercised over society. According to Clapham, this is 'accepted as normal behaviour, condemned only in so far as it benefits someone else rather than oneself'.[23] The failure to understand that such systems are an alternative type of governance (and I am certainly not approving of them) that works for some people—some very important and influential people—in Africa is a major lacuna in the EU's overall 'partnership' strategies.

Of course, the turn to 'good governance' by the EU can be related to both the dominance of technocratic neoliberal thinking and a refusal to acknowledge that European policies have not worked in Africa to promote development. Certainly, the refusal by Brussels to acknowledge that policies have not worked is central to the emergence of the 'good governance' discourse within the EU's development rhetoric. Instead of questioning their own prescriptions, European elites have sought to advance 'good governance' as a necessary precondition for reforms to *finally* work, deftly ignoring the elephants in the room—gross levels of subsidisation to Europe's farmers and the effective blocking of much of Africa's export potential by EU policies *and* the reality of neo-patrimonial forms of governance (cheerily supported by key EU states such as the UK in places such as Uganda or Sierra Leone and by France in most, if not all, francophone states).

The turn to 'good governance' itself reflected the conviction among major global institutions that neoliberalism was the only way forward and that what had been wrong was not the content of various assistance programmes, but rather their implementation and wider institutional setting in the borrowing states. Why this emerged sprang from the institutional culture and specifically the hegemony of narrow-minded economists. As Weaver notes regarding the World Bank, 'governance and anticorruption issues ran headfirst into the economistic, technocratic, and apolitical features of the Bank's intellectual culture'.[24] After all, there existed 'the dominance of neoclassically trained economists within the Bank...[many] recruited from academia with little or no experience in government and with little interest in or appreciation of noneconomic factors affecting development'.[25]

The result, Fatton noted, was that policy advice was 'based on a series of deeply flawed assumptions' which:

> posit that development can be 'private-driven,' and that African bourgeoisies can suddenly have a change of heart and become the engine of the take-off, whereas these bourgeoisies have never shown any commitment to sustained productive investment. They posit that privatization leads necessarily to rational economic decisions and that private agents are inherently more virtuous and efficient than public servants, whereas revenues derived from the sale of state assets can be stolen and squandered, and private agents are bent on defending their own selfish interests rather than the collective good. They posit that democratic governance is compatible with the imposition of fiscal austerity in an environment which is already suffering from acute material deprivation, whereas SAPs' huge social costs are unlikely to be tolerated by docile and

passive populations. Finally, they posit that trade liberalization will promote more efficient African economies whereas Africa's small industrial base is incapable of withstanding and surviving foreign competition without public protection.[26]

The above accounts for the often distinct naivety that the EU operated from in its dealings with large parts of the continent. As Claude Ake noted, 'one of the most amazing things about the literature on development in Africa is how readily it assumes that everyone is interested in development and that when [African] leaders proclaim their commitment to development and fashion their impressive development plans and negotiate with international organizations for development assistance, they are ready for development and for getting on with it'.[27] This is a major problem for the EU in crafting coherent and long-term developmental relationships, as per the EU's stated foreign policy goals *vis-à-vis* NEPAD, although short-term commercial exchanges of mutual benefit to African elites and European corporations are evidently possible.

Having said that, despite rhetorically supporting NEPAD, the EU has not seen the initiative as the channel for financial resources or new co-operation instruments. Rather, the EU contributes collectively with other donors and with the G-8 to existing initiatives with existing and additional resources: 'While NEPAD sets out the right goals, European cooperation with Africa will continue to take place through the existing contractual instruments (MEDA, Cotonou and the South Africa agreement), as well as international commitments taken in the framework of the Millennium goals, the Doha/ WTO process, the third United Nations Conference on the Least Developed Countries, the Durban Conference process, Monterrey, Johannesburg and other multilateral initiatives'.[28]

In fact, the EU's support for NEPAD has been conditional and varied. The UK (under the prime ministership of Tony Blair) was the most active supporter of NEPAD during the period when it was taken most seriously.[29] However, this was not to last long and succumbed to wider scheming, something which the French were also adept at.

Business as usual

When NEPAD was launched in 2001, the British were initially the most enthusiastic. In contrast, the French sought to sabotage the initiative via its client state, Senegal. Senegal's President Abdoulaye Wade had sought to present his own 'recovery plan' at the Franco-Africa Summit in Yaoundé, Cameroon in January 2001. This was at a time when the Millennium Africa Recovery Plan (MAP), the precursor to NEPAD was being showcased around Africa by Mbeki, Olusegun Obasanjo of Nigeria and Abdelaziz Bouteflika of Algeria. The MAP was 'designed to present a common front when Africa deals with the developed world, seek aid and investment in return for good governance, and unite African countries against social and economic problems like AIDS. On the other hand, the Omega Plan, drawn up by the

Senegalese president, set goals and define[d] financial means to narrow infrastructural gaps'.[30]

Only hard bargaining managed to prevent Wade's (ie the French) Omega Plan from sabotaging African unity before it had even begun, particularly when Wade began claiming that his plan was 'a practical initiative for overcoming Africa's economic difficulties' while asserting that the MAP was 'more of a manifesto'.[31] Of note, and highly revealing, the South African Department of Foreign Affairs admitted that 'the three original MAP Presidents [only] became aware of the Omega Plan for the first time at the World Economic Forum in Davos on 30 January 2001.[32] The French ambush of Africa's latest recovery plan almost succeeded.

Given that French policy towards Africa is notoriously self-interested, it was unsurprising that Wade's plan (or was it Chirac's?) was highly problematic. It involved obtaining repayable treasury bonds from the developed world to finance what was essentially a pan-continental infrastructure scheme which, Wade readily admitted and advertised, would favour Western contractors and businesses. Letting the cat out of the bag, Wade specifically referred to the benefits that French businesses would accrue from his 'development plan':

> Take the case of France. Their interest [in the Omega Plan] is that French firms...would benefit. After all, French companies could be the ones called on to build thousands and thousands and thousands of kilometres of roads in Africa. Oh yes, I will show how the West will benefit...two-thirds of the resources I'm talking about would go to Western companies to carry out the work.[33]

However, because, according to Wade, 'it was inconceivable to appear divided in front of the international community [Africa] had to speak out in a single voice. Therefore, after 48 hours of long and intense discussions in Pretoria, on July and 3, 2001, [it was] agreed to combine the two projects [Omega and MAP]'.[34] This meeting, attended by the five core MAP Steering Committee countries (South Africa, Nigeria, Algeria, Senegal and Egypt) and also involving the UNECA Executive Secretary and representatives from the OAU, developed what was known as MAP Final Draft 3 (b), which, with various adjustments, was later converted into NEPAD.

While not wishing to valorise the British, London's policies towards NEPAD were at least not as immediately brazenly cynical as those of the French. Expressed concerns over Africa's situation galvanised London to embark on a high-profile campaign advocating specific remedies for Africa— largely because Britain held the chairmanship of both the G-8 and the European Union in 2005.[35] Note that this was one year after the launch in 2004 of the Blair Commission for Africa and 'follow[ed] a trend started at the G-8 meetings in Kananaskis in Canada in June 2002 and Evian, France, two years ago' where Africa was placed on the G-8 agenda.[36] However, the desire by Blair to hijack/sideline NEPAD within a few years of its launch posed problems, notably around the Commission for Africa, also known as the 'Blair Commission'.

The Blair Commission for Africa was set up early 2004 to 'take a fresh look at the challenges Africa faces in the context of the global forces in play in the 21st century'.[37] Blair's Commission was supposed to discuss Africa's development challenges—all of which were more or less within NEPAD's remit and which at the time raised issues related to NEPAD's future. Indeed, one commentator averred that the 'new Commission signal[ed] impatience and lack of confidence with Africa's home-grown development paradigm'.[38] Another African commentary noted:

> NEPAD's take-off was sabotaged by Tony Blair's Commission on Africa, with glitzy media hype in Western capitals touting superficial solutions to African problems. Were NEPAD's technocrats blind to these manoeuvres aiming at overshadowing and eclipsing NEPAD? Why did they not speak vehemently against the propping up of the Commission on Africa when NEPAD existed as a vehicle to propound the same issues the Commission sought to publicise and achieve?[39]

The China variable

Having said all the above, the entry of the Chinese into Africa may make NEPAD—and even the EU's governance projects—irrelevant. Chinese economic and political activities in Africa are growing at exponential rates and this expansion of Chinese involvement is arguably the most momentous development on the continent since the end of the Cold War.[40] The People's Republic of China is now Africa's second most important trading partner, behind the USA but ahead of France and the UK. Along with the rise in Sino-African activity have come accusations that China is a new 'colonising' power, exploiting Africa's natural resources, flooding the continent with low-priced manufactured products while turning a blind eye to Africa's autocrats.[41] Senior EU politicians have enunciated this view: for instance, Karin Kortmann, Parliamentary State Secretary in the German Development Ministry, declared in November 2006 that 'Our African partners really have to watch out that they will not be facing a new process of colonization' in their relations with China.[42] But equally, 'thanks to the Chinese' a French official has commented, 'we [have] rediscovered that Africa is not a continent of crises and misery, but one of 800-million consumers'.[43]

It is true that at the moment there appears to be some divergence between EU and Chinese policy aims regarding governance and that this at times suggests a convergence between Beijing and certain types of African leaders. But this can only ever be temporary in nature if China wishes to have a long-running and stable relationship with Africa. China is like all other actors in Africa—it needs stability and security in order for its investments to flourish and for its connections with the continent to be coherent.[44] EU nations have had to learn the hard way that propping up dictators willy-nilly is not sustainable nor desirable (even if this continues), and China will likewise learn this as its relations unfold. As Obiorah notes, 'After an initial phase of snapping up resource extraction concessions, it is almost conceivable that

China will be compelled by instability and conflict in Africa to realise that its long term economic interests are best served by promoting peace in Africa and that this is most likely to come about by encouraging representative government in Africa rather than supporting dictators'.[45] This has started to happen:

> China's changing calculation of its economic and political interests has partly driven this shift. With its increased investments in pariah countries over the past decade, China has had to devise a more sophisticated approach to protecting its assets and its citizens abroad. It no longer sees providing uncritical and unconditional support to unpopular, and in some cases fragile, regimes as the most effective strategy.[46]

Thus, while in the current period there sometimes appears to be divergence, there can ultimately only be growing convergence with EU policy aims—maybe not with regard to democracy, but certainly with regard to governance and security and, by implication, a greater connection to the downside of supporting regimes that undermine development and China's own notions of human rights.

Furthermore, China's integration into the global economy and the concomitant responsibilities that have come with this greater incorporation necessitate structural and systemic reforms for Beijing, particularly through increasing membership of multilateral bodies. In the long term these could conceivably have an impression on Beijing in the development of a regime that incorporates increased respect for the rule of law and a better safeguarding for universal human rights.[47] For instance, Beijing's key commitments pertaining to its membership of the World Trade Organization (WTO) comprise responsibilities to advance the transparency, consistency and standardisation of China's legal system. And it is more than obvious that over the past 20 years or so, Beijing has signed up to and ratified a growing number of international instruments pertaining to human rights and labour as it embeds itself in various multilateral regimes. The task for EU policy makers is to encourage such developments, not to perpetually criticise Beijing: 'The Western countries should accept that they are not any longer in a position to prevent the rise of China and other actors of global change. The objective should be to design a strategy toward China that does not only constrain competition, but develop common commitments on how to deal together on pressing global challenges.'[48]

Finally, the Chinese have actually been quite explicit in their support for NEPAD. At the second Forum on China–Africa Cooperation, Beijing agreed to, 'strengthen cooperation with Africa on priority sectors identified under the New Partnership for Africa's Development (NEPAD)'.[49] Setting the governance strictures to one side, NEPAD is fundamentally a neoliberal project aimed at opening up African markets and developing liberalised economies. Just as China has, since 1978, pursued the capitalist path to development, so too Beijing is now *de facto* encouraging Africa to likewise accept and advance the precepts of liberalised capitalism. Clearly there are material interests in the Chinese elites encouraging African states to open up their markets, but this does place a different twist on the much-hyped (within Africa) notion that China presents an alternative 'model' for the continent, one somehow qualitatively different from the West's. In fact, China is, in the sense of being a model for Africa, little more than a metaphor for a non-Western path to development. That the objective conditions in Africa are hugely different from those that China encountered (and continues to encounter) in its quest for capitalist growth appears to escape the notice of many African intellectuals. The fact that China is not the West appears to be good enough for many. What escapes the notice of such commentators is that both the EU and China are, at least in the economic realm, advocating almost identical policies—and policies that have hitherto been rejected by many African intellectuals as 'neo-colonial' and exploitative.

Conclusion

A major problem in evaluating NEPAD and the EU's engagement with it is that the project was so vague and so all-encompassing and NEPAD's Secretariat so adept at moving the goalposts as to what it was *supposed* to be, that criticising it was rather like trying to pin jelly to a wall.[50] Early on in its history an (unnamed) foreign diplomat in Pretoria was quoted as stating, 'NEPAD is like, I don't know what you call it in English...it's like foam'.[51] Later, an African commentator noted that:

> NEPAD, in its different capacities as institution, secretariat, ideological manifestation, bargaining chip and validation instrument amongst many others, has served different purposes to different groups of people both within and outside the African continent. This effectively renders 'NEPAD' intangible and consequently, impossible to coherently analyse and critique. If indeed such an exercise is carried out, it cannot help but be equally lacking in analytical coherence and substance as it will be based on a foundation that is constantly changing and undefined to the extent of being non-existent. The dialectic of thesis, antithesis and synthesis can therefore not be used with regards to the thesis-deficient NEPAD.[52]

Yet there are some points we can make. With regard to the EU's endorsement of NEPAD, it is surely naïve to expect elites, whose own governance modus operandi is based on privatised patronage (in EU eyes, malgovernance) and the prohibition and erosion of democracy, to begin implementing and operating by the rubric of the EU's definition of 'good governance'. To do so would not only damage their own holds on power but reduce their ability to maintain lucrative linkages with the external world. Furthermore, the discursive framework of NEPAD—that external actors have the power to change Africa for the better—was a flawed assumption. 'The vast majority of NEPAD staff time [went] into persuading donors and international bodies. Comparatively little went into examining how NEPAD would achieve its other goal: changing the behaviour and direction of African government policy.'[53] This naivety was remarkable. 'The plan's unstated operational theory was that countries would be invited to conferences that would develop continental plans and, as a consequence of this participation, return home and change national policy'.[54] But if the governance structures of neo-patrimonialism work for the elites, why should they change them?

Indeed, in the context where two quite different—in fact, incompatible—notions and practices of governance were encountering each other, depending on one to somehow replace the other voluntarily, even if that goes against the material interests of key actors, was nonsensical. From the perspective of the EU, depending upon the whims of elites within governments who practice and benefit from 'alternative' governance processes was never likely to work. Just as importantly, nor could such a 'partnership' be detached from a critical restructuring of Africa's global economic linkages and EU trade policies. Besides, as mentioned above, with the rise of China in Africa (as well as other 'new' actors, such as Brazil, India, Iran, Malaysia, etc), the leverage of the EU—arguably even the very point of NEPAD—has been reduced, although both China and the EU desire the same goals in Africa—stability and predictability for their investments alongside liberalised markets.

Where NEPAD fits into all of this is questionable. Six years after its launch, Abdoulaye Wade 'announced his unofficial disaffiliation from NEPAD, attributing his disillusionment to its embarrassingly dismal performance against a backdrop of what he termed its monumental funding'.[55] Later, in mid-2008, the inaugural meeting of the NEPAD Coordinating Unit convened. This Unit was established by the African Union to oversee the integration of NEPAD into the processes and structures of the AU. This was, in itself, both a good and a bad thing. It was good because in doing so NEPAD gained pan-African legitimacy from the continent's highest intergovernmental body. Without such support, the status and direction of NEPAD had been problematic. Yet, in gaining such legitimacy, NEPAD opened itself up to possibly crippling handicaps. This was most notable in having to pander to the politics of the lowest common denominator in trying to ensure pan-African solidarity and unity, with characters such as Muammar Gaddafi of Libya seeking to shape the discourse in his own particular way.

From the start and despite denials to the contrary, NEPAD's promoters were eager to try and keep the project out of the grip of the AU. In the main this was because the project's initiators were 'very keen that it should not become subject to the slow and cumbersome procedures of [AU] decision-making. They were wary of the dangers of it being derailed by the interference of small, ill-governed countries wanting to ensure that their voices were heard and their rulers paid off'.[56]

With NEPAD's founders, Thabo Mbeki and Olusegun Obasanjo out of the picture, it appears that NEPAD has died a death, for all practical purposes. And, indeed, it is extremely difficult to point to any notable, concrete (as opposed to rhetorical/symbolic) results. The chief executive officer of NEPAD, Ibrahim Assane Mayaki, has confessed that 'when I go at the level of countries, the first question I am asked is what is NEPAD doing?'[57] In fact, eight full years after NEPAD's foundation, 'the pitiful state of democracy in Africa was highlighted when the organisers of [the Ibrahim Prize for Achievement in African Leadership] said that they had decided not to give out the award this year' because the Prize 'has apparently run out of suitable candidates'.[58] Where this leaves the EU in its 'partnership' with NEPAD and the AU, grounded in ostensible commitments to 'good governance' is anyone's guess.

Of course, this is not the full story and where the EU's claimed 'partnership' sits in a milieu marked out by outrageous subsidies and agricultural barriers to African trade is a moot point, and one generally ignored in discussions of the EU's support for NEPAD. An African newspaper put it thus:

> [NEPAD] assumed African nations functioned in a vacuum, as though their destiny and its crafting were exclusively in the hands of African governments. Overnight, the economic dictators of the West had been transformed by NEPAD into eager 'partners' of development, ignoring the realities of aid and conditional lending within the strangling international trade and financial systems already functional in all African countries.[59]

Oxfam has estimated that cotton subsidies by the USA and the EU in 2002 caused a loss of up to $300 million in revenue to the African continent, which is more than the total debt relief ($230 million) approved by the World Bank and the IMF under the enhanced highly indebted poor countries (HIPC) Initiative to nine cotton-exporting countries in West and Central Africa. Because many African countries are so dependent upon commodities, the continued high level of subsidies and barriers to trade practised by the EU has stimulated a growing call for some type of reform so as to allow exports from Africa to develop. Access to EU markets is a fundamental problem for African exporters, particularly as the bulk of trade barriers are in agriculture, which is where Africa has an arguable comparative advantage.

Indeed, how African agricultural exporters can hope to compete in the West when it is estimated that Western nations pay their farmers $350 billion per year (or nearly $1 billion a day) in subsidies is clearly problematic. This obviously further leads to underdevelopment and the associated governance problems that come with the territory. Discussing how this might be addressed *vis-à-vis* the EU's governance agenda with regard to Africa and NEPAD is however, outside the remit of this article, though it hints at the hypocrisy of Brussels in confronting China in Africa with accusations of exploitation and neo-colonialism, and also in lecturing Africa's leaders on their (admittedly profound) flaws. Making sure that Brussels' own house was in order with regard to its engagement with Africa would be a much better way for the EU to have exerted its energies, rather than pinning one's collective hopes to quixotic voluntarism as exemplified by NEPAD.

Notes

1 See I Taylor, *NEPAD: Towards Africa's Development or Another False Start?*, Boulder, CO: Lynne Rienner, 2005.
2 See I Taylor, 'The "Mbeki Initiative": towards a post-orthodox New International Order?', in P Nel, I Taylor & J van der Westhuizen (eds), *South Africa's Multilateral Diplomacy and Global Change: The Limits of Reform*, Aldershot: Ashgate, 2001.
3 S Panebianco & R Rossi, *EU Attempts to Export Norms of Good Governance to the Mediterranean and Western Balkan Countries*, Jean Monnet Working Papers in Comparative and International Politics 53, October 2004, p 6.
4 European Union, 'The European Consensus on Development', Joint Statement by the Council and the Representatives of the Governments of the Member States Meeting within the Council, the European Parliament and the Commission, *Official Journal of the European Union*, 24 February 2006, C46/01, Annex I.
5 Statement by Minister Plenipotentiary Ole E Moesby, Deputy Permanent Representative of Denmark to the UN, on behalf of the European Union at the Ad Hoc Committee of the Whole of the General Assembly for the Final Review and Appraisal of the Implementation of the United Nations New Agenda for the Development of Africa in the 1990s: Agenda Item 41 (New York), 25 September 2002.
6 European Union, 'NEPAD and the African Union', *Newsletter of the European Union Delegation to the African Union*, Addis Ababa, September 2002.
7 F Grannell, 'The European Union and the New Partnership for Africa's Development (NEPAD)', *The Courier ACP–EU*, 194, September–October 2002, p 28.
8 See P Nel & I Taylor, '"New Africa", globalisation and the confines of elite reformism: "getting the rhetoric right", getting the strategy wrong', *Third World Quarterly*, 23(1), 2002, pp 163–180.
9 At http://www.nepad.org/AboutNepad/sector_id/7/lang/en, accessed 4 September 2009.
10 European Union, 'NEPAD and the African Union'.
11 KY Amoako, 'NEPAD: making individual bests a continental norm', *UN Chronicle*, 40(1), 2003.
12 M Baaz, *The Paternalism of Partnership: A Postcolonial Reading of Identity in Development Aid*, London: Zed Books, 2005.
13 *East African* (Nairobi), 2–8 July 2007.
14 G Gerhart, 'Africa' (review of books), *Foreign Affairs*, 80(6), 2001, p 195.
15 *East African*, 2–8 July 2007.
16 P Chabal, 'The quest for good governance and development in Africa: is NEPAD the answer?', *International Affairs*, 78(3), 2002, p 462.
17 C Ake, 'How politics underdevelops Africa', in A Adedeji, O Teriba & P Bugembe (eds), *The Challenge of African Economic Recovery and Development*, London: Frank Cass, 1991, p 316.
18 M Bratton & N van de Walle, 'Neopatrimonial regimes and political transitions in Africa', *World Politics*, 46(4), 1994, pp 453–489.
19 R Fatton, 'Bringing the ruling class back in: class, state, and hegemony in Africa', *Comparative Politics*, 20(3), 1988, p 36.
20 This has always been a source of personal wonder and amusement when interviewing EU officials across Africa.
21 International Monetary Fund, *The Role of the IMF Governance Issues: Guidance Note*, 25 July 25 1997, p 2.
22 Commission of the European Communities, *Governance and Development*, Communication from the Commission to the Council, the European Parliament and the European Economic and Social Committee, COM(2003) 615 final, 20 October 2003, para 4.
23 C Clapham, *Third World Politics: An Introduction*, London: Croom Helm, 1985, p 49.
24 C Weaver, *Hypocrisy Trap: The World Bank and the Poverty of Reform*, Princeton, NJ: Princeton University Press, 2008, p 115.
25 *Ibid*, p 102.
26 R Fatton, 'Civil society revisited: Africa in the new millennium', *West Africa Review*, 1(1), p 4.
27 Ake, 'How politics underdevelops Africa', p 319.
28 Grannell, 'The European Union and the New Partnership for Africa's Development', p 29.
29 *Ibid*.
30 *This Day* (Lagos), 23 July 2001.
31 *Daily News* (Gaborone), 28 June 2001.
32 Department of Foreign Affairs, *NEPAD: Historical Overview*, Pretoria: DFA, 2003.
33 Quoted in O Quist-Arcton, 'A "continental strategy" for building Africa infrastructure needed' (Interview with Abdoulaye Wade), *allAfrica.com*, 8 February 2001, at http://www.allafrica.com, accessed 12 November 2009.
34 A Wade, 'Africa, an outcast or a partner?', *African Geopolitics*, 6, 2002, pp 49–56.

35 See I Taylor '"Advice is judged by results, not by intentions": why Gordon Brown is wrong about Africa', *International Affairs*, 81(2), 2005, pp 299–310.
36 A Vines, 'Commission for Africa: into Africa', *World Today*, 61(3), 2005, pp 22–23.
37 *Star* (Johannesburg), 29 March 2004.
38 *Business Day* (Johannesburg), 24 March 2004.
39 *East African*, 2–8 July 2007.
40 See I Taylor, *China's New Role in Africa*, Boulder, CO: Lynne Rienner, 2009; and Taylor, *China and Africa: Engagement and Compromise*, London: Routledge, 2006.
41 See I Taylor & Xiao Yuhua, 'A case of mistaken identity: "China Inc" and its "imperialism" in sub-Saharan Africa', *Asian Politics and Policy*, 1(4), 2009, pp 709–725; and I Taylor 'Beyond the new "two whateverisms": China's ties in Africa', *China aktuell: Journal of Current Chinese Affairs*, 3, 2008, pp 181–195.
42 *Guardian*, 16 November 2006.
43 *Business Day*, 19 October 2007.
44 I Taylor, 'China's oil diplomacy in Africa', *International Affairs*, 82(5), 2006, pp 937–959.
45 N Obiorah, 'Who's afraid of China in Africa?', in F Manji & S Marks (eds), *African Perspectives on China in Africa*, Cape Town: Fahamu, 2007, p 40.
46 S Kleine-Ahlbrandt & A Small, 'China's new dictatorship diplomacy: is Beijing parting with pariahs?', *Foreign Affairs*, 87(1), 2008, pp 38-39.
47 S Breslin & I Taylor, 'Explaining the rise of "human rights" in analyses of Sino-African relations', *Review of African Political Economy*, 115, 2008, pp 59–71.
48 Jing Gu, J Humphrey & D Messner, 'Global governance and developing countries: the implications of the rise of China', *World Development*, 36(2), 2007, p 288.
49 *Xinhua News* (Beijing), 17 December 2003.
50 I had personal experience of this after the Danish Ministry of Foreign Affairs invited me to engage with the NEPAD Secretariat at a workshop in Copenhagen in 2005. Every single criticism of NEPAD was rejected by its Chief Executive on the grounds that 'that was not what NEPAD was about'; or that critics had 'misinterpreted' the project (with hints that such misinterpretation was deliberate and probably inspired by 'Afro-pessimism'). This was the case even when critiques were directly quoting from the NEPAD document. Eventually an exasperated Danish official declared the workshop exercise a waste of time.
51 Quoted in *Business Day*, 6 December 2002.
52 I Motsi, *NEPAD: The Unveiling of an Urban Legend*, Briefing Paper 28, Centre for International Political Studies, 2005, p 4.
53 R Herbert, *Time to Rethink NEPAD*, Braamfontein: South African Institute of International Affairs, 2008.
54 *Ibid*.
55 *East African*, 2–8 July 2007.
56 A De Waal, 'What's new in the "New Partnership for Africa's Development"', *International Affairs*, 78(3), 2002, p 467.
57 *Voice of America*, 20 October 2009.
58 *The Times*, 20 October 2009.
59 *East African*, 2–8 July, 2007.

The EU and Southeastern Europe: the rise of post-liberal governance

DAVID CHANDLER

ABSTRACT *This article suggests that EU governance in Southeastern Europe reproduces a discourse in which the failures and problems which have emerged, especially in relation to the pace of integration and the sustainability of peace in candidate member states such as Bosnia-Herzegovina, have merely reinforced the EU's external governance agenda. On the one hand, the limitations of reform have reinforced the EU's projection of its power as a civilising mission into what is perceived to be a dangerous vacuum in the region. On the other hand, through the discourse of post-liberal governance, the EU seeks to avoid the direct political responsibilities associated with this power. Rather than legitimise policy making on the basis of representative legitimacy, post-liberal frameworks of governance problematise autonomy and self-government, inverting the liberal paradigm through establishing administrative and regulatory frameworks as prior to democratic choices. This process tends to distance policy making from representative accountability, weakening the legitimacy of governing institutions in Southeastern European states which have international legal sovereignty but lack genuine mechanisms for politically integrating society.*

The EU's discourse of governance enables it to exercise a regulatory power over the candidate member states of Southeastern Europe[1] while evading any reflection on the EU's own management processes, which are depoliticised in the framing of the technocratic or administrative conditions of enlargement. In this way responsibility for the integration process and any problems which might arise are seen to have their roots in the institutional frameworks (both formal and informal) which are held to reproduce non-rational, non-liberal, or politically 'immature' outcomes in the autonomous political processes of Southeastern European elites and their interaction with their societies.[2] The discourse of governance reinterprets the limits to the EU's external attempts at social and political engineering of its 'near abroad' as indications that the EU should try harder and be more 'hands on' in its assistance to external support for institutional change, often referred to as state building.[3] In this discourse the problem is the autonomy or the sovereignty of candidate states, rather than their lack of independence to make and implement their own policies.

The post-liberal discourse of governance is very different from the modern liberal discourse of government. While government presupposes a liberal rights-based framing of political legitimacy in terms of autonomy and self-determining state authority, the discourse of governance focuses on technical and administrative capacity, or the way of rule, rather than the representative legitimacy of policy making or its derivational authority.[4] This shift is vital to understanding the discursive framework in which the EU can export good governance and claim a legitimate authority to judge the capacities of new member and of candidate states in Southeastern Europe. The discourse of governance is, in this respect, one in which the external engagement of the EU is seen as a prerequisite for policy progress rather than as an exception to the norm in need of special justification, and one where the legitimacy of this intervention, and of the policy prescriptions attached to it, is judged in technical or administrative terms rather than liberal democratic ones.

The governance discourse critiques sovereignty, not on the basis of a liberal discourse of external intervention, undermining formal political and legal equality, but on the basis of the need for external expertise to develop and build capacity in the institutions of rule. In the terminology of influential policy analysts Claire Lockhart and Ashraf Ghani this external governance assistance does not undermine sovereignty, rather it supports it through overcoming the 'sovereignty gap': the technical and administrative weaknesses of Southeastern European new members and candidate states.[5] The European Union has become the exporter of governance *par excellence* through the enlargement process, in which candidate states have been member-state built.[6]

The EU has been keen to promote itself as a policy leader in the field of governance and this has been taken up supportively by academic commentators, keen to emphasise that the EU is unique as a policy actor, exercising 'soft power', 'normative power', or building a 'voluntary empire'.[7] In this way the EU's exercise of power and influence is contrasted positively to the 'neocolonial' or 'hard power' approaches of the USA or of the individual member states. This article seeks to problematise some of these assumptions about the EU's governance discourse on Southeastern Europe and suggests that the technocratic and administrative legitimisation of external intervention is not beyond criticism in both normative and practical policy terms.

The article briefly reviews the EU's governance framework, both in terms of the institutionalist paradigm and the mechanisms of implementation in Southeastern Europe, operationalised through the rubric of member-state building, and traces their development since 1999, particularly in relation to the Stabilisation and Association process. It seeks to highlight briefly how the EU has denied its power in the very processes of exercising it, through:

- presenting its diktat in the language of 'partnership' and country 'ownership';
- internationalising the mechanisms of its domination by engaging a multitude of external states and international organisations;

- internationalising or Europeanising the candidate states' core institutions of governance; and
- engaging with and attempting to create a policy-advocating 'civil society'.

It concludes by considering some of the limitations to the post-liberal governance discourse of member-state building.

The institutionalist paradigm

The West European states, collectively operating as the EU, could not avoid being the determining influence in the political and economic affairs of Southeastern Europe with the end of the Cold War. The problem that the EU faced was how to manage this position of power and influence. According to the report of the International Commission on the Balkans, chaired by former Italian prime minister Guiliano Amato, *The Balkans in Europe's Future*:

> If the EU does not devise a bold strategy for accession that could encompass all Balkan countries as new members within the next decade, then it will become mired instead as a neo-colonial power in places like Kosovo, Bosnia and even Macedonia. Such an anachronism would be hard to manage and would be in contradiction with the very nature of the European Union. The real choice the EU is facing in the Balkans is: Enlargement or Empire.[8]

This quotation sharply sums up the dilemma facing the EU, which appeared to face two unpalatable options: either to leave the Southeastern European states to manage their own affairs and problems or to take on an increasingly formalised responsibility of managing them themselves. The response of the EU has been to develop a 'Third Way', a method of intervention and regulation, but one that does not formally undermine the sovereignty and legal independence of Southeastern European states. This third way approach is that of the post-liberal discourse of governance: external regulation without formal responsibility for governing and policy making in the region. In this way the governance discourse of enlargement has enabled discussion of EU engagement to be framed outside the traditional understandings of sovereignty-based international relations: either respecting sovereign autonomy or coercively intervening to undermine sovereignty in the establishment of protectorate relations.

The discourse of governance asserts that it is supportive of autonomy and sovereignty but as a policy aim or policy goal to be achieved in the future.[9] This framework enables interventionist practices and conditionalities to be posed as capacity building in the Southeastern candidate states rather than as impositions denying or undermining their sovereignty. The policy practices bound up with the discourse of governance are those of state building.[10] Whereas traditional liberal discourses presupposed sovereignty and political autonomy as the condition of statehood, the governance discourse sees statehood as separate from sovereignty (seen as the capacity for good governance). The institutionalist approach of governance understands the problems at economic, social and political levels as a product of poor institutional frameworks, which have been unable to constrain actors' pursuit of self-interest in irrational or destabilising ways. This discourse operates at the formal levels of state institutions and the informal level of civil society.

The formal level of state institutions

Institutionalist approaches to governance are legitimised on the basis that the autonomy of state-level political processes is potentially dangerous and destabilising. The starting assumption with regard to member-state building in Southeastern Europe was that external engagement was necessary for both the interests of the European Union and for the citizens of Southeastern European states themselves. The European Commission asserted that:

> The lack of effective and accountable state institutions hampers the ability of each country to co-operate with its neighbours and to move towards the goal of closer integration with the EU. Without a solid institutional framework for the exercise of public power, free and fair elections will not lead to representative or accountable government. Without strong institutions to implement the rule of law, there is little prospect that states will either provide effective protection of human and minority rights or tackle international crime and corruption.[11]

The problems identified in the governance sphere were not with the formal mechanisms of democratic government or the electoral accountability of government representatives but were concerns that went beyond procedural questions of 'free and fair elections' to the administrative practices and policy choices of governments and the attitude, culture and participation levels of their citizens. Where the traditional liberal agenda focused on processes rather than outcomes, and free and fair elections where seen to be the main indicator of representative and accountable government, under the post-liberal framing of governance institution building was now held to be the key to democratic development. According to the Commission, strengthening state institutions was vital for 'assuring the region's future, being as relevant to human rights and social inclusion as it is to economic development and democratisation'.[12]

The EU's approach to institutional governance reform has been described as implying no less than the 'reforming and reinventing [of] the state in Southeastern Europe'.[13] As the European Stability Initiative observed:

> A new consensus is emerging among both regional and international actors that the most fundamental obstacle to the advance of democracy and security in South Eastern Europe is the lack of effective and accountable state institutions. Strengthening domestic institutions is increasingly viewed as the key priority across the diverse sectors of international assistance, as relevant to human rights and social inclusion as it is to economic development and democratisation.[14]

The international institutions, involved in stabilising and integrating the Southeastern European states within European structures,[15] have consistently viewed the governance agenda as their central concern in the region. Today the argument is still often repeated that many states in the region lack sufficient capacity and suffer from historical 'path dependencies' which have undermined the relations between states and their societies.[16] One typical expression of this framing was that of Valentin Inzko, the Austrian official serving as the EU's High Representative in Bosnia when, in August 2009, he put the lack of political progress down to the fact that he felt that Bosnia suffered 'from a "dependency syndrome" that dates back centuries, to when it was part of the Ottoman Empire'.[17]

The informal level of civil society

In the discourse of governance the concept of civil society is used quite differently from the conceptualisation in traditional political discourses of liberal modernity. Whereas, for traditional conceptions of civil society, the autonomy of civil society as a sphere of association and citizenship was seen as a positive factor, for the EU, civil society is seen as problematic and in need of external intervention and regulation. Civil society highlights the problematic nature of autonomy, understood as irreducible differences which risk conflict if they are not regulated via the correct institutional mechanisms. In the distinctive use of difference in this context of external engagement the concept of civil society is used in ways which reflect and draw upon pre-modern concepts problematising and essentialising difference, especially the pre-existing discourses of race and culture.

Regarding civil society the European Commission was even more forthright in its condemnation of the aspiring Southeastern European members involved in the Stabilisation and Association process:

> None of the countries can yet claim to have the level of vibrant and critical media and civil society that is necessary to safeguard democratic advances. For example, public and media access to information, public participation in policy debate and accountability of government and its agencies are aspects of civil society which are still largely undeveloped in all five of the countries.[18]

In this case the potential accession states from the region could apparently not even make a 'claim' that they could safeguard 'democracy' in their states without external assistance in the form of civil society capacity building. In fact, the Commission was clearly concerned as much by society in the region as by government, arguing that the aim of its new programmatic development was necessarily broad in order 'to entrench a culture ... which makes forward momentum towards the EU irreversible'.[19]

The way in which civil society relates to earlier framings of race and especially of cultural distinctions can be seen in the understanding of the problems of ethnic or regional divisions within Southeastern European societies. Here civil society is seen as weak or problematic and as undermining external attempts to reform and improve governance. Education is often highlighted as especially important in terms of transforming societal informal institutional structures. For example, Claude Kiffer, who runs the

Organisation for Security and Co-operation in Europe (OSCE) education department in Bosnia, suggests that 'the absence of genuine education reform designed to bring future citizens together undermines all other reforms so far ... The system is producing three sets of citizens who do not know anything about the others and have no intercultural skills.'[20] David Skinner of Save the Children further argues that education systems are problematic in the region as they apparently fail to 'produce citizens with critical thinking skills'.[21]

The good governance agenda, with its institutionalist emphasis on state-level institution building and civil society development, became established in the 1990s, reflecting the regulatory power which the EU had over the region, enabling external institutions to take an active interest in questions which were previously seen to be ones of domestic political responsibility. This transformation in relations of power and influence is a crucial determinant for the governance discourse and in explaining the post-liberal interventionist thrust of external policy making. The Commission argued that its focus on building the capacity of state institutions and civil society development reflected not only the importance of this question and the clear needs it had identified, 'but also the comparative advantage of the European Community in providing *real added value* in this area'.[22] It would appear that the Southeastern European states were fortunate in that their wealthy neighbours to the West had not only identified their central problems but also happened to have the solutions to them already at hand.

Co-production of sovereignty

In the governance agenda sovereignty is no longer understood as something that inheres to state institutions *per se*, but rather as a variable quality or capacity for good governance. For those tasked with building the 'sovereignty' or the governance capacity of other states, the traditional liberal discourse, which assumed sovereign autonomy to be a positive quality, has little purchase. Stephen Krasner, Robert Keohane, Ashraf Ghani and Clare Lockhart and other observers have commented positively on the EU's approach to the 'co-production' of the sovereignty of Southeastern European states, or the EU model of 'shared sovereignty' or 'conditional sovereignty'.[23] This post-liberal framing of sovereign rights and legitimacy has been shaped by the governance discourse of 'partnership' and 'country ownership'. Such concepts have been central to the Stabilisation and Association Process (SAP) which was launched in May 1999 to cover Albania, Bosnia-Herzegovina, Croatia, Macedonia, Serbia and Montenegro.

The SAP is the cornerstone of the EU policy of exporting its governance agenda through 'anchoring the region permanently to the development of the EU itself'.[24] This 'anchoring' is seen as crucial to the encouragement of reforms in the governance sphere, relating to the rule of law and democratic and stable institutions. The legitimacy of the EU's relationship of regulation is based on two grounds: the recognition by Southeastern European elites of the need to reform to meet the governance prescriptions of the EU; and the

EU's offer to provide financial assistance, with the promise of EU membership at some point in the future. The policy of aid in return for the EU's regulatory control over the reform process was underpinned by the CARDS (Community Assistance for Reconstruction, Development and Stabilisation) assistance programme providing €4.65 billion over 2000–06. In 2007 this process was streamlined as the Pre-Accession Assistance Programme (available to candidate countries and potential candidates in the region) with €11.5 billion available from 2007 to 2013.[25] The legitimacy of this buying of external influence is bolstered by the promise of EU integration, ie 'on a credible prospect of membership once the relevant conditions have been met'.[26]

In 2000 the EU Zagreb Summit endorsed the SAP objectives and conditions, namely the prospect of accession on the basis of the Treaty on European Union and the 1993 Copenhagen criteria, the CARDS assistance programme, and the countries' undertaking to abide by the EU's conditionality and to participate fully in the SAP process. Ahead of the EU–Western Balkan summit in Thessaloniki in 2003 the General Affairs and External Relations Council adopted the Thessaloniki agenda for moving towards European integration, strengthening the SAP by introducing new instruments to support reform and integration efforts, including European Partnerships, this time including Kosovo, as governed under the auspices of UN Security Council Resolution 1244, within its remit.[27] The European Council argued that, for the Southeastern European states, the process of formulating the SAP contract would be 'both pedagogical and political'.[28] The 'pedagogical' aspect of the process highlights the relationship of subordination involved. As the EU reported, this process: 'has proved an effective means of focusing authorities' minds on essential reforms and of engaging with them *in a sustained way to secure implementation*'.[29]

The European Commission emphasised that there is 'a close *partnership* with SAP countries'.[30] This partnership was held to start by involving countries closely in the programming, including discussions on CARDS and Pre-Accession Assistance strategies; countries would also be involved in ongoing dialogue on developing annual action plans. The European Commission strongly emphasised the importance of country 'ownership':

> This partnership helps promote each country's sense of *ownership* over Community assistance that is crucial if it is to have the desired impact on the ground. This national commitment is all the more important for ... institution building, which require the countries to undertake reforms if the assistance is to be effective.[31]

Country ownership is clearly central to the EU SAP. However, it is clear that the promotion of 'ownership' was being pushed by the EU itself and does not involve any real equality of input over policy guidelines. While the formal regulatory mechanisms emphasise 'partnership' and 'country ownership', at the informal level real ownership is exercised by the European Commission, which guides donor co-ordination and works closely with the major international institutional actors, such as the World Bank.[32] For example, once the Stabilisation and Association Agreements (SAAs) were signed the relationship of regulation became fully institutionalised (the SAAs are legally binding international agreements).³³

The first SAA agreement was signed with Macedonia in April 2001 and entered into force in 2004. The second, with Croatia, was signed in October 2001 and entered into force in 2005. Albania signed up to the formal process of negotiating the SAA in 2003 and Serbia and Montenegro and Bosnia-Herzegovina in November 2005. The agreements were 'the principal means to begin to prepare themselves for the demands that the perspective of accession to the EU naturally entails'.³⁴ These demands were determined by the EU and considered to be so onerous that the Southeastern European states would need the additional encouragement of conditionality:

> The Stabilisation and Association Agreements, then, are posited on respect for the conditionality of the Stabilisation and Association process agreed by the Council. But they also bring with them a dynamic means of operationalising that conditionality and give the EU the leverage necessary to get the countries to adopt genuine reforms with a view to achieving the immediate objectives of the agreements. The mechanisms of the Agreements themselves will enable the EU to prioritise reforms, shape them according to EU models, to address and solve problems, and to monitor implementation.³⁵

The EU attains the necessary 'leverage' over states in the region through conditionality at three levels—the SAP, programme and project levels. At the SAP level, lack of progress in the reforms advocated by the EU in the economic, political and social spheres can lead to financial assistance being frozen or 'granted through other means'.³⁶ If the EU chooses, it can invoke 'programme conditionality', threatening to close certain aid programmes if the country concerned fails to satisfy the external administrators with regard to 'specific reform targets or adoption of sectoral policies'.³⁷ 'Project level conditionality' can apply to ensure that the candidate state meets 'specific conditions' judged to be related to the project's success.

The SAP is a contractual relationship. But a contract made between two unequal parties, with only one party being the judge of whether the conditions of the contract are met and in a position to coerce the other. From the EU perspective, the political strategy towards the region 'relies on a realistic expectation that the contract it enters into with individual countries will be fulfilled satisfactorily'.³⁸ The contracts commit the Southeastern European states to a relationship of subordination to EU mechanisms. They establish formal mechanisms and agreed benchmarks which enable the EU to work with each country towards meeting the required standards and focus attention on key areas of EU governance concern.³⁹

CARDS programmes of assistance, the major external aid associated with the SAP, focused clearly on EU-defined priorities. The first priority institution-building area in terms of overall CARDS support is:

> Familiarisation of the *acquis communautaire* as countries start to move their legislation—especially on areas covered under the SAA—more into line with the

approaches used inside the EU. This will focus on core *acquis* issues relating to the internal market.[40]

This is followed by civil service reform to develop 'administrative procedures in conformity with EU standards', fiscal and financial management reforms, trade and customs regulation and reform of the legal and administrative framework of justice and home affairs.[41]

The European Commission's desire to impose a pre-established governance agenda of institutional reform seems to assume that there is a 'one size fits all' method of strengthening Southeastern European government institutions as it enforces its 'leverage' over the region through a number of similar mechanisms of conditionality with the emphasis upon EU managerial control and 'co-ordination' of external directives, together leaving little doubt that the SAP process is far from one of 'partnership'. Yet the 'partnership' element has been central to keeping the EU's options open with regard to the membership process. As Christopher Bickerton notes, partnership does not just conceal the power inequalities involved in the process of integration, preventing candidate states from negotiating the transitional measures adopted by existing members. It also helps to mitigate tensions and uncertainties of existing member states about enlargement by creating a flexible framework in which the vicissitudes of internal EU institutional wrangling can be played out as problems with the pace of capacity building and ownership in the applicant states.[42]

The process of relationship management with the candidate countries in the region has been much more interventionist and regulatory than the enlargement process that involved the states of Central Eastern Europe. Allegedly the Southeastern European states are too weak to be left to their own devices in meeting the conditions of the accession process. The more 'hands-on' approach of the SAP is held to be essential for the EU to replicate the success of the enlargement process in earlier rounds. Here, where states are weaker, state building is part of the enlargement process itself. For the process of state building the EU needs to have much more leverage than in relation to the Central Eastern European states. From the perspective of the EU administration the reforms being insisted upon are in Southeastern European states' own interests; they are held to be legitimate policy goals in their own right and so cannot be left to publics to decide upon. In these circumstances EU conditionalities operate as a process of relationship management rather than merely establishing the end goals of membership of the EU club.

The centrality of conditionality in the Stabilisation and Association process in Southeastern Europe is rarely fully drawn out. There is an assumption that conditionality is explicitly projecting the EU's norms and values in a way which promotes democracy and strengthens state institutions. In fact, the reality is very different. Accession states have formally decided to accede to the EU and, in this respect, their decision is a voluntary and autonomous one. However, the decision to sign up to the Stabilisation and Association process blurs the clarity of the relationship between the EU and aspirant states. This is because the accession states are signing up to a process where the conditionality is an ongoing one. The democratic and voluntary aspect of the process, in effect, ends with the signing of the agreement as the ongoing steps and conditions are managed by bypassing the democratic political process. From the position of the EU the candidate countries only need to make one democratic decision, which is to subordinate themselves to the accession process. The process of aligning policy with the needs of the EU *acquis* then allows little room for democratic consideration as the policy process becomes an external one, where the external advisers state why policy reforms need to be made and when they need to be achieved, leaving the specific content up to local authorities, albeit with external advice and support.

It is important to realise that the incremental use of conditionalities is not some technical process, it is entirely political. When the EU is considering which 'benchmarks' are important or what level of reforms are necessary for the next stage, a large number of factors come into play, including 'enlargement fatigue', which tends to add further conditions to satisfy member states which are more hostile to enlargement; broader policy concerns with security or crime and corruption; and specific views with regard to the perceived needs of state building in particular aspirant states. Incrementalised conditions are designed to ensure that the process of EU relationship management continues: this blurs the clarity of goals with a focus on the means. In other words, the process of external state building takes centre stage.

Governance not government

In many ways the relationship of inequality between elected representatives in the region and the external regulatory bodies, such as the EU, is highlighted in the international regulation of Bosnia and Kosovo. Bosnia and Kosovo, rather than standing out as exceptions because of the restrictions on local sovereignty and self-government—thereby institutionalising a relationship of inequality and external domination—in fact indicate with greater clarity the problems of post-liberal governance, at the levels of institutional reform and civil society intervention, in the context of an unequal 'partnership'. In both Bosnia (under the administrative regulation of the international Office of the High Representative) and Kosovo (where the highest civilian power is the International Civilian Representative)—both these positions being 'double-hatted' with the position of EU Special Representative (EUSR)—there are elected governments at local, regional and state levels. In both cases the international administration is held to be part of a contractual process moving towards 'ownership', self-government and integration into European structures.[43]

In Bosnia the EU is in the process of winding down the executive powers of the High Representative and the key question is how conditionality can be used to provide the leverage previously provided by the threats of dismissals and direct imposition by the Office of the High Representative.[44] The SAP is seen to be contractually tying-in and committing politicians to work on the EU road. Conditionality is not about final membership conditions, which are open-ended because of uncertainty over enlargement criteria—which depend on a number of political considerations, not some abstract set of technical or administrative factors. Conditionality is a process of relationship management which aims at incremental progress to ensure that reforms happen without stand-offs between politicians and EU administrators. The conditionality of the SAP is seen to be about the day-to-day management of the accession and reform process, with the EU officials wary of conflict if they ask for 'too much too soon'. This delicate process of reform management transforms the political centre from the domestic sphere to the international one. The EU is not just deciding upon its own standards for new members; the EU policy engagement in the states of the region and the EU Special Representatives (EUSR) are important political factors in the societies which they seek to manage, attempting to make delicate political decisions on how to move the reform process forwards.

Here the distinction between 'hard' and 'soft' powers in the context of the EU's relationship with Southeastern European states is not of fundamental importance. Once tied into the SAP, the alleged 'pull of Brussels' (EU conditionality) is no different from, for example, the 'push from Bonn' (the executive powers of the Office of the High Representative). The EUSR does not need to use executive powers once the policy process is institutionalised and incremental conditionality is used to oversee the policy process, setting the timetable for reforms and the policy content. While the fact that Bosnian politicians themselves vote for the requirements of EU accession is vital for the EU's own credibility, the fact that policy is presented to the legislature as a *fait accompli* makes the policy process little different when viewed from the domestic perspective.[45] Whether the policy is brought with the 'hard' threat of dismissals or with the 'soft' threat of funding withdrawals and the stalling of the accession process, there is still little opportunity for political parties to debate upon policy alternatives. The external framework of policy making means that political parties negotiate with the international administrator behind closed doors rather than with each other in public.[46]

This process of political management under the auspices of the SAP, or the 'soft power' pull of Brussels, results in not just an externally driven political process but in one that is openly manipulative. Rather than clarifying what EU membership will involve, the pressure is for elites to evade open or public discussion and instead to attempt to buy social acquiescence. The strategic use of conditionalities also means that the EU openly seeks to turn political issues into technical ones in order to massage and facilitate the reform process.[47] This was clear in Bosnia when police reform was billed as a technical necessity and conditional for signing the SAA, at a time when there was no agreed EU framework for centralised policing.[48] This was an attempt to reshape the Dayton framework and weaken the powers of the Bosnian Serb entity but framed as a technical necessity. This instrumental and manipulative use of conditionality can also be seen in ongoing discussions to use human rights requirements to reform the tri-partite voting for the

Bosnian presidency. Rather than openly state policy goals, which would be controversial, the dynamic is to push controversial reforms under the guise of technical or administrative necessity. The political shaping of Western Balkan society by external managers tends to degrade the entire political process, highlighted by the hollowing out of the opportunities for domestic debate and engagement, encouraging the collaboration of political elites and external administrators against the wishes and aspirations of citizens of West Balkan states.

It is in this context that the post-liberal conception of the role of civil society becomes important. The EU argues that it is more democratic than elected representatives and has shared interests with the citizens of Southeastern European states. For example, opinion polls in Bosnia show that the overwhelming majority of the population support joining the EU; this is the case for each of the three main ethnic constituencies.[49] For the EU its interests are therefore the same as those of the Balkan peoples: there is a mutual interest in a better future of peace, stability and prosperity. The claim is that the EU is therefore not forcing anything on anyone.

However, the passive opinion poll support for the EU is not reflected in major political party positions. The national question still plays a defining role for many Southeastern European states for fairly obvious reasons. Rather than take on board the realities of the region, EU officials argue that the EU needs to 'help bridge the gap' between political elites and the people. This 'gap-bridging' is held to be the task of civil society. Civil society groups are funded and encouraged to talk about single issues which the EU is keen to promote—from the importance of small and medium enterprises to issues of jobs, crime, corruption and healthcare. The EU argues that its missions and Special Representatives listen to the people and civil society, while the elected politicians do not.

This 'democratic' discourse, which portrays the EU as the genuine representative of the people against their illegitimate or immature politicians, fits well with the allegations that politicians do not have the citizens' public interests at heart and therefore must be motivated by private concerns of greed and self-interest. It also tends to discount the votes expressed in elections as being the product of elite manipulation or electoral immaturity. The process of conditionality around an external agenda is then seen to be thwarted or blocked by the processes of domestic representation (much as the Irish electorate were seen to be irrationally blocking the Lisbon treaty, implying that the votes of the public should count for less than the consensus of international experts).

This elitist discourse then results in a manipulative view of conditionality, where political decision making seeks to evade public accountability. In Bosnia EU experts and political elites talk about a 'window of opportunity' for reforms; this window is alleged to be after the last municipal elections in October 2008 and before the next state-level elections in 2010. A process of manipulation develops where politics is actively excluded from the public sphere and decision making is a matter of elite negotiation with Brussels. In short, the EU is reproducing itself in Southeastern Europe. EU member-state building in the region is a clear example of the limitations of the post-liberal governance discourse. Where states have a tenuous relationship to their societies, the relationship management of the EU sucks the political life from societies, institutionalising existing political divisions between ethnic or national groups by undermining the need for public negotiation and compromise between domestic elites.

The externally driven nature of the policy process means that political elites seek to lobby external EU actors rather than engage in domestic constituency building. Even more problematically, the fact that it is in political elites' and EU officials' interests to keep the process of relationship management going means that local political elites are increasingly drawn away from engaging with their citizens (in a similar way to political elites in member states). Rather than exporting democracy and legitimising new state structures, the process of EU member-state building in Southeastern Europe is leading to a political situation in which the voters and the processes of electoral representation are seen to be barriers to reform rather than crucial to it.

The post-liberal state

States that are not designed to be independent political subjects in anything but name are a façade without content. States without political autonomy may have technically sound governance and administrative structures on paper but the atrophied political sphere hinders attempts to reconstruct post-conflict societies and overcome social and political divisions. The states created, which have international legal sovereignty but have ceded policy-making control to external officials in Brussels, lack organic mechanisms of political legitimation as embodiments of a collective expression of the will of their societies. Their relationship of external dependency upon the EU means that the domestic political sphere cannot serve to legitimise the political authorities or reconstruct their societies.

Bosnia is the clearest case of a new type of post-liberal state being built through the EU enlargement process of distancing power and political responsibility. To all intents and purposes Bosnia is a member of the European Union; in fact more than this, Bosnia is the first genuine EU state where sovereignty has in effect been transferred to Brussels. The EU provides its government, the international High Representative is an EU employee and is the EU's Special Representative in Bosnia. This EU administrator has the power to impose legislation directly and to dismiss elected government officials and civil servants. EU policy and 'European Partnership' priorities are imposed directly through the European Directorate for Integration.[50] The EU also runs the police force, taking over from the United Nations at the end of 2002, and the military, taking over from NATO at the end of 2004, and manages Bosnia's negotiations with the World Bank. One look at the Bosnian flag—with the stars of the EU on a yellow and blue background chosen to be in exactly the same colours as used in the EU flag—demonstrates that Bosnia is more EU-orientated than any current member state.[51] However, the EU has distanced itself from any responsibility for the power it exercises over Bosnia; formally Bosnia is an independent state and member of the United Nations and a long way off meeting the requirements of EU membership.

After 14 years of state building in Bosnia there is now a complete separation between power and accountability.[52] This clearly suits the EU, which is in a position of exercising control over the tiny state without either admitting it into the EU or presenting its policy regime in strict terms of external conditionality. Bosnia is neither an EU member nor does it appear to be a colonial protectorate. Bosnia's formal international legal sovereignty gives the appearance that it is an independent entity, voluntarily engaged in hosting its state-capacity-building guests. Questions of aligning domestic law with the large raft of regulations forming the EU *aquis* appear as ones of domestic politics. There is no international forum in which the contradictions between Bosnian social and economic demands and the external pressures of Brussels' policy prescriptions can be raised.

However, these questions are not ones of domestic politics. The Bosnian state has no independent or autonomous existence outside the EU 'partnership'. There are no independent structures capable of articulating alternative policies. Politicians are subordinate to international institutions through the mechanisms of governance established, which give EU bureaucrats and administrators the final say over policy making. The Bosnian state is an artificial one; but it is not a fictional creation. The Bosnian state plays a central role in the transmission of EU policy priorities in their most intricate detail. The state here is an inversion of the sovereign state central to liberal modernity. Rather than representing a collective political expression of Bosnian interests—expressing self-government and autonomy ('Westphalian sovereignty' in the terminology of state builders)—the Bosnian state is an expression of an externally driven agenda.

The more Bosnia has been the subject of external state building, the less it has taken on the features of the traditional liberal state form. Here the state is a mediating link between the 'inside' of domestic politics and the 'outside' of international relations, but rather than clarifying the distinction it removes the distinction completely. The imposition of an international agenda of capacity building and good governance appears internationally as a domestic question and appears domestically as an external, international matter. Where the liberal paradigm of sovereign autonomy clearly demarcated lines of policy accountability, the post-liberal paradigm of international governance and state building blurs them. In this context domestic politics has no real content. There is very little at stake in the political process. In fact, political responsibility for policy making disappears with the removal of the liberal rights-based framework of political legitimacy.[53]

Conclusion

For external state builders the subordination of politics to bureaucratic and administrative procedures of good governance is a positive development.

In functional terms they argue that sovereignty, and the political competition for control of state power that comes with it, is a luxury that Southeastern European states often cannot afford. Robert Keohane, for example, argues that many states now negotiating EU ties are 'troubled societies' plagued by economic, social and ethnic divisions, which means that elections can be highly problematic 'winner-take-all' situations. In these states unconditional sovereign independence is a curse rather than a blessing and conflict can be prevented by enabling 'external constraints' on autonomy in exchange for institutional capacity building.[54]

Post-transition and post-conflict states, such as those in Southeastern Europe, stand in desperate need of a state-building project which can engage with and reconstruct society around a shared future-orientated perspective. What they receive from European Union state builders is external regulation, which has, in effect, prevented the building of genuine state institutions that can engage with and represent social interests. These weakened states are an inevitable product of the technical, bureaucratic and administrative approach exported under the paradigm of post-liberal governance.

Notes

1 This article focuses on the pre-accession states, Albania, Bosnia-Herzegovina, Croatia, Macedonia, Serbia, Montenegro and Kosovo.
2 For example, see the UK Shadow Foreign Secretary, William Hague's view of the need to extend the EU's 'strong outside pressure' to overcome the political blockages to reform in Bosnia, in N Morris, 'Bosnia is back on the brink of ethnic conflict, warns Hague: Shadow Foreign Secretary fears "Europe's black hole" is slowly falling apart again', *Independent*, 12 August 2009, at http://www.independent.co.uk/news/world/europe/bosnia-is-back-on-the-brink-of-ethnic-conflict-warns-hague-1770638.html, accessed 18 September 2009.
3 See D Chandler, *International Statebuilding: The Rise of Post-Liberal Governance*, London: Routledge, 2010.
4 European Commission, *European Governance: A White Paper*, Brussels, 25 July 2001, at: http://eur-lex.europa.eu/LexUriServ/site/en/com/2001/com2001_0428en01.pdf, accessed 18 September 2009. For a development of the policy discourse of governance, see, for example, the seminal World Bank papers highlighting the shift towards institutionalist approaches: *Sub-Saharan Africa: From Crisis to Sustainable Growth: A Long-Term Perspective Study*, Washington, DC: World Bank, 1989; *Governance and Development*, Washington, DC: World Bank, 1992; *The State in a Changing World: World Development Report 1997*, New York: Oxford University Press, 1997; and *Assessing Aid: What Works, What Doesn't, and Why*, New York: Oxford University Press, 1998.
5 A Ghani & C Lockhart, *Fixing Failed States: A Framework for Rebuilding a Fractured World*, Oxford: Oxford University Press, 2008.
6 See, for example, F Trauner, 'From membership conditionality to policy conditionality: EU external governance in South Eastern Europe', *Journal of European Public Policy*, 16(5), 2009, pp 774–790; H Grabbe, *The EU's Transformative Power: Europeanization through Conditionality in Central and Eastern Europe*, Basingstoke: Palgrave, 2006; and M Leonard, *Why Europe will Run the 21st Century*, London: HarperCollins, 2005.
7 See, for example, I Manners, 'Normative power Europe: a contradiction in terms?', *Journal of Common Market Studies*, 40(2), 2002, pp 235–258; H Sjursen (ed), 'Special Issue: What Kind of Power? European Foreign Policy in Perspective', *Journal of European Public Policy*, 13(6); and R Cooper, *The Breaking of Nations: Order and Chaos in the Twenty-First Century*, London: Atlantic Books, 2003.
8 International Commission on the Balkans, *The Balkans in Europe's Future*, 2005, p 11, at http://www.cls-sofia.org/en/books/the-balkans-in-europe-s-future-28.html, accessed 18 September 2009.
9 See Michel Foucault's discussion of the development of institutionalist approaches in the critique of liberal assumptions of the autonomous subject in inter-war Germany, especially the links between the Frankfurt school of critical theory and the Freiburg school of ordo-liberalism, both heavily influenced by the phenomenology of Edmund Husserl. M Foucault, *The Birth of Biopolitics: Lectures at the Collège de France 1978–1979*, Basingstoke: Palgrave Macmillan, 2008, p 120.

10 For institutionalist approaches the problem is not the economic and social relations *per se* but the formal and informal institutions of the societies concerned, which are held to prevent or block the market from working optimally. See the theoretical framing developed in DC North and RP Thomas, *The Rise of the Western World: A New Economic History*, Cambridge: Cambridge University Press, 1973; DC North, *Structure and Change in Economic History*, New York: Norton, 1981; and North, *Institutions, Institutional Change and Economic Performance*, Cambridge: Cambridge University Press, 1990.
11 European Commission, *Regional Strategy Paper 2002–2006: CARDS Assistance Programme to the Western Balkans*, 2001, p 11, at http://www.reliefweb.int/library/documents/2001/ec_balkans_22oct.pdf, accessed 18 September 2009.
12 *Ibid*. See also H Storey, 'Human rights and the new Europe: experience and experiment', *Political Studies*, 43, 1995, pp 131–151.
13 EastWest Institute and European Stability Initiative, 'Democracy, security and the future of the Stability Pact for South Eastern Europe: a framework for debate', 2001, p 18, at http://www.esiweb.org/pdf/esi_document_id_15.pdf, accessed 18 September 2009.
14 *Ibid*, p 18.
15 The EU's process of governance regulation of Southeastern Europe has involved close integration with a large number of non-EU actors, such as the OSCE, UN agencies and the international financial institutions, and a variety of informal and *ad hoc* institutional experiments, with leading examples being the Contact Group, the EU-led Stability Pact, the Peace Implementation Council (for Bosnia) and the International Steering Group (for Kosovo).
16 See, North, *Institutions, Institutional Change and Economic Performance*, pp 93–94.
17 C Whitlock, 'Old troubles threaten again in Bosnia: 14 years after war, leaders suggest US should step in to rewrite treaty', *Washington Post*, 23 August 2009, at http://www.washingtonpost.com/wp-dyn/content/story/2009/08/22/ST2009082202479.html?sid=ST2009082202479, accessed 18 September 2009.
18 European Commission, *Regional Strategy Paper 2002–2006*, pp 10–11.
19 European Commission, *The Stabilisation and Association Process for South East Europe: First Annual Report*, COM(2002)163 final, 4 April 2002, p 8, at http://eur-lex.europa.eu/LexUriServ/LexUriServ.do?uri=COM:2002:0163:FIN:EN:PDF, accessed 18 September 2009.
20 A Cerkez-Robinson, 'Bosnia's ethnic divisions are evident in schools', Associated Press, 22 August 2009, at http://www.google.com/hostednews/ap/article/ALeqM5jtMzf4gX7WCrEY0Zz7aMNZV7uP3gD9A82CJG0, accessed 18 September 2009.
21 *Ibid*.
22 European Commission, *Regional Strategy Paper 2002–2006*, p 9, emphasis added.
23 R Keohane, 'The ironies of sovereignty: the European Union and the United States', *Journal of Common Market Studies*, 40(4), 2002, pp 743–765; S Krasner, 'The case for shared sovereignty', *Journal of Democracy*, 16(1), 2005, pp 69–83; and Ghani & Lockhart, *Fixing Failed States*.
24 European Commission, *The Stabilisation and Association Process and CARDS Assistance 2000 to 2006*, European Commission Paper for the Second Regional Conference for South East Europe, 2001, p 3, at http://ec.europa.eu/enlargement/archives/seerecon/region/documents/ec/ec_sap_cards_2000–2006.pdf, accessed 18 September 2009.
25 European Commission, *Instrument for Pre-accession Assistance (IPA)*, at http://ec.europa.eu/enlargement/how-does-it-work/financial-assistance/instrument-pre-accession_en.htm, accessed 18 September 2009.
26 European Commission, *The Stabilisation and Association Process and CARDS Assistance 2000 to 2006*, p 3.
27 See, for example, European Commission, *Kosovo (under USCR 1244) 2005 Progress Report*, SEC(2005)1423, 9 November 2005, at http://europa.eu.int/comm/enlargement/report_2005/pdf/package/sec_1423_final_en_progress_report_ks.pdf, accessed 18 September 2009.
28 European Union, *Review of the Stabilisation and Association Process*, European Union General Affairs Council Report, 11 June 2001, No 9765/01, at http://www.consilium.europa.eu/uedocs/cms_data/docs/pressdata/en/misc/09765.en1.html, accessed 18 September 2009.
29 *Ibid*, IIIc, emphasis added.
30 European Commission, *The Stabilisation and Association Process and CARDS Assistance 2000 to 2006*, p 7, emphasis in the original.
31 *Ibid*, emphasis in the original.
32 *Ibid*, p 8
33 European Commission, *The Stabilisation and Association Process for South East Europe*, p 4.
34 European Commission, *The Stabilisation and Association Process and CARDS Assistance 2000 to 2006*, p 3.
35 European Union, *Review of the Stabilisation and Association Process*, III.

36 European Commission, *Regional Strategy Paper 2002–2006*, p 24.
37 *Ibid*, p 25.
38 European Commission, *The Stabilisation and Association Process and* CARDS *Assistance 2000 to 2006*, p 3.
39 *Ibid*.
40 European Commission, *Regional Strategy Paper 2002–2006*, p 37.
41 *Ibid*, p 38.
42 C Bickerton, 'Rebuilding states, deconstructing statebuilding', paper presented at the SAID Workshop, University of Oxford, 28 April 2005, at http://www.said-workshop.org/Bickerton.paper.doc, accessed 18 September 2009. See also J Heartfield, 'European Union: a process without a subject', in CJ Bickerton, P Cunliffe & A Gourevitch (eds), *Politics without Sovereignty: A Critique of Contemporary International Relations*, London: UCL Press, 2007, pp 131–149; and H Grabbe, 'Europeanisation goes east: power and uncertainty in the EU accession process', in K Featherstone & CM Radelli (eds), *The Politics of Europeanism*, Oxford: Oxford University Press, 2003.
43 See, for example, W van Meurs & S Weiss, *Qualifying (for) Sovereignty: Kosovo's Post-status Status and the Status of EU Conditionality*, Discussion Paper, 6 December 2005, Guetersloh: Bertelsmann Stiftung, 2005; and D Chandler (ed), *Peace without Politics? Ten Years of International Statebuilding in Bosnia*, London: Routledge, 2006.
44 'Little chance of Bosnia joining EU by 2014', *B92*, 22 August 2009, at http://www.b92.net/eng/news/region-article.php?yyyy=2009&mm=08&dd=22&nav_id=61301, accessed 18 September 2009.
45 See P Ashdown, 'The European Union and statebuilding in the Western Balkans', *Journal of Intervention and Statebuilding*, 1(1), 2007, pp 107–118.
46 D Farrell, 'Democracy promotion, domestic responsibility and the impact of international intervention on the political life of Republika Srpska', unpublished PhD thesis, National University of Ireland, Maynooth, January 2008.
47 G Venneri, 'The EU "hands-off" statebuilding: from Bosnia-Herzegovina to Kosovo', paper presented at the International Studies Association's 49th Annual Convention, San Francisco, 26 March 2008.
48 See European Stability Initiative, *The Worst in Class: How the International Protectorate Hurts the European Future of Bosnia and Herzegovina*, Berlin: ESI, 2007, at http://www.esiweb.org/pdf/esi_document_id_98.pdf, accessed 18 September 2009; and T Muehlmann, 'Police restructuring in Bosnia-Herzegovina: problems of internationally-led security sector reform', *Journal of Intervention and Statebuilding*, 2(1), 2008, pp 1–22.
49 See, for example, the Oxford Research International report for the United Nations Development Programme, *The Silent Majority Speaks: Snapshots of Today and Visions of the Future of Bosnia and Herzegovina*, 2007, at http://www.undp.ba/download.aspx?id=1127, accessed 12 October 2009.
50 See, for example, the 280-page document outlining the timetable for implementing the EU's medium priorities, European Partnership for Bosnia and Herzegovina, *Medium Term Priorities Realisation Programme*, Sarajevo: European Directorate for Integration, nd.
51 See further J Poels, 'Bosnia and Herzegovina: a new "neutral" flag', *Flagmaster*, 98, 1998, pp 9–12
52 See Chandler, *Peace without Politics?*
53 See Friedrich Ebert Stiftung, *Arithmetic of Irresponsibility—Political Analysis of Bosnian Domestic and Foreign Affairs*, Sarajevo: FES, 2005.
54 Keohane, 'The ironies of sovereignty', pp 755–756. See also R Paris, *At War's End: Building Peace after Civil Conflict*, Cambridge: Cambridge University Press, 2004, pp 187–194.

The EU in Central Asia: successful good governance promotion?

KATHARINA HOFFMANN

ABSTRACT *A reappraisal of security and economic interests has led to increased engagement by the European Union with Central Asia in the past few years. As a new foreign policy tool the EU adopted a new partnership strategy for Central Asia in 2007. The strategy aims to integrate both interest-based and governance-related policy ambitions. In the two years since the strategy was adopted activities concerning the implementation of good governance-related initiatives are still rather weak. This article discusses the obstacles and prospects for good governance promotion in Central Asia. The prospects for external good governance promotion in stable authoritarian environments are limited. Domestic economic pressure increases the willingness of the Central Asian incumbent governments to enter into international agreements and widens the scope of external good governance promotion. Yet the prioritisation of interest-based policy objectives and the reluctance to employ conditionalities on the part of the EU provide an opportunity for the Central Asian regimes to limit their concessions and feign reforms. Initiatives focusing on grassroots levels appear to be the most promising in terms of the diffusion of ideas of good governance and democracy.*

Until recently Central Asia hardly existed on the map of European foreign policy. Only during the early years of the 21st century did the European Union start paying more attention to the region, intensifying its financial engagement and readjusting its foreign policy tools for the area. The *Strategy for a New Partnership* was adopted by the European Council in 2007 as a core foreign policy instrument.[1] The EU's new engagement was motivated by the new strategic relevance of Central Asia, as EU enlargement had brought it closer to the borders of the Union and the region's vast supply of energy resources was being recognised. Accordingly, the EU's foreign policy ambitions in the region are motivated by both interest-based issues and value-based policy aims like good governance and democracy promotion.

The strengthening of 'democracy, human rights, the rule of law and good governance' is presented as one of three priority areas of the strategy. However, in the first two years since adoption of the strategy, implementation efforts and results concerning the promotion of good governance have been weak. Set against this background, this article discusses the obstacles and prospects for good governance promotion in the framework of the latest EU strategy for the five former Soviet republics Kazakhstan, Kyrgyzstan, Tajikistan, Turkmenistan and Uzbekistan.

The EU's Central Asia strategy depicts good governance in a rather technocratic way, focusing on administrative reform and transparency of public finances. Yet it is emphasised that good governance, the rule of law, democratic process, civil society and respect for human rights are fundamentally intertwined.[2] For these reasons, the article focuses both on the wider context of good governance and on the technocratic use of the term. It discusses efforts to implement good governance and democracy-related projects formulated in the strategy rather than the impact the EU's approach has had on the general governance performance of the countries under study, since it is difficult to assess the impact of external action after only two years. Based on theoretical considerations it is argued that the scope for the external promotion of good governance in an authoritarian environment like Central Asia is in any case very limited.

EU good governance projects are aimed at both the level of government and that of society. Thanks to the relative stability of the regimes in Central Asia and the EU's economic and strategic interests, the EU lacks the appropriate instruments for successful good governance and democracy promotion at the government level. In the past two years the Central Asian states have made concessions in several governance-related areas. Yet these are motivated rather by the need for international contacts than compliance with good governance principles and tend to be organised in a way that limits their impact on the political regime and society. Projects directed at grassroots level appear to have better prospects for success.

The second section of the article discusses some theoretical considerations related to the external promotion of political reforms in authoritarian environments and provides an overview of the political regimes in the region. The next three sections analyse the EU's engagement with Central Asia and discuss the process of strategy implementation with regard to good governance promotion. The article ends with some concluding observations.

External impact on political reform

In its *Strategy for a New Partnership*, the EU emphasises that 'lessons learnt from the political and economic transformation of Central Eastern Europe' are considered to be helpful for the 'development and consolidation of stable, just and open societies, adhering to international norms'.[3] In the case of Central Eastern Europe the EU's external democratisation policy was targeted at regimes that were already in the process of transition. Furthermore, countries were embedded in the enlargement process, which allowed the EU to impose strong conditionalities. Given that the five Central Asian countries can hardly be considered regimes in transition and that the EU does not provide clear incentives for compliance, one needs to ask how helpful the lessons learnt from the transformation of Central Eastern Europe actually are with regard to Central Asia.

What does the theory of external influence on political reform tell us about the scope of externally stimulated transitions to democracy and good governance? Regarding external promotion of political reform, first of all diffuse processes have to be distinguished from concrete strategic attempts to trigger political reform. Both mechanisms are complementary but their impact differs depending on the political environment. Geoffrey Pridham has argued that norm diffusion as an indirect process of democracy promotion has a high potential to foster political change. The spread of ideas on democracy and good governance is expected to challenge the legitimacy of non-democratic regimes and to open a window of opportunity for democratic reform.[4]

Conditions for the success of concrete agendas to stimulate political reform have been discussed since the very beginning of the transition debate. Dankwart Rustow, one of the first scholars of 'transitology', has proposed the rather vague advice that democracy promoters should 'force, trick, lure or cajole non-democrats into democratic behaviour'.[5] His basic idea is that the cost–benefit calculus of non-democratic actors needs to be influenced. Continued adherence to non-democratic norms should be made more costly than acceptance of the costs of change to a democratic set of norms. Changing elites' cost–benefit assessment is expected to lead ultimately to democratisation. According to this analytical approach, external actors are advised to employ various tools of democracy promotion—including political dialogue and negotiation, capacity building, strategic advice, and conditionality—that will make continuation of non-democratic governance costly for domestic political elites.

When does non-democratic rule get too costly for non-democratic leaders and when would the institution of democratic processes become a viable alternative? Domestic factors, including the strength of the non-democratic regime and structural characteristics of the given society, determine whether a regime is able to withstand international democratisation pressures.[6] More precisely, Henry Hale has argued that the power of the incumbent government and the role of the national elite are crucial predictors of political change. Analysing the dynamics of the so-called 'colour revolutions' in the post-Soviet space, he concluded that political change was accompanied by international and internal pressures for democratisation but should ultimately be understood as a process set in motion by national political elites in response to those pressures.

Locating himself in the literature on neo-patrimonialism, Hale argues that the core dynamics of regime change depend on the relation between the elites and the incumbent government. Only when the incumbent government loses its popularity and power elites start to form new coalitions is a process triggered that may result in political change. The logic of power maintenance in neo-patrimonial regimes seriously limits regimes' willingness for political reform that is aimed at good governance and the participation of societal actors, if the incumbent government and political elites are strong. Elements of good governance such as transparency, participation and the strengthening of formal institutions would undermine the basis for rule and power maintenance. Despite all this, Hale argues that incumbent governments may be open to certain learning processes. Because of the need for integration into the international economy and political arena and the need for incumbent governments to prevent regime change, non-democratic governments in the post-Soviet space reacted to the international support given to democratisation movements. This did not lead to democratisation of the countries concerned, however. On the contrary, governments attempted to weaken or co-opt civil society organisations and made limited concessions to international democratisation efforts as long as they could still be controlled by the regime.[7]

In a nutshell, the theoretical approaches presented in this section emphasise that, whereas the long-term impact of the diffusion of democratic norms on society and political elites appears to be relatively effective, the outcome of direct strategies of democracy promotion is highly dependent on regime stability and the power to stimulate non-democratic regimes to adopt democratic principles. Concessions made by non-democratic governments need to be evaluated carefully, since they could be little more than liberal window dressing. In order to evaluate both the strength of the regimes and the EU's potential to exert pressure on the governments of Central Asia, the following section presents a short overview of the regimes in the region.

Political regimes in Central Asia

On the basis of the Freedom House democracy index, one needs to be sceptical about the claim that the Central Asian states are undergoing a process of transition. Apart from Kyrgyzstan, which is labelled a 'semi-consolidated authoritarian regime', all the countries in the region are categorised as 'consolidated authoritarian regimes'. Nevertheless a discussion of some characteristics of regime stability, liberalisation efforts, economic performance and the countries' internal pressure to co-operate with international actors is helpful to evaluate the environment in which the EU is trying to promote good governance.

Over the past decade scholars have increasingly been applying the concept of neo-patrimonialism to characterise the political regimes of Central Asia. The main elements of the term—personalised power, monopolisation of resources at the regime's centre, the predominance of informal institutions and controlled access to political power—are clearly applicable to the countries in question.[8] After the breakdown of the USSR all five Newly Independent States have adopted some principles of democratic rule into their constitutions. Despite this political change, the political and economic system of the countries is still fundamentally shaped by the Soviet legacy. This is hardly surprising given the continuity of governments and elites. Kyrgyzstan was the only country to undergo more fundamental political change in the so-called 'tulip revolution', but even this has had hardly any democratising effect.[9] Most governments used existing clan structures and the erosion of formal institutions that had been created in the Soviet period to build up a system of governance revolving around personalised power.

The presidents of Turkmenistan, Kazakhstan and Uzbekistan, in particular, conceived personalised power in a very traditional way when they appointed their relatives to key economic and political positions.[10] But also in post-tulip-revolution Kyrgyzstan kinship and clientelist relations are vital when it comes to the distribution of positions in the regime.[11] Their role in the privatisation of state-owned enterprises gave the presidents the opportunity to strengthen their regimes. While the degree of privatisation varies from country to country—with Tajikistan being the most reluctant in this regard and Kyrgyzstan performing quite well—the political and economic sectors remain strongly intertwined in all Central Asian countries. Even if economic actors are not formally tied to the state, informal ties ensure control on part of the regime.

Presidential and parliamentary elections are among the most popular institutions to feign democratic intentions. The presidents of Kazakhstan, Tajikistan and Uzbekistan have made sure that limits to presidential terms have been abolished, but still continue to organise elections. Other candidates do formally participate in such elections, but incumbent presidents are usually re-elected with 80% to 90% of the votes. In 2006 Turkmenistan saw the smooth installation of a presidential candidate designated by his predecessor. The transfer of the presidency to Gurbanguly Berdimukhamedov after Sarparmurat Niyazov's sudden death was accompanied by position re-shuffles, but did not lead to visible conflicts within the regime. This succession process indicates how strong Turkmenistan's regime actually was. In contrast to Turkmenistan's experience, elections in Kyrgyzstan in July 2009 led to protests in the capital Bishkek. Nevertheless, such protests hardly affected the regime and president Bakiev stayed on for a new term.[12] In Tajikistan the 1990s had been characterised by a high degree of political instability, but president Rakhmon has managed to stabilise his regime in recent years.

Regardless of their degree of authoritarian performance all regimes under scrutiny have relied relatively successfully on logics of governance and power maintenance that defy principles of transparency and political participation. Accordingly, there is not much sign of civil society in most of these countries, although civil society organisations exist at least formally. The environment for civil society activities is most favourable in Kyrgyzstan. The relative openness of the country in this regard is not only reflected in the relatively large number of protests in Kyrgyzstan: non-governmental organisations were even granted a certain influence on fundamental issues like the revision of the constitution.[13]

The Kazakh regime has relied on the co-optation of civil society organisations—a tendency that has notably increased since 2005 in reaction to the 'colour revolutions' taking place in the post-socialist space. The governmental initiation of non-governmental organisations is a common strategy.[14] The Kazakh initiative to establish an official dialogue between civil society organisations and the government was interpreted widely as an instrument to control non-governmental activities rather than a possibility for broader societal participation.[15]

Turkmenistan's society has experienced limited liberalisation during the past few years after the disappearance of president Niyazov's authoritarian regime. Liberalisation efforts expressed themselves mainly in socioeconomic and educational reform. Despite the adoption of an amendment to the constitution in 2008 aimed at strengthening the role of parliament and allowing for a multiparty system, the country has known hardly any effective political liberalisation.[16] The authoritarian rule of Turkmenistan's president Berdimukhamedov has been facilitated by the regime's extraction of rents from natural gas production and oil export. On the one hand, high rents are an effective instrument to prevent serious unrest in society. On the other hand, they allow the country to stay relatively isolated from the global economy and hence be less affected by the global financial crisis. Berdimukhamedov seems to be more open to international co-operation than his predecessor, a position that appears to be inspired in large part by disagreements with Russia over gas exports. Nevertheless, Turkmenistan often appears to be nothing more than a silent observer in most international fora.[17]

In comparison to Turkmenistan, Kazakhstan's profile on the international stage is relatively weak and the country is struggling hard to be accepted internationally as a regional leader. Its strong economic growth of the past few years may have served as a basis for regime stability as well as international recognition. Despite the fact that the country took over the chairmanship of the Organisation for Security and Co-operation in Europe (OSCE) in 2010 there are few signs of compliance with democratic principles.[18] Uzbekistan's foreign policy can best be described as a movement back and forth between the eastern and western vector, while the country is eager to obtain a leading position in the region.[19] President Karimov recently turned to his Western partners again mainly because of the economic situation facing the country.[20]

In similar but less powerful ways both Tajikistan and Kyrgyzstan have attempted to balance their foreign policy allegiance between Russia and Western actors, as they badly need economic support.[21] Tajikistan's economic performance in particular is very poor and enormous socioeconomic problems have arisen because of this. The country is highly dependent on its neighbours Uzbekistan and Turkmenistan in terms of energy supply. Its reliance on international assistance for the completion of planned hydropower plants and for general economic support is the main incentive for Tajikistan to engage in co-operation with Western actors.[22]

By way of conclusion, it is evident that the regimes of all these Central Asian countries, and *a fortiori* Turkmenistan, Uzbekistan and Kazakhstan, appear to be fairly stable. Economic pressure combined with leadership ambitions on the international stage have made the countries more sensitive to international co-operation and opened a window of opportunity for concrete good governance promotion strategies. Yet ambitions regarding governance quality are limited by the internal logics of power maintenance of the relatively strong authoritarian regimes. The predominance of clientelism implies that even the technocratic elements of good governance, revolving around transparency in administration, may pose substantial challenges to Central Asian regimes. International pressures are much more intense in the case of Tajikistan and Kyrgyzstan, where the scope for external influence on governance practices does consequently seem to be wider.

The European Union in Central Asia

The above discussion indicated that the scope for EU good governance and democracy promotion is very limited in Turkmenistan, Uzbekistan and Kazakhstan and only a little bigger in Tajikistan and Kyrgyzstan. Against this background the application of EU instruments for governance-related reform would seem to be crucial for the prospects of EU good governance promotion in this region. A more detailed overview of the design and implementation of EU instruments is needed in order to provide clarity on this issue.

The EU's external relations are driven by its self-conception as a soft power anxious to spread its fundamental ideas and norms throughout the world. As outlined in the EU Security Strategy the overall ambition is 'to promote a ring of well governed countries' in the EU's neighbourhood in order to increase the security of the EU.[23] Accordingly, good governance takes a prominent position on the EU agenda for Central Asia. The *Strategy for a New Partnership*, however, was meant to be a comprehensive policy tool incorporating and integrating both value-based ambitions and interest-driven stakes in the region. The promotion of values and the safeguarding of interests require different mechanisms of negotiation and implementation. When analysing the success or failure of EU good governance promotion in the relatively stable authoritarian environment of Central Asia, the crucial question is how these two components interact. Are they complementary or contrasting and how are they weighed? The following analysis of the development of EU engagement with Central Asia provides some insight into EU priorities.

During their first years of independence the Central Asian states did not receive much attention from the European Union. In comparison with the Eastern European states both the financial and political engagement with Central Asia were rather weak. Until 2001 EU–Central Asia relations were subsumed under the EU external policy instrument for post-Soviet states, the so-called bilateral Partnership and Cooperation Agreements (PCAs). This instrument mainly focused on economic co-operation and trade and paid only secondary attention to good governance and democratic rule.

Initially bilateral PCAs had been negotiated with Kazakhstan, Kyrgyzstan, Uzbekistan and Turkmenistan only. The violent conflict in Tajikistan prevented a similar process with that country until a ceasefire agreement had been concluded in 1998. By that time the PCAs for Kazakhstan, Kyrgyzstan and Uzbekistan had already come into force. Turkmenistan's general reluctance to engage in international relations and its problematic human rights situation slowed down the process of negotiation with that country significantly. A PCA with Turkmenistan was eventually signed in 1998. Despite the fact that they were agreed over a decade ago, the PCAs of Tajikistan and Turkmenistan are still in the process of ratification by the EU member states.

The PCAs consist of three parts: 'political dialogue', 'co-operation' and 'trade'. The overwhelming majority of activities and common aims relate to trade and economic co-operation. Despite the fact that the PCAs are based on compliance with the principles of democracy, human rights and the rule of law, the wording remains vague when it comes to the concrete promotion of these principles in the Central Asian context. The PCA documents exhibit little more than the ambition to support ongoing political change and strengthen the countries' link with the democratic community through political dialogue. Taking the post-war situation in Tajikistan into account, the political dialogue is intended to cover primarily co-operation against terrorism and the proliferation of weapons of mass destruction. Political dialogue was planned at the ministerial and parliamentary level at a rather low frequency.

Other institutional frameworks for stabilising bilateral co-operation had also been envisaged.[24] Yet, in the case of Kazakhstan, Kyrgyzstan and Uzbekistan, such instruments have hardly served to frame bilateral relations, as these were characterised much more by ad-hoc and issue-based initiatives. The central instrument to back up co-operation as projected in the PCA was the Technical Aid to the Commonwealth of Independent States (TACIS) fund launched in 1991. Between 1991 and 2001 assistance funds of some €419 million were allocated to the five Central Asian countries. Uzbekistan and Kazakhstan received the largest share (€167 million), while Turkmenistan and Tajikistan have not received more than €50 and €8 million, respectively. Total EU assistance to Central Asia up to 2001 amounted to €970 million, the biggest part of which was spent on humanitarian support for Tajikistan and Kyrgyzstan in the 1990s.[25] Trade flows between the EU and Central Asia remain rather limited. Companies from various EU member states tried to gain a foothold in the region's mineral and oil commodities in the early 1990s. Their success, however, has been rather limited.[26] The EU's minor interest in the region is reflected additionally in the absence of EU representation in the region. The first EU delegation office in Central Asia was established in Kazakhstan only in 2001. Among the EU member states only Germany and the UK maintain consulates in all five countries.[27]

Overall 2001 marked a watershed in EU–Central Asia relations. As a result of the international focus on terrorism after '9/11', the Central Asian states came to be viewed in a different light and EU engagement with the region received a boost. Security considerations and the region's energy resources have been shaping the new agenda. The initial event in this regard was the war in Afghanistan, which suddenly attributed new strategic importance to Central Asia. On the one hand, military co-operation with Kyrgyzstan and Uzbekistan became vital for those EU member states involved in Operation

Enduring Freedom, as they needed access to military bases in the region. On the other hand, EU and member state commitment to the region increased as a result of fears about the relative weakness of the state in Tajikistan and the spread of Islamic extremism in Tajikistan and Uzbekistan, and concomitant concerns about the spread of terrorism and organised crime to the states bordering Afghanistan.[28] Such concerns gained importance especially after the EU's Eastern enlargement, which reduced the geographic distance between the EU and Central Asia. These considerations led the EU to more-or-less abandon the idea that Central Asia belonged to the Russian sphere of interest and encouraged it to establish closer ties with countries in the region.[29]

A further step in the EU's interest in Central Asia was triggered by the need to diversify energy supply to the EU. Fuelled by the Russia–Ukraine gas crises that started in 2006 and culminated in the winter of 2009 in shortages of gas supply in EU countries, the EU increased its efforts to speed up the building of the Nabucco gas pipeline, which is meant for the transportation of gas from Kazakhstan, Turkmenistan and Uzbekistan.[30]

The newly recognised importance of the region for the EU led to the gradual formulation of a comprehensive approach to Central Asia, accompanied by increased financial engagement. The first step in the process was the formulation of the *Strategy Paper for Central Asia 2002–2006*. This strategy aimed to improve the democratic process and respect for human rights, and to assist the Central Asian countries with the transition to a market economy. Further, the EU wished to contribute to greater security and the elimination of sources of political and social tension, as well as to a better environment for trade and investment. The EU allocated €150 million from the TACIS budget to implement this strategy over a three-year period.[31] The EU's latest strategy for Central Asia, adopted in 2007, increased the financial commitments to Central Asia. The new strategy contains a budget of €750 million for the period 2007–13.

The account of increased EU engagement with Central Asia so far has shown that the EU has been motivated mainly by security and economic interests. Even though governance-related components have always been part of EU ambitions, stronger emphasis had been placed on economic co-operation. The prominence of economic relations reflected the Central Asian states' reluctance to engage in political reform. The minor role of good governance promotion in the PCAs was, therefore, hardly surprising.

The latest EU document, *Strategy for a New Partnership*, seems, however to reflect a rather new take on the issue of governance and democracy promotion in Central Asia. This strategy proposes seven areas of co-operation that are, at least formally, equally important. Economic and security-related issues like promotion of 'economic development', 'trade and investment', 'energy and transport links' and 'combating common threats and challenges' are accompanied by the softer value-based clusters 'human rights, rule of law, good governance and democratisation', 'youth and education' and 'intercultural dialogue'. In addition to these broad areas of co-operation, three so-called flagship initiatives are highlighted that all relate to good governance in a wider perspective. The 'European education initiative' and the 'e-silk-highway' both aim at capacity building and improved access to information. The 'European rule of law initiative' is designed to foster judicial reform by dialogue at a political as well as an expert level and long-term co-operation projects between Central Asia and European institutions.[32] Bilateral and multilateral dialogue, which is the most important EU soft power instrument, is foreseen on energy co-operation and respect for human rights. One-quarter of the total budget is allocated to the priority area 'Support for good governance and economic reform'.[33] Co-operation and assistance in the areas mentioned above are to be implemented, *inter alia*, by public–private partnership initiatives, technical assistance, and the twinning and seconding of EU and Central Asian government staff.

The multitude of envisioned projects and instruments is meant to serve the EU's economic, security and norm-based interests all at the same time. Economic interests mentioned in the strategy relate to the improvement of the investment climate in the region, improved access to EU markets and energy-related co-operation. The combating of terrorism, drug trafficking and organised crime rank first within the domain of security. The overall aim with regard to governance is to contribute to the 'development and consolidation of stable, just and open societies, adhering to international norms'. The term 'good governance' is conceived in a rather technical way in the strategy as it refers primarily to effectiveness and transparency of administration. Focus areas of the EU approach include the promotion of civil society, human rights and the democratic process, judicial reform and rule of law as well as public administration.[34] Projects concerning good governance and related issues are envisaged both at the level of government and society. Whereas the 'European rule of law initiative' and the 'human rights dialogue' would include high-level politicians and practitioners on both sides, capacity-building projects are included to address non-governmental actors at the local level. Education-related initiatives focus on international exchange programmes and enhanced access to information.

In an attempt to strengthen the value-based components of the strategy, the EU has introduced notions of conditionality. Enhanced co-operation on security and economic matters is made dependent on the region's performance in relation to democratic and governance reform.[35] The EU's leverage on these issues is, however, rather weak. The EU's attempts to increase the costs of non-compliance with the norms on democratisation and governance were important steps, since in the past the regimes had hardly demonstrated an interest even in the more technocratic aspects of the good governance agenda, as was pointed out above. Although it is difficult to tell after only two years, effective usage of conditionalities seems to depend on the consistent application of the rules in order effectively to increase the costs of non-compliance for the regimes concerned. The following section explores the implementation of the new EU strategy for Central Asia and highlights its priorities and successes in the area of governance.

Strategy implementation: facing autocrats

After a very slow start a relatively high number of projects has been launched in the framework of the EU's Central Asia strategy. These projects indicate that the EU is placing emphasis on implementation and that Central Asian states are willing to co-operate with the EU. Implementation of the strategy appears to be most advanced with regard to interest-based issues. Some general features can be observed in relation to the implementation of projects in the cluster 'human rights, rule of law, good governance and democratisation'. Implementation of projects in that area started reluctantly and seems to be successful predominantly in countries that are faced with greater internal pressure for international co-operation. In general, projects are limited to rendering technical support and transferring knowledge by using a seminar format. Furthermore, conditionalities are hardly ever followed by actions, a situation that weakens the effectiveness of EU instruments. As is argued below, this situation is largely the result of the prioritisation of stable long-term economic relations by the EU.

The formulation of the EU's strategy for Central Asia was accompanied by a general change in the approach towards the Central Asian democratic deficit. Instead of the application of hard conditionalities, involving the imposition of sanctions in cases of fundamental human rights violations, a new formula of 'norm diffusion by steady dialogue' was introduced. In recognition of the fact that Central Asian states are not very dependent on their relations with Western Europe and in response to several cases of unilateral withdrawal from projects by Central Asian states, the EU wished to make sure that the five states would be ready to talk.

The 'human rights dialogue', the 'European rule of law initiative', the 'European education initiative' and the governance-related projects took shape only by the end of 2008. As a first step projects were set up to support non-state-actors, local authorities and civil society initiatives. Tajikistan, and to a lesser extent Kyrgyzstan and Kazakhstan, have been the main partners in these projects. In all cases the overwhelming part of the budget was spent on technical equipment. A large proportion of the projects addressed government agencies, and only a few involved societal actors.

The 'civil service reform and good governance' programme in Tajikistan, for example, supplied the Civil Service Department with office equipment to improve the implementation of civil service tasks. In a similar way, the support of health management and public finance management in the country remained confined to the provision of communication systems. Projects aimed at transferring knowledge appear to be less frequent at this stage. Some examples of such projects are to be found in Tajikistan and Kyrgyzstan, where advice is being provided in the area of the law on pensions and social protection. Projects on HIV/AIDS and general health protection have been launched to support non-governmental actors and local authorities in Tajikistan. Finally, seminars were held in this country to improve journalists' knowledge of economics.[36]

The basic framework for exchange of expertise and knowledge transfer to foster reform in Kazakhstan is the joint EU–Kazakh Support for the Development of the Policy Dialogue Advice Programme (PDAP). The main instruments of knowledge transfer are seminars that present best-practice options from the EU. Engagement from the Kazakh side seems to be fairly limited.[37] Legal and policy support is also being provided to strengthen the position of lawyers in Kazakhstan and to promote judiciary reform in Kyrgyzstan. The judiciary in these countries is supported, moreover, by providing better access to Interpol.[38] This step has been criticised by human rights organisations since the project may be abused for the persecution of human rights activists. It seems justifiable to conclude that the implementation of projects on governance and administrative reform so far appears to be limited to providing material support and rather superficial knowledge transfer, whereas hardly any project has addressed issues of capacity building for non-governmental organisations.

At the grassroots level the 'youth and education' cluster seems to occupy a more central role. Most activities are part of the Erasmus Mundus and Tempus programmes or are supported by the European Training Foundation.[39] The projects focus on international exchange in higher education and the opening and improvement of the educational system. Moreover the 'e-silk highway', a platform intended to improve access to relevant resources for Central Asian academics, is in the process of realisation.

Initiatives that focus on co-operation with the Central Asian governments are at risk of not going beyond the declaratory level, as the examples of the 'European law initiative' and the 'human rights dialogue' indicate. The former initiative was launched more than one year after the adoption of the Central Asia strategy, and aims to enhance political dialogue and co-operation between judicial institutions and the administration of the EU and its Central Asian partners in a predominantly multilateral framework. Until today, however, implementation results have hardly matched the high ambitions. Most progress is visible in the establishment of a political dialogue at the ministerial level. During a ministerial conference in 2008 the partners agreed to hold two follow-up conferences, in Bishkek and Tashkent, in 2009. The Bishkek conference was postponed, which seems to indicate that the Central Asian states are reluctant to adopt the format that had been proposed. The tendency to avoid controversial issues and concentrate on common interests, which was highlighted earlier in the article, applies to this issue as well. The dialogue has concentrated hitherto on commercial and trade-related reforms of the legal and judicial system rather than on reforms affecting governance and democracy directly. Observers rate the effect of this initiative and related projects very low as they argue that the political dialogue is only another 'political talking shop undermining the EU's commitment to back up strategic priorities with practical action'.[40]

The impact of the human rights dialogues can be assessed in a similar way to the European law initiative. Experiences in this area, in particular, demonstrate that, on the one hand, Central Asian governments are willing to make only limited concessions and, on the other hand, the EU is not ready to apply its conditionalities. The establishment of the human rights dialogues had already taken place before the adoption of the EU's new Central Asia strategy. The EU agreed to hold an *ad hoc* dialogue with Turkmenistan in 2005. The EU and the Central Asian states agreed to upgrade the dialogue from an *ad hoc* to a regular event at a ministerial conference in April 2008. The dialogue includes meetings at different political levels as well as civil society and media seminars.[41]

The Uzbek reaction to the first human rights dialogue in 2007 provides an illustration of the impact of the instrument. For the dialogue the EU had proposed to include a wide range of topics, including freedom of opinion, of the media and individual cases of human rights violations. Although Uzbekistan accepted the dialogue, it managed to limit attendance at the dialogue to low-level politicians. Human rights activist and civil society representatives were not admitted. The Uzbek strategy demonstrated a merely formal commitment to democracy promotion tools such as the human rights dialogue, as well as the country's ability to effectively weaken the impact of the instrument. From an Uzbek perspective the fact that the dialogue took place was not without result. Both Uzbek foreign minister Vladimir Norov and representatives of the EU referred to the dialogue as a positive development in the country's human rights performance, and for the EU it was an argument that enabled it to lift its sanctions on Uzbekistan.[42]

An Uzbek–EU media conference planned for the spring of 2008 showed similar dynamics. The conference had been proposed by the Uzbek government in response to the EU decision to freeze the sanctions. First scheduled for May 2008, the conference was postponed at very short notice to June 2008. This step prevented international human rights organisations attending. Following an EU appeal to the Uzbek government, the conference was rescheduled for October 2008. At that time international groups were invited but Uzbek journalists and civil society groups were excluded from participating in the conference.[43]

Other roundtables and projects related to human rights show similar patterns.[44] Before the human rights dialogue in Uzbekistan in 2009 international human rights organisations appealed to the EU to avoid this format as the dialogues would be a tokenistic event that authoritarian regimes could use to deflect criticism.[45] The ambitions of the Uzbek government to keep discussions on sensitive topics like human rights issues as marginal as possible were expressed by foreign minister Norov in a recent bilateral EU–Uzbek meeting. He emphasised the equality of the partners in the EU–Uzbek relationship and argued that the agenda should not be set unilaterally by the EU, with the aim of preventing sensitive democracy-related issues being raised.[46] Finally, the Uzbek government's resolve to avoid value-based debates is reflected in a report of the 19th Economic Forum that brought together international experts to discuss EU–Central Asian relations. A session dedicated to authoritarianism and religious extremism in Central Asia was apparently cancelled as a result of interventions by the Uzbek delegation.[47]

Overall, most initiatives in the EU–Central Asia relationship seem to have been inspired by (economic) security concerns. As part of the EU's Border

Management Programme in Central Asia (BOMCA) and its Central Asia Drug Action Programme (CADAP), which had been established in 2003 and 2004, several projects have been initiated to provide technical equipment and training for border control and anti-drugs activities. Efforts in Kazakhstan and Kyrgyzstan focus mainly on training projects, while the activities in Tajikistan, Uzbekistan and Turkmenistan concentrate on material support.[48] The projects focus on predominantly technical issues, and this implies that the divergence of security concepts applied by the EU and Central Asian states do not stand in the way of intensive co-operation.[49] Similar engagement can be observed in the field of energy. The Interstate Oil and Gas Transport to Europe (INOGATE) and Transport Corridor between Europe and Asia (TRACEA) programmes serve as frameworks for initiatives concerning regional co-operation, infrastructure and environmental problems in the domain of oil and gas. Bilateral memoranda of understanding on energy co-operation have been signed between the EU and Kazakhstan and Turkmenistan. The EU seems unconcerned about the unwillingness of Kazakhstan, Turkmenistan and Uzbekistan to collaborate in certain other areas, and seems motivated primarily by the wish to get these countries to participate in the Nabucco Pipeline project, which is meant to reduce the EU's dependence on Russian gas. An important event in this regard was the participation of the three states in the EU Energy Summit in Prague in 2009. Even though none of the Central Asian countries signed the final declaration of the summit their mere presence was seen as an important step towards future co-operation.[50]

This section has demonstrated that the implementation process of the EU's Central Asia strategy with regard to governance reform is conditioned by the compliance of the Central Asian regimes. Turkmenistan and Uzbekistan, which both have a rather strong bargaining position, are hardly involved in good governance, rule of law and human rights initiatives. To the extent that these countries do get involved in such initiatives, they appear to be well able to emasculate these. Crucially they have prevented initiatives from going beyond seminar level and involving non-governmental actors. Weak ambitions on the part of the EU to enforce conditionalities further widen the scope for the Central Asian regimes to benefit from co-operation with the EU and prevent changes that might challenge their power. Given the ability of the Central Asian regimes to control and co-opt initiatives focused on non-governmental actors, a more powerful strategy would be to emphasise activities relating to the transfer of ideas of good governance and democracy in society. In that light the international dimension of the educational component of the Central Asia strategy and its objectives on 'intercultural dialogue' could be advanced.

Conclusion

This article has discussed EU policies with regard to the promotion of good governance in Central Asia by focusing on the recent *Strategy for a New Partnership*. In line with the strategy governance was considered in a wider perspective, including the rule of law, civil society and administrative reform. The overview of the two years' experience with the strategy provided evidence that regional partners have engaged rather reluctantly with the values promoted by the European Union. Nevertheless, there seems to be much potential for co-operation between the EU and its Central Asian partners in areas where common interests are evident. Due to diverging governance and security conceptions, agreement is not expected to emerge easily with regard to the values and norms embraced by the partners.

As emphasised by analytical approaches to external democracy promotion, both the strength of non-democratic regimes and the extent to which external parties possess instruments for exerting pressure on those regimes are important predictors for the success of external action. An analysis of the political and economic situation in the Central Asian countries indicated that the authoritarian regimes in Turkmenistan, Uzbekistan and Kazakhstan are relatively stable and only marginally dependent on their relationship with the EU. Moreover, their political systems are highly reliant on personalised power and informal processes in political and economic decision making. This means that even rather technical good governance projects focusing on improved transparency in administration would be challenging to the regimes. It was shown that Turkmenistan and Uzbekistan have scarcely become involved in any projects targeting administrative or judicial reform. Kazakhstan appears to be more open in this regard. In any case, given the minor involvement of Kazakh partners in most projects, the EU's Central Asia strategy is not expected to have great impact in this country. As a consequence of their unstable economic situation, Tajikistan and Kyrgyzstan seem to be significantly more susceptible to EU initiatives, but even these countries have participated in few projects focusing on non-governmental actors, human rights or fundamental legal reform.

It seems quite likely that the Central Asian states will be able to ignore critical governance-related initiatives from the European Union, given that the latter's strategy does not seem to place equal emphasis on interest- and value-based elements. This article has argued that Europe's engagement with Central Asia is driven mainly by economic and security interests—for this reason, the EU's ambition to establish stable, long-term relations with countries in the region is strong and tends to override value-based considerations of the European strategy on Central Asia. Even though compliance with principles of democracy and good governance is officially a condition for strengthened partnership with the EU, the EU seems to be rather generous in the assessment of the Central Asian states' efforts in this regard. The EU's approach, in which the 'carrots' for the authoritarian Central Asian regimes are small and conditions are not applied stringently, runs the risk of losing its credibility. The EU's attempt to merge value- and interest-based considerations into one strategy is problematic as this practice leads to the watering down of the value-based approach and fails to produce a comprehensive and consistent foreign policy strategy. In the highly authoritarian environment of Central Asia, the enhancement of international exchange and people-to-people contacts might be more successful, as this might lead to a spread of values concerning governance and democracy in the region.

Notes

1 European Union, *The EU and Central Asia: Strategy for a New Partnership*, Brussels: European Union, 2007.
2 European Commission, *Regional Strategy Paper for Assistance to Central Asia for the Period 2007–2013*, Brussels: European Commission, 2007, p 30.
3 European Union, *The EU and Central Asia*, p 1.
4 G Pridham, 'The international dimension of democratisation: theory, practice and inter-regional comparisons', in G Pridham, E Hering & G Sandford (eds), *Building Democracy: The International Dimension of Democratization in Eastern Europe*, London: Leicester University Press, 1994, pp 8–29.
5 DA Rustow, 'Transition to democracy: towards a dynamic model', *Comparative Politics*, 2(3), 1970, pp 337–363.
6 J Zielonka, 'Foreign made democracy', in J Zielonka & A Pravda (eds), *Democratic Consolidation in Eastern Europe: International and Transnational Factors*, Oxford: Oxford University Press, 2001, p 517.
7 T Carothers, 'The backlash against democracy promotion', *Foreign Affairs*, 85(2), 2006, pp 55–68.
8 SN Eisenstadt, *Traditional Patrimonialism and Modern Neopatrimonialism*, Beverly Hills, CA: Sage, 1973.
9 P Jones Luong, *Institutional Change and Political Continuity in Post-Soviet Central Asia: Power, Perceptions and Pacts*, Cambridge: Cambridge University Press, 2002, p 9.
10 *Eurasia Insight*, 7 July 2007; and A Ilkhamov, 'Neopatrimonialism, interest groups and patronage networks: the impasses of the governance system in Uzbekistan', *Central Asian Survey*, 26(1), 2007, p 75.
11 International Crisis Group, *Kyrgyzstan: A Deceptive Calm*, Asia Briefing 79, 14 August 2008, p 5, at http://www.crisisgroup.org/home/index.cfm?id=5627, accessed 1 October 2009.
12 N Ababakrivo, 'Election in Kyrgyzstan: Bakiyev again', *Central Asia–Caucasus Analyst*, 19 August 2009.
13 B Pannier, 'Kyrgyzstan', in *Nations in Transit: Democratization from Central Europe to Eurasia*, Washington, DC: Freedom House, 2007, p 10.
14 *RFE/RL Newsline*, 22 July 2009.
15 B Dave, 'Kazakhstan', in *Nations in Transit: Democratization from Central Europe to Eurasia*, Washington, DC: Freedom House, 2008.
16 C Durdiyeva, 'Turkmenistan adopts a new constitution', *Central Asia–Caucasus Analyst*, 15 October 2008.
17 L Anceschi, 'Analyzing Turkmen foreign policy in the Berdimukhamedov era', *China and Eurasia Quarterly*, 6(4), 2008, p 39.
18 A Schmitz, *Kasachstan: Neue Führungsmacht im postsowjetischen Raum?*, SWP-Studie 7, 2009.
19 U Halbach, *Usbekistan als Herausforderung für westliche Zentralasienpolitik*, SWP-Studie 26, 2006.
20 *RFE/RL Newsline*, 13 July 2009.
21 *RFE/RL Newsline*, 11 February 2009.
22 *RFE/RL Newsline*, 12 March 2009.
23 Council of the European Union, *A Secure Europe in a Better World: European Security Strategy*, Brussels, 12 December 2003, p 8, at http://www.consilium.europa.eu/uedocs/cmsUpload/78367.pdf, accessed 4 September 2009.
24 See European Commission, *EU's Relations with Central Asia*, at http://ec.europa.eu/external_relations/central_asia/index_en.htm, accessed 12 November 2009.
25 See European Commission, *Trade: Central Asia*, at http://ec.europa.eu/trade/creating-opportunities/bilateral-relations/regions/central-asia/index_en.htm, accessed 12 November 2009.
26 A Matveeva, *EU stakes in Central Asia*, Chaillot Paper 91, Paris: Institute for Security Studies, 2006, p 83.
27 European Commission, *Strategy Paper 2002–2006 and Indicative Programme 2002–2004 for Central Asia*, 2002, p 54, at http://ec.europa.eu/external_relations/central_asia/rsp/02_06_en.pdf, accessed 1 October 2009.
28 A Cooley, 'Principles in the pipeline: managing transatlantic values and interests in Central Asia', *International Affairs*, 84(6), pp 1173–1188.
29 N Kassenova, 'The EU in Central Asia: strategy in the context of Eurasian geopolitics', *Central Asia and the Caucasus*, 4(46), 2007, p 98.

30 *RFE/RL Newsline*, 8 May 2009.
31 European Commission, *Strategy Paper 2002–2006*.
32 European Commission, *EU Rule of Law Initiative for Central Asia*, 28 November 2008, at http://ec.europa.eu/external_relations/central_asia/docs/factsheet_law_en.pdf, accessed 1 October 2009.
33 European Union, *Central Asia Indicative Programme 2007–2010*, at http://ec.europa.eu/external_relations/central_asia/rsp/nip_07_10_en.pdf, accessed 12 November 2009.
34 Council of the European Union, *A Secure Europe in a Better World*, p 21.
35 European Union, *The EU and Central Asia*, p 5.
36 European Commission's Delegation to Kazakhstan, Kyrgyzstan and Tajikistan, *EU Promotes Economic Awareness of Media in Tajikistan*, at http://delkaz.ec.europa.eu/joomla/index.php?option=com_content&task=view&id=648&Itemid=43&lang=en, accessed 12 November 2009.
37 Support for the Development of the Policy Dialogue Advice Programme (PDAP), *The EU Experts Consult Anti-monopoly Agency of the RK*, at http://www.supportpdap.kz/en/news/index.php?ID=1879, accessed 12 November 2009.
38 Interpol, *Launch of EU-funded Project to Expand INTERPOL Tools in Central Asia*, at http://www.interpol.int/Public/ICPO/PressReleases/PR2009/PR200922.asp, accessed 12 November 2009.
39 ETF Project, *National Qualifications Framework*, at http://www.etf.europa.eu/web.nsf/pages/Project_NQF_EN?opendocument, accessed 12 November 2009.
40 R Isaacs, *The EU's Rule of Law Initiative in Central Asia*, EUCAM Policy Brief 9, August 2009, p 4.
41 European Commission, *EU Human Rights Dialogues with Central Asian Countries*, 2008, at http://ec.europa.eu/external_relations/central_asia/docs/factsheet_hr_dialogue_en.pdf, accessed 1 October 2009.
42 *RFE/RL Newsline*, 16 September 2008, 9 April 2008. At a more recent meeting of the European Council, the human rights situation in Uzbekistan was still being criticised. The Council recalled the fact that the intensity of co-operation is bound up with the human rights situation in the country, but did not decide on any concrete measures against Uzbekistan. See Council of the European Union, *Council Conclusions on Uzbekistan*, 2971st External Relations Council meeting, Luxembourg, 27 October 2009, at http://www.consilium.europa.eu/ueDocs/cms_Data/docs/pressData/en/gena/110783.pdf, accessed 12 November 2009.
43 *RFE/RL Newsline*, 2 October 2008.
44 S Ismailov & B Jarabik, *The EU and Uzbekistan: Short-term Interests versus Long-term Engagement*, EUCAM Policy Brief 8, July 2009, p 1.
45 Human Rights Watch, *Human Rights Watch Concerns on Uzbekistan*, 8 June 2009, at http://www.hrw.org/en/news/2009/06/08/human-rights-watch-concerns-uzbekistan-0, accessed 1 October 2009.
46 *RFE/RL Newsline*, 15 September 2009.
47 *RFE/RL Newsline*, 10 September 2009.
48 The European Union's Border Management Programme in Central Asia, *The European Union's Border Management Programme in Central Asia Hands over Refurbished Training Centre of the State Border Service to Turkmenistan*, at http://bomca.eu-bomca.kg/en/news/?news=105, accessed 12 November 2009.
49 N Kassenova, *The New EU Strategy towards Central Asia: A View from the Region*, CEPS Policy Brief 148, 2008, p 2; and *RFE/RL Newsline*, 2 June 2009.
50 *RFE/RL Newsline*, 12 May 2009.

Investigating the Two Faces of Governance: the case of the Euro-Mediterranean Development Bank

KARIM KNIO

ABSTRACT *The literature on governance has recently witnessed a growing tension between a techno-managerial account of governance and a power-sensitive approach. This article argues that the downgrading of power relations by the techno-managerial approach is significantly problematic and counter-productive. Building on the case of the Euro-Mediterranean Development Bank, the article shows how the EU's articulation of the techno-managerial approach has had serious negative implications. On the one hand, it re-emphasised the embedded long-term power asymmetries that have characterised the EU's general governance attitude relationship with its Mediterranean partners. On the other hand, it compromised the credibility of EU policies in addressing and pressing for further reforms in the Mediterranean region.*

Since the beginning of the 1990s, the governance literature has gained increasing importance among development practitioners and academics. There are various explanations of this ascendancy. The end of the Cold War, the proliferation of non-governmental organisations and the emergence of relatively new concepts and practices, such as human intervention and human rights, are some of the driving forces behind this popularity.[1] These developments have also produced new conceptualisations that no longer associated the term 'governance' with the state and the machinery of government, but incorporated various sorts of networks and informal institutions that co-exist and interact with the public sector in an organised community.

Unsurprisingly the governance concept has been defined in different ways depending on the field of study it was used in. In public administration, for example, governance referred more to questions about the way in which public bureaucrats steer inter- and intra-organisational networks in processes of public sector reform,[2] while its usage in the field of international relations was more or less a critique of the once dominant neo-realist paradigm that perceived states as the principal unit of analysis.[3] Similarly governance was conceived as a novel way to capture state–civil society interactions in the field of comparative politics,[4] while the literature springing from new institutional economics (NIE) associated it with the process of institutional design, in which the institutionalisation of property rights is one of the key determinants of long-term economic performance.[5] Next to having different usages, the term has also been used in conjunction with various adjectives: good, bad, global, regional, local, corporate and sectoral. The variety of adjectives is witness to the breadth of the subject matter, as well as to the complexity and interdependence of debates that have followed.

Yet the debate surrounding the nature of governance and its analytical framing remains a fundamental issue that cuts across all these intricate differences. As Hout and Robison have pointed out in a recent publication,[6] two distinctive approaches to governance can be detected virtually across all fields. The first one, often associated with the World Bank, major international donor organisations and national developmental agencies, tends to define and treat governance as a technocratic construction focusing on concerns about the design, sequencing, implementation and enforcement of institutional reforms. In this vein governance epitomises a 'techno-managerial' fix targeting the institutional engineering of mechanisms of anti-corruption, decentralisation, accountability, transparency, and the rule of law, and aiming to complement and strengthen the efficiency of market institutions. Consequently this instrumental view of governance, it has been argued, leads to a certain degree of blindness, providing a platform to circumvent direct political issues in societies.

The second approach is a power-relations perspective *par excellence*. In this view the notion of governance contains an acute understanding of 'conflicts over power and wealth underpinning the establishment of authority in market societies'.[7] The problems surrounding processes of institutional reform are not simply attributed to government capacity or to weak institutions. Such problems are, rather, taken to reflect power dynamics embedded in social and political relations. For this reason governance, according to this analysis, implies a direct engagement with the politically contentious issues existing in a polity.

In this article I show that the European Union's economic governance strategy in its Euro-Mediterranean policies is a good reflection of the first approach presented above. Drawing on the interesting case of the Euro-Mediterranean Development Bank, which the European Commission has repeatedly failed to establish, I demonstrate how the two analytical approaches to governance are reflected in the policy deliberations of this process. I argue that the eventual prioritisation of the first 'technical' approach over the 'power-sensitive' one has created two problems for the EU. The first concerns the nature of the EU's governance approach to the Mediterranean. The fragility of the argument is highlighted by the EU's attempts to attribute the slow pace of reforms to problems of implementation on the part of the Mediterranean partners (MPs). The second problem relates to the credibility of the EU's overall strategy in the region as it exposes the

Union's constraints in anchoring reforms and in bringing the MPs' economies closer to the Single Market.

The next section illustrates why the first analytical approach to governance is inherently 'power insular', referring to examples from the Euro-Mediterranean background. The third section presents a case study of the Euro-Mediterranean Development Bank, before the article is concluded with a discussion of the two problems outlined above.

Why governance as 'techno-managerialism' is 'power insular'

The shift from 'government' to something beyond the realm of governments has significant implications for the manner in which governance is conceptualised. If governance is to be understood generally as the setting, application and enforcement of the rules of the game, as Kjaer has argued,[8] then the institutional grounding of the term is unavoidable. The study of governance has benefited from the distinction between formal and informal institutions made in the neo-institutionalist literature in the social sciences. This approach has resulted in a way of theorising in which institutions mattered again after having been neglected for several decades in the individualist ontology of behavioural and rational choice approaches. The neo-institutionalist counter-revolution itself, however, soon evolved into a broad church of thinking, encompassing at least eight variants across various fields of study. While some of these variants can be seen as complementary, others were specifically formulated to challenge the conceptual and practical tenets of certain variants of neo-institutionalism.[9]

The theoretical underpinnings of the 'techno-managerial' account of governance have been clearly inspired by the literature on the NIE and its equivalent in the field of political science, rational-choice institutionalism (RCI). Both theoretical approaches address the serious limitations of the assumptions of a frictionless world, inherent to previously dominant neo-classical economics and rational choice theory. Although some have argued that NIE and RCI only extended the theoretical range of the previous orthodoxy,[10] many prominent scholars in the field have insisted that the new lines of theorising contain some fundamental starting points that set them apart from earlier approaches.[11] The focus on processes of change, continuity and long-term economic performance were key themes in this regard.

Continuity, change and economic performance in NIE/RCI

One of the most important contributions of the new institutional economics and rational-choice institutionalism was their challenge to the rationality assumption inherent in the previous orthodoxy. Douglass North, for instance, vehemently opposed the 'instrumental rationality' proposition of neo-classical economics and emphasised the importance of what he called 'mental models'. In so doing, he elaborated on how perceptions of reality shape our daily practices and understanding of rules, norms and values. The mental models exemplify why 'lock-in' or 'path-dependency' effects occur and persist over time, even when the will for reform or change is apparent. In his own words, 'history demonstrates that ideas, ideologies, myths, dogmas and prejudices matter'.[12] Given the essential distinction between formal and informal institutions, Denzau and North argued that reform will generally be easier in formal institutions than in informal ones, because of the time lag associated with adjusting mental models in the latter. From this perspective, the process of institutional change is understood to be inevitably incremental.[13]

Further, the NIE/RCI literature clearly indicated that the process of institutional change is not only gradual, but also conscious. Key to this argument is the analytical separation between, and the concomitant interaction of, institutions and organisations. North's seminal contributions to the literature make a distinction between (formal and informal) institutions, seen as aggregations of rules that define how the game (human interaction) is played, and organisations, which consist of groups of individuals guided by the pursuit of common objectives in different spheres (politics, the economy, society, or education). This analytical distinction comes with a Giddens-like line of argumentation, according to which institutions shape and condition the creation of organisations, while organisations, which invest in the development of skills, knowledge and technology for their own survival, are the source and driving force of institutional change. For North:

> the organisations that come into existence will reflect the opportunities provided by the institutional matrix. That is, if the institutional framework rewards piracy then piratical organisations will come into existence; and if the institutional framework rewards productive activities then organisations—firms—will come into existence to engage in productive activities.[14]

If the process of change is propelled by the synchronisation between organisations and institutions, then the institutional anchoring of incentives that protect and safeguard property rights is the core of NIE/RCI's understanding of medium- and long-term economic performance. Since the institutional framework, or matrix, comprises opportunities and constraints by which organisations or players are rationally bounded, 'one gets efficient institutions by a polity that has built-in incentives to create and enforce efficient property rights'.[15] In this perspective property rights are the central economic institutions in society. Their implementation, however, is not restricted to the economic realm but also involves the political system and the norms that co-exist with it.[16]

With regard to the political system, the literature emphasises how incremental institutional engineering makes the rules of formal institutions that enforce property rights more transparent, accountable, predictable and streamlined.[17] Moreover, the literature addresses the incentive structure that causes rationally bounded actors to comply with the 'new' rules: the more rational it is for players to stick to the rules of the game that enforce property rights, the better economic performance will result in the long run.[18]

These and similar ideas from the work of North and Ostrom are reflected in many World Bank publications on good governance, anti-corruption and decentralisation policies.[19]

NIE/RCI and 'power insularity'

Despite its popularity, the NIE/RCI literature has not remained without criticism. For example, normative institutionalism opposes the 'logic of consequentiality' that is an important element of the NIE/RCI tradition, and proposes, instead, the 'logic of appropriateness', according to which actors are contextually and culturally norm-driven.[20] Historical institutionalism pays more attention to the legacy of the past, and to how policy choices, made when institutions are created, have a determining effect on the trajectory of these policies. In so doing, it presents an amalgam of 'calculus' and 'sociological' logics of institutional behaviour.[21] In addition, research stemming from the field of network analysis has provided yet another variant—network institutionalism—that does not necessarily challenge the ontological premises of RCI but criticises its neglect of policy networks and epistemic communities in its institutional analysis.[22]

The academic challenges to NIE/RCI, whether relating to ontological or methodological differences or both, involves primarily the mechanics of institutional analysis, and not so much the fundamental issues associated with the genesis of institutions. Here the mechanics of institutional analysis refers to the understanding of how institutions are defined and how they operate, as well as to the way in which political behaviour and important themes such as institutional continuity, change and performance are studied. The emphasis of NIE/RCI, as well as of the variants of institutionalism that have been referred to briefly above, on institutional tinkering implies that their analyses are silent about where institutions come from, how they are formed, whose interests they serve, and how they are legitimised.

The upshot of the NIE/RCI's argument is that 'economic' and 'political' institutions should be designed carefully—in effect, these are concretised in reference to the institutionalisation of property rights. Apart from the creation of typologies on the sources of variation in property rights over time and space, NIE/RCI analyses have paid little attention to how these rights were created in the first place, whose interests they serve and how they have evolved in different spatio-temporal settings.[23] The silence concerning such formation/post-formation questions has led to the emergence of an array of institutional approaches that aimed to essentialise power relations as a yardstick for the study of institutions (thysmology).

In economic sociology, for example, interest-based institutionalism explicitly views institutions as models of dominant interests in society. According to this perspective, actors who are pursuing their own interests are seen to 'orient themselves' strategically to relevant institutions instead of 'following the rules' laid down by these institutions, as would be argued by NIE/RCI scholars. Interest-based institutionalism seeks to move beyond an analysis of the rules of the game *per se* by focusing on the power dynamics related to their existence.[24] In a similar fashion the French regulation school approaches institutions as an *ensemble* representing major interests in society. The school focuses on the variation of growth regimes under capitalism(s) and how these are institutionalised on the basis of different power configurations, in both a spatial and temporal sense.[25] Finally, constructivist institutionalism emphasises the independent causal role of 'ideational' and 'discursive' factors in its analysis of institutional formation and post-formation dynamics. Here institutions are conceived to be in a permanent state of disequilibrium as a result of the permanent construction/deconstruction of ideas and their appropriation by human agency.[26]

There are evident ontological, epistemological and methodological differences between the institutionalist approaches discussed in the preceding paragraph. Nevertheless, they are different from NIE/RCI and other forms of institutional theories because of the central place that power relations occupy in their institutional analysis. As argued by Hout and Robison, all of this does not imply that techno-managerial approaches to governance do not deal with, or are not aware of, politics, conflicts and power relations.[27] Yet the way in which this approach explains and illustrates governance processes leads to the removal of power consideration from its analytical and policy repertoire.

The next three sections serve to show how the institutionalisation of an investment facility organisation, proposed as a particular option in the policy deliberations on the creation of a Euro-Mediterranean Development Bank (EMDB), exemplifies the techno-managerial approach to governance. By contrast, the institutionalisation of a full-scale multilateral development bank, presented as a second option during the same deliberations, would have reflected a more power-sensitive approach to governance. Given that the first option prevailed in the negotiations, the political significance and implications of this development for the EU's involvement in the Mediterranean region are discussed in more detail.

Economic governance in recent EU Mediterranean policies: a brief background[28]

The European Mediterranean Partnership (EMP)

The EMP was launched in the mid-1990s in an attempt to reinvigorate the EU's static Mediterranean policies. Central elements of the EU's new approach were the consolidation of reciprocal trade concessions and the regulation of the increasing illegal immigration flows to the Union. In 1995 the 15 EU member states met 12 MPs[29] in Barcelona and agreed to create a partnership based on three objectives.[30] The Barcelona Declaration mentioned as key objectives:

- establishment of an area of peace and stability reinforced through political and security dialogue (political and security chapter);

- construction of a zone of shared prosperity, and establishment of a free trade zone in order to integrate Mediterranean partners into this new regional partnership (economic and financial co-operation chapter); and
- bringing together civil societies in the region (social dialogue and co-operation in humanitarian affairs).

The economic and financial chapter of the declaration envisaged the creation of a Euro-Mediterranean free trade area by 2010. As an instrument to alleviate the anticipated socioeconomic costs resulting from the transition process, the EU set up the MEDA funds[31] which were endowed with €9772 million for the 1995–2006 period. The EU used a standard mix of policies identical to those normally recommended by the World Bank and the IMF as part of their reform packages. The reforms included the elimination of tariff and non-tariff barriers to trade in manufactured goods and services, prioritisation of the development of the private sector, establishment of an appropriate institutional and regulatory framework for a market economy capable of attracting foreign direct investment, creation of social safety nets, and consolidation of sound macro economic management.[32]

The European Neighbourhood Policy (ENP)

The ENP is a relatively new policy (March 2003) that covers geographically countries that were drawn closer to the EU after the recent Eastern enlargement in May 2004. It covers Armenia, Azerbaijan, Belarus, Georgia, Moldova, the Ukraine, and the non-EU members of the EMP. The objective of the policy is to share the benefits of the recent EU enlargement (stability, security and well-being), and prevent the emergence of new dividing lines between the enlarged Union and its new neighbours. Through this policy the EU wants to offer its neighbours the chance to participate in various activities through close political, security, economic and cultural co-operation. In order to reach its goals, the Commission proposed a new instrument: jointly agreed Action Plans, which contain a set of common priorities, defined together with the partner countries.[33] The Action Plans reflect a commitment to shared values revolving around the respect for human rights, minority rights, rule of law, good governance, promotion of good neighbourly relations, principles of market economy, sustainable development, and co-operation in certain key foreign policy areas. The pace with which the EU develops its links with the partners is made dependent on the extent to which the values are effectively shared and respected.[34]

The ENP's economic approach offers MPs the opportunity to get access to the EU internal market on condition of a greater regulatory and legislative convergence with the *acquis communautaire*. It also offers them more opportunities to participate in a number of EU programmes (education, training, research and innovation), and to access instruments to improve their physical infrastructure (energy, transport, environment and information society). These programmes are seen as further incentives or 'additional carrots' to achieve deeper economic integration, as they are in line with the approach adopted already under the EMP. All specific tailor-made action plans signed with the MPs act as further endorsements of already existing Association Agreements, but ENP plans are far more specified and contain clearer road maps for policy implementation. In line with this, they encourage convergence with EU regulatory standards as opposed to the harmonisation process envisaged previously under the EMP. In support of the activities the EU has created the European Neighbourhood and Partnership Instrument (ENPI), which is endowed with €12 billion for the period from 2007 to 2013.[35]

The Barcelona Initiative (2005)

In acknowledgment of the multiple difficulties that accompany the process of policy implementation and the delicate socioeconomic situation of most MPs, the EU launched a new initiative to reinvigorate the EMP during a meeting held in Barcelona in November 2005 in celebration of the 10th anniversary of the process. For the purpose of this meeting the European Commission drafted a detailed work programme proposal that was fully endorsed by the Foreign Affairs ministers' summit in Barcelona. The proposal aimed to place the EMP in line again with its declared 2010 objectives, and to enable MPs to meet the challenges they were facing across all the 'Barcelona' political, economic and social chapters.[36]

In relation to the economic and financial co-operation chapter, the European Commission found that the partnership had been successful in achieving a Euro-Mediterranean free trade area in industrial goods, but fell short of expanding its overall scope. The Commission argued that progress towards a number of the goals set out in the Barcelona Declaration had been somewhat slow. This had been partly because of the occasional reluctance of many MPs to commit themselves to some principles to which they had signed up, the difficulties caused by continuous conflicts in the region, and the lack of consensus on particular reforms. The Commission contended that, in a context of increasing political and economic interdependence, the EMP had been characterised by a certain lack of economic assertiveness on the part of the MPs, which hindered them from reaping the fruits of economic reform and economic and trade liberalisation. In order to overcome these difficulties, the Commission maintained that:

> partners should now take the necessary measures to expand the scope of this core free trade area, in deepening trade liberalisation in agriculture and fish products and in further opening markets to new areas such as services ... Mediterranean Partners are encouraged to make full use of the Economic Dialogues provided for in the Association Agreement in order to consolidate progress in macroeconomic stabilisation and growth policies, as indicated in the ENP Action Plans.[37]

In sum, the EU five-year strategy for reform, endorsed by all MPs, sought to consolidate the economic approach laid down in the EMP and ENP.[38] From this perspective, most of the items on the reform agenda were similar to previous policies, with the exception of a proposal made by the Commission for the possible creation of a Euro-Mediterranean Development Bank (see below).

The Barcelona Process: Union for the Mediterranean (2008)

Influenced by the French presidency in the second half of 2008, the Union for the Mediterranean (UM) is a recent Euro-Mediterranean policy, the principles of which were approved by the European Council in March 2008 and publicly launched during the Paris Summit of 13 July 2008. The UM seeks to build on the achievements of the Barcelona Process especially in terms of promoting multilateral and bilateral relations, but also addresses the shortcomings and difficulties encountered with this project. Key to the qualitative and quantitative change intended by this policy is the reassertion of the political co-ownership of the Barcelona process and its visibility *vis-à-vis* its citizens.[39]

In order to address the issue of co-ownership, the UM proposed the introduction of a co-presidency (with one president representing the EU and the other consensually representing the MPs) that should be 'compatible with the provisions on the external representation of the EU in the Treaty of the European Union and the Treaty establishing the European Community'.[40] In addition, the UM suggested the setting up of a Brussels-based committee composed of representatives from all EU member states, MPs, and the European Commission (the so-called 'Joint Permanent Committee') in order to enhance the visibility of the framework. The UM is envisaged to be only a multilateral partnership for regional and transnational projects (fighting pollution of the Mediterranean Sea, citizen protection against natural disasters, the establishment of maritime and land highways, and solar energy plans) with the aim of increasing the potential for regional integration and cohesion. In this sense the UM builds on and reinforces the other Euro-Mediterranean policies and should not be seen as a completely separate institutional development.[41] Similar to the Barcelona initiative of 2005, the economic dimension of the UM specifically encourages the strengthening of the Euro-Mediterranean Investment and Partnership Facility (FEMIP),[42] which is analysed further in the next section.

The Euro-Mediterranean Development Bank

As was indicated above, the creation of a Euro-Mediterranean free trade area by 2010 is one of the EU's major targets for the region. The countries in question would need to ensure high levels of economic growth in order to offset the various social and fiscal problems prompted by the process. The MPs are not exceptional given their high level of trade dependence *vis-à-vis* the EU and the general protectionist nature of their trade regimes before the inception of the EMP. Building on a consensus among the European Council, the Commission and the European Investment Bank (EIB) that the Mediterranean's long-term economic development relies on private sector development and investment, the Laeken European Council (14–15 December 2001) invited the Council and the European Commission to examine the setting up of a Euro-Mediterranean Development Bank.[43]

In response to the request from the Council, the European Commission drafted a proposal in 2002 that embraced the idea of creating an EMDB, and suggested, after considering several funding options, the establishment an EIB-owned subsidiary dedicated to support the Mediterranean Partners.[44] The Ecofin (economic and financial ministers operating under the EU Council of Ministers) and European Council meeting endorsed the proposal in 2002 and decided to strengthen the EIB's existing involvement with the region by creating the Facilité Euro-Méditerranéenne d'Investissement et de Partenariat (FEMIP), a financial facility dedicated to private sector development in the EMP. In addition, the meeting concluded that a decision on the transformation of FEMIP into an EIB subsidiary should be considered after one year.[45]

In anticipation of the Ecofin meeting of November 2003, the Commission prepared a communication in which it presented two options for decision making. The first was the further development of the newly established FEMIP, with a private sector development mandate. In this scenario FEMIP would remain a department within the EIB, where it would be managed by EIB staff members, and would be included in its statute and financial policies. Financially the facility would operate mainly from Council lending mandates, Community budget guarantees and contributions from the EC budget for technical assistance to support its risk capital operations and interest rates subsidies for environmental projects. According to the first scenario, the headquarters would remain in Luxembourg, with the possibility of establishing a few regional offices.[46]

The second option involved the establishment of an EIB-owned subsidiary. In this scenario the new subsidiary would have its own staff, statute, financial policies, and a private sector development mandate. The number of staff would be substantially larger in this case to reflect the resource-intensive development of the subsidiary's private sector operations. In addition, the new subsidiary would be expected to offer a broad range of financial products, and have a profile similar to that of multilateral development banks, with a particular financial standing and a capital base aimed at securing a best creditor status and a triple A rating. Its operations would be centrally managed from its headquarters, with an important role provided for local country offices. Although the EIB would retain a majority shareholding position in this subsidiary, the capital base would be open to EU member states, the European Community and the MPs. The governance framework of this subsidiary would mirror its shareholding structure.[47]

After a lengthy period of deliberation, during which the Commission studied the feasibility of both scenarios with the standard Extended Impact Assessment tool,[48] it concluded that both options would provide a substantial contribution to private sector development in the region. The Commission favoured the second option for a variety of factors. First, it argued that this option would have a higher degree of flexibility in addressing private sector needs because of its less risk-averse profile. Second, private sector financial needs would be better met in this scenario given the broader range of the state-of-the-art financial products that it would be equipped with. Third, capitalisation costs would be relatively lower than in the first scenario, because there would be a wider range of potential financial donors. Equally importantly, the commission held that the second option would increase the ownership and the visibility prospects of the EMP, so that it would provide MPs with a stronger incentive to consolidate the process of economic reform. The Commission indicated, further, that most MPs were in favour of this scenario. The commission argued that it would settle for the first option if the Council were to veto its proposal, but would attempt to use FEMIP as a transitional stage towards the implementation of an EIB-owned subsidiary.[49]

The Ecofin meeting of November 2003 did not endorse the Commission's proposal, and decided that it would review the FEMIP mandate after another three years, on the basis of a reassessment of its progress. In line with its preferences, the Commission tried to keep the second option open, and tabled it as one of the reforms for rejuvenating the process of economic reform under the Barcelona 2005 Initiative.[50] In December 2006 the Ecofin meeting rejected the EMDB proposal for a third consecutive time and opted to strengthen FEMIP's budget, operations and modality.[51] Between October 2002 and December 2008 the facility has invested €8.5 billion in the Mediterranean, with a focus on supporting the private sector and creating an investor-friendly environment in the region.[52]

The two faces of governance and their implications

Policy processes are characterised by the repeated up- and downgrading of particular policy options, as a consequence of the varying influences on policy makers. In this regard there is nothing surprising about the manner in which the EMBD process has unfolded. Nevertheless, the most interesting part of the case study of the EMDB results from the interplay between the two approaches (or faces) of governance that were discussed earlier in this article. Indeed, the two scenarios considered in the previous section were both plausible outcomes of the policy process, and seemed to offer clear incentives for players to deepen the process of economic reform within the EU's Euro-Mediterranean policy.

The first option was considered to be more technical and managerial, in the sense that it aimed to create an institution— FEMIP—endowed with some financial capacity to assist MPs in developing their private sector and in removing the obstacles that impeded the growth of their economies. In other words, enabling Mediterranean entrepreneurs to launch their privately owned small- and medium-sized enterprises means that such actors should be enabled to secure their newly acquired property rights *vis-à-vis* their own states (involving establishment, registration, licences and patents). This approach would put more pressure on the Mediterranean states to facilitate the creation of a business-friendly environment with a regulatory framework revolving around clear, accessible, predictable and transparent rules.

The institutionalisation of such rules is expected to produce positive spill-over effects. On the one hand, they would provide Mediterranean entrepreneurs with incentives to be innovative and dynamic in a competitive market environment. On the other hand, they would enhance the investment credibility of the economy in question, especially when the new regulatory framework was fully based on the *acquis communautaire*. This should encourage the inflow of foreign direct investment into the MPs, and should consequently contribute towards higher levels of economic growth. The rationale behind this option fundamentally rests on the institutionalisation of property rights and the design and sequencing of incentives that derive from them. More interest-related issues, concerning the nature of these economic activities, and the players who are involved with investment ventures, are not addressed explicitly in this option for the EMDB process.

The second option, in contrast, involves a more power-sensitive approach for a variety of reasons. First, the envisaged development bank would be more independent in its operations and status, implying that the bank would have more than a narrow private sector mandate and would incorporate various types of developmental activities that are needed to guide the process of transition, including public–private investment ventures. Second, by opening up the bank's capital base to EU member states, the European community and the MPs, the EU would strengthen its political presence in the region and anchor its commitment *vis-à-vis* its Mediterranean counterparts.

Third, and more importantly, the broadening of the bank's capital base would add a notion of ownership to the process, as it would give the MPs a stake in the constitution and formation of the bank. This would imply that the bank could be a platform for MPs, and that it would not only address private sector issues, but also the broader priorities of Mediterranean governments, with a view to economic growth and overall development policies. In this regard the notion of ownership is intrinsically linked with the institutionalisation of a 'Mediterranean voice' within the bank. This would make sure that the institutionalisation of the development bank is not driven solely by EU concerns and interests but relates also to the needs of the MPs. In a nutshell the securing and safeguarding of property rights constitute only part of the second scenario, as the latter focuses on the establishment of the bank and takes account of the wider political context influencing this formation process.

The eventual prioritisation of the 'technical-managerial' option over the 'power-sensitive' has serious implications for the EU. The first implication is that the EU's commitment to the partnership and the nature of its governance structure can be seriously questioned. Without going into detail about the specific reasons that prevented the Council from approving the EMBD on three consecutive occasions, it is clear that Euro-Mediterranean relations are not high on the EU's agenda. The lack of progress and the slow pace of reforms undertaken by MPs cannot be attributed solely to problems of implementation or the lack of political will. Instead, the major obstacle lies in the way these policies were formed and implemented.

For example, Youngs has shown that MPs have had little influence on the content of the EU's Mediterranean policies, and that they were faced with a 'take-it-or-leave-it' scenario before the inauguration of the EMP.[53] Further, Joffe has shown how the EU has constantly been pushing MPs to implement further reforms during the early days of the EMP, but turned a blind eye to certain problems that were too politically sensitive for the Union itself (in particular, the liberalisation of agricultural markets).[54] Similarly, when the EU introduced the concept of ownership in the context of the ENP, many scholars pointed out how the tailor-made action plans were in essence insensitive to the context and reflective of the EU's interests and its perceptions of development.[55] In addition to the chronic problems of functional governance, the depth of political, economic and social restructuring envisaged by the EMP/ENP, accompanied by the MPs' non-eligibility for EU membership, highlights a gulf between perceptions, expectations and interests that is not sustainable in the long run. For all these reasons, the rejection of the 'power-sensitive' policy option for the EMDB accentuates the asymmetrical power relations embedded in the EU–Mediterranean partnership and hurts the credibility of the EU in advocating reforms in the region.

On a similar level the credibility of a policy cannot only be grasped in reference to its nature and substance. It also relates to the ability of a policy to bring about compliance from the players in question. Given the EU's reluctance to institutionalise a fully fledged development bank, it is doubtful whether the MPs will comply with the EU's requests for further reforms. The agenda on the liberalisation of services, which is considered a key area of reform by the EU, could easily become a major topic of resistance for the MPs.[56]

As was argued above, the Barcelona 2005 initiative originated in the EU's dissatisfaction with the slow progress on the EMP agenda during 10 years of negotiations and implementation. The attention to the services agenda in the initiative of 2005 got further momentum with the appearance of a joint World Bank/European Commission publication in the same year.[57] In this study the liberalisation of services was considered the vehicle for deeper integration of the two sides of the Mediterranean. It was argued that the removal of tariff and non-tariff barriers would yield substantial economic welfare benefits, since the services sector accounts for 57 per cent of GDP in eight MPs. The study also highlighted how the deepening of liberalisation of the so-called backbone services (telecommunications, transport, financial services and electricity) would anchor the MPs further into the Single Market, as they would need to achieve partial or complete regulatory harmonisation with EU standards. A study performed by Müller-Jentsch argued for partial harmonisation rather than the complete adoption of the *acquis communautaire*. A later document from the European Commission, however, emphasised the benefits that would follow from full adoption of the *acquis*, as this would produce greater confidence in the structure of MPs' markets and boost their ability to attract foreign direct investment.[58]

Even though the deadline set for the launch of the free trade area with the MPs is approaching fast (2010), progress on this agenda is unsurprisingly slow. A recent European Commission communiqué about the status of implementation within the ENP indicated that even the four MP front runners (Egypt, Jordan, Morocco and Tunisia) were lagging behind on this important reform agenda.[59] Clearly, MPs' resistance to the liberalisation of services relates to many factors and has its roots in the period before the initiation of the EMBD process. Nevertheless, the two processes are not unrelated. After all, FEMIP directly deals with financial backbone services, and the development of the private sector in economies with a substantial services sector is at the heart of FEMIP's mandate. If the EU were to refrain from politically institutionalising an EMBD and opt for a less committed technical approach, how could it realistically expect MPs to advance an already problematic process of services liberalisation that would entail a loss of regulatory sovereignty? All the above leads me to conclude that the prioritisation of the techno-managerial approach over the power-sensitive one will further exacerbate existing problems within the partnership rather than offer a solution to those problems.

There is no doubt that the logic of techno-managerial governance applies to and offers a solution for certain collective action problems. Yet the tendency inherent in this approach to sideline power analysis or, in other words, to artificially separate the 'technical-managerial' from the 'political', leads to a failure to recognise the deep-rooted dynamics at play behind policies and institutions. The EU's preference for the techno-managerial over the power-sensitive option is symptomatic of its general governance approach towards the MPs, and is likely to reduce its credibility and appeal. If the Union is honest about its engagement with the Mediterranean region, an alternative 'governmentality' needs to be adopted that not only pays lip service to power considerations in policy deliberations but takes these seriously.

To end the article on a more optimistic note, it seems that the EU's recent approach to the Union for the Mediterranean differs from earlier functional approaches to governance, as the UM proposal has the intention to rectify embedded power asymmetries. Although it is difficult to build an argument on such a relatively recent development, the progress of the UM is a potentially interesting area for future research.

Notes

1 TG Weiss 'Governance, good governance and global governance: conceptual and actual challenges', *Third World Quarterly*, 21(5), 2000, pp 795–814.
2 RAW Rhodes 'Governance and public administration', in J Pierre (ed), *Debating Governance: Authority, Steering and Democracy*, Oxford: Oxford University Press, 2000, pp 54–90.
3 JN Rosenau, 'Governance in the twenty-first century', *Global Governance*, 1(1), 1995, pp 13–43.
4 G Hyden 'Operationalising governance for sustainable development', in JE Jreisat *Governance and Developing Countries*, Leiden: Brill, 2002, pp 13–32.
5 DC North, 'The New Institutional Economics', in J Harriss, J Hunter & CM Lewis (eds), *The New Institutional Economics and Third World Development*, London: Routledge, 1995, pp 15–24.
6 W Hout & R Robison, 'Development and the politics of governance: framework for analysis', in Hout & Robison (eds), *Governance and the Depoliticisation of Development*, London: Routledge, 2009, pp 1–11. See also R Robison 'Strange bedfellows: political alliances in the making of neo-liberal

governance' and W Hout 'Development and governance: an uneasy relationship', in Hout & Robison, *Governance and the Depoliticisation of Development*, pp 15–28, 29–43.
7 Hout & Robison, 'Development and the politics of governance', p 5. See also Hout's introductory article in this issue.
8 AM Kjaer 'Introduction: the meaning of governance', in Kjaer (ed), *Governance*, Cambridge: Polity, 2004, pp 1–18.
9 See E Ostrom, 'An agenda for the study of institutions', *Public Choice*, 48, 1986, pp 3–25. Cf BG Peters, *Comparative Politics: Theory and Methods*, Basingstoke: Macmillan, 1998.
10 EG Furubotn & R Richter, *Institutions and Economic Theory: The Contribution of the New Institutional Economics*, Ann Arbor, MI: University of Michigan Press, 2005, pp 1–45.
11 See the work of O Williamson, D North and J Stiglitz. For a good summary on this debate, see C Ménard & MM Shirley, 'Introduction', in Ménard & Shirley (eds), *Handbook of New Institutional Economics*, Heidelberg: Springer, 2008, pp 1–18.
12 DC North, *Institutions, Institutional Change and Economic Performance*, Cambridge: Cambridge University Press, 1990, p 362.
13 A Denzau & DC North, 'Shared mental models: ideologies and institutions', *Kyklos*, 47(1), 1994, pp 3–31.
14 DC North, 'Economic performance through time', *American Economic Review*, 84(3), 1994, p 361.
15 North, *Institutions, Institutional Change and Economic Performance*, p 140.
16 See D Acemoglu & S Johnson, 'Unbundling institutions', *Journal of Political Economy*, 113(5), 2005, pp 949–995. See also D Acemoglu, S Johnson & JA Robinson, *Institutions as the Fundamental Cause of Long-Run Growth*, National Bureau of Economic Research Working Paper 10481, Cambridge, MA: NBER, 2004.
17 O Williamson, 'The New Institutional Economics: taking stock, looking ahead', *Journal of Economic Literature*, 38, 2000, pp 595–613. See also DC North, *Understanding the Process of Economic Change*, Princeton, NJ: Princeton University Press, 2005.
18 See E Ostrom, *Governing the Commons: The Evolution of Institutions of Collective Action*, Cambridge: Cambridge University Press, 1990.
19 For instance, World Bank, *World Development Report: The State in a Changing World*, Oxford: Oxford University Press, 1997, pp 99–109; and World Bank, *Managing Development: The Governance Dimension—A Discussion Paper*, Washington, DC: World Bank, 1991, pp 1–23.
20 JG March & JP Olsen, 'The new institutionalism: organisational factors in political life', *American Political Science Review*, 78, 1984, pp 738–749; and March & Olsen, 'Institutional perspectives on political institutions', *Governance*, 9, 1996, pp 247–264.
21 PA Hall & RCR Taylor, 'Political science and the three institutionalisms', *Political Studies*, 44(4), 1996, pp 936–957; and PA Hall, 'Policy paradigms, social learning and the state: the case of economic policy-making in Britain', *Comparative Politics*, 25(3), 1993, pp 185–196.
22 C Ansell, 'Network institutionalism', in RAW Rhodes, SA Binder & BA Rockman (eds), *The Oxford Handbook of Political Institutions*, Oxford: Oxford University Press, 2006, pp 75–89.
23 C Hay, 'Ideas, interests and institutions in the comparative political economy of great transformations', *Review of International Political Economy*, 11(1), 2004, pp 204–226.
24 R Swedberg, 'The tool kit of economic sociology', in BR Weingast & DA Wittman (eds), *The Oxford Handbook of Political Economy*, Oxford: Oxford University Press, 2006, pp 937–950.
25 B Jessop, 'Capitalism and its future: remarks on regulation, government and governance', *Review of International Political Economy*, 4(3), 1997, pp 561–581.
26 *Ibid*, p 565.
27 Hout & Robison, 'Development and the politics of governance', p 5.
28 This is an updated version of a section that appeared in K Knio, 'Governance, politics and the Euro-Mediterranean partnership: problems of implementation or policy design?', in Hout & Robison, *Governance and the Depoliticisation of Development*, pp 77–91.
29 The 12 MPs are Algeria, Cyprus, Egypt, Israel, Jordan, Lebanon, Malta, Morocco, Palestinian Authority, Syria, Tunisia and Turkey. Libya has observer status under the Euro-Mediterranean Partnership agreements. Since joining the EU in 2004 Cyprus and Malta have no longer been MPs. Israel and Turkey are technically MPs but are in a *sui generis* position. Israel is not eligible for many EU funds since it is considered to be a semi-developed economy. Turkey is also not eligible for funding because of its current negotiations with the EU in relation to potential future membership. See European Commission, *Information Notes on the Euro-Med Partnership*, Luxembourg: Office for Official Publications of the European Communities, 2002.
30 In 2005 migration was added as the fourth chapter under the Barcelona Process, reflecting the gradually increasing importance of this agenda in recent years. See European Commission, *Ministerial Conclusions of the first Euro-Mediterranean Ministerial Meeting on Migration*, 19 November 2007, at http://www.eu2007.pt/UE/vEN/Noticias_Documentos/20071119Conclusoeseuromed.html, accessed 2 December 2009.

31 After the French *mesure d'ajustement* (adjustment measure).
32 D Hunt, 'Development economics, the Washington Consensus and the Euro Mediterranean Partnership Initiative', in G Joffé (ed), *Perspectives on Development*, London: Frank Cass, 1999, pp 16–38.
33 European Commission, *Wider Europe-Neighbourhood: A New Framework for Relations with our Eastern and Southern Neighbours*, COM(2003)104 final.
34 European Commission, *A Strong European Neighbourhood Policy*, COM(2007)774 final, 2007.
35 *Ibid*.
36 European Commission, *Tenth Anniversary of the Euro-Mediterranean Partnership: A Work Program to Meet the Challenges of the Next Five Years*, Communication from the Commission to the Council and the European Parliament, 2005.
37 *Ibid*, pp 5, 9.
38 *Ibid*, p 13.
39 The members of the UM are all EU member states, the European Commission, the MPs, observer status countries under the Barcelona Process (Albania, Libya, Mauritania) and other Mediterranean coastal states (Bosnia and Herzegovina, Croatia, Monaco and Montenegro). See European Commission, *Barcelona Process: Union for the Mediterranean*, COM(2008)319 final.
40 European Commission, *Tenth Anniversary of the Euro-Mediterranean Partnership*, p 6.
41 *Ibid*, p 2.
42 *Ibid*, p 9.
43 European Commission, *Shaping Support for Private Sector Development in the Mediterranean*, SEC(2003), ECFIN/366, p 2.
44 European Commission, *A New Euro-Mediterranean Bank*, SEC(2002)218.
45 European Commission, *Shaping Support for Private Sector Development in the Mediterranean*, p 2.
46 *Ibid*, p 5.
47 *Ibid*.
48 Extended Impact Assessments are tools used by the European Commission to improve the policy development process. They examine the main choices and potential impacts of a particular policy decision from an *ex-ante* perspective. In so doing, they identify the likely positive and negative impacts of a potential policy action, enable informed policy judgments and identify tradeoffs between competing policy targets. The criteria used by the Commission in this study focus on: risk profile, intensity of resources, corporate culture, partnership, interaction with local economic reforms, long-term political commitment and visibility and overall costing. See *ibid*, pp 9-15. See also European Commission, *Communication of the Commission on Impact Assessment*, COM(2002)276; and European Commission, *Commission Work Programme 2003*, COM(2002)0590, Annex 2.
49 European Commission, *Shaping Support for Private Sector Development in the Mediterranean*, p 14.
50 European Commission, *Tenth Anniversary of the Euro-Mediterranean Partnership*, p 13.
51 European Commission, *Barcelona Process*, p 9.
52 See FEMIP's website at http://www.eib.org/projects/regions/med/index.htm, accessed 2 December 2009.
53 R Youngs, 'The Barcelona Process after the UK presidency: the need for prioritization', *Mediterranean Politics*, 4(1), 1999, pp 1–24.
54 G Joffé, *The Euro-Mediterranean Partnership: Two Years After Barcelona*, Royal Institute of International Affairs Briefing Paper 44, London: Chatham House, 1998, pp 1–4.
55 G Escribano, *Europeanisation without Europe? The Mediterranean and the Neighbourhood Policy*, European University Institute Working Papers, Robert Schuman Centre for Advanced Studies 2006/19, 2006, pp 1–20.
56 European Commission, *The Barcelona Process: Ten Years On*, Luxembourg: Office for Official Publications of the European Communities, 2005.
57 D Müller-Jentsch, *Deeper Integration and Trade in Services in the Euro-Mediterranean Region: Southern Dimensions of the European Neighbourhood Policy*, Washington, DC: World Bank, 2005.
58 See European Commission, *Strengthening the European Neighbourhood Policy*, COM(2006)726 final.
59 European Commission, *Implementation of the European Neighbourhood Policy in 2008*, COM(2009)188/3, pp 3-7.

Global Europe, Guilty! Contesting EU neoliberal governance for Latin America and the Caribbean

ROSALBA ICAZA

ABSTRACT *This article examines bi-regional governance between the European Union and Latin American and Caribbean countries as a source of social resistance and contestation. The analysis focuses on the contributions of a bottom-up and informal mechanism of litigation, the Permanent People's Tribunals against European Multinationals and Neoliberalism, to cognitive justice and as a challenge to the notion of neoliberal governance. It questions the underlying assumptions regarding global/regional governance and resistance in the literature on international relations and international political economy, and the type of development and regionalism promoted by EU institutions and governments in Latin America and the Caribbean. The article calls for a problematisation of the resistance that is mobilised through the Tribunals, which is not free of tensions but, nonetheless, contributes through practices of cognitive justice to unveiling the fragmented, and hence, contested, nature of EU neoliberal governance for Latin America and the Caribbean countries.*

In 1999 the European Union and Latin American and Caribbean (LAC) countries launched a Strategic Partnership as a new comprehensive approach to govern their transatlantic interactions. This partnership aimed at transforming the EU's relationship of co-operation with LAC countries, which had been dominated by the giving of development aid, into one based on three main components: political dialogue, co-operation and trade. Since then this governance framework has been facing opposition from sectors of civil society in Europe and LAC countries, which are challenging its development sustainability and democratic credentials. As was to be expected, lobby campaigns directed at local, national and supra-state authorities for a reform of the partnership followed, parallel to the creation of a mechanism for citizen participation within and outside official decision-making mechanisms.

Research has shown that this social mobilisation eventually stimulated a shift in the approach of the European Commission and some LAC governments to address the concerns with democracy and sustainability voiced by civil society organisations. Changes included procedural reforms in official decision-making mechanisms and the creation of corporate social responsibility schemes.[1] More recently, in 2006, the launch of the so-called Global Europe strategy by the European Commission seemed, for many of the same actors, to enhance the imbalance between investor rights and responsibilities. The strategy, and the official responses previously described, have created a certain eagerness among social movements and civil society networks in Europe and LAC to find ways of organising and mobilising that could potentially dismantle and/or roll back what is seen as an essentially neoliberal and corporation-friendly form of bi-regional governance.

This article investigates the contributions that the Permanent People's Tribunals against European Multinationals and Neoliberalism (hereafter, Tribunals) have made to expose human rights violations and violations of environmental standards by multinational corporations (MNCs) based in the EU or their subsidiaries in LAC countries. The Tribunals were officially launched in Vienna in 2006 by the network Enlazando Alternativas.[2] This article is not an assessment of the impacts that these Tribunals have had on particular policy outcomes within EU–LAC bi-regional governance frameworks. It has a different objective and looks at the attempts made by the Tribunals to identify power and authority holders as duty bearers. Most importantly, the article contributes to the questioning of the essentially neoliberal nature of the EU's external and development policies. In so doing, it offers an account of the role that social resistance might play in unveiling the fact that the governance reforms accompanying the EU–LAC bi-regional frameworks have never been uncontested and have been far from all-encompassing. The Tribunals' most fragile but emancipatory contribution to social justice is their exposé of an oppressive capitalist, patriarchal, racialised global system that nonetheless is far from being a *fait accompli*.[3]

The view of governance that is emphasised in this contribution does not only concern its 'polycentric', multilevel nature, but also its often neglected but equally significant subjection to permanent contestation and negotiation, both of which take place formally and informally among multilateral institutions, public–private institutions, corporations, civil society organisations and policy networks.[4] In this perspective bi-regional governance refers to the arrangements, rules and institutions steering EU–LAC interactions, of which the EU–LAC strategic partnership is only one example, but one that has permanently been contested and renegotiated. These ideas are developed in the following three sections. The next section examines the international relations (IR) and international political economy (IPE) literature on 'global governance' and explores the possibility of developing some general arguments regarding resistance to neoliberal bi-regional governance. The third section focuses on recent developments in EU–LAC bi-regional governance. The fourth section presents the Tribunals' experiences, focusing on their attempts to question EU neoliberal governance for LAC. This analysis is performed by examining the position papers and documents produced by the Tribunals; it is supported by fieldwork activities, including participant observation at the Tribunals' sessions in Vienna (2002) and Guatemala (2008) and by interviews with their organisers and participants.

Resistance as questioning: global governance under neoliberalism

Over the past decades IR and IPE analyses have connected the emergence of global governance to the transformation of 'traditional' forms of state authority and sovereignty.[5] In this post-Wesphalian governance era the state seems increasingly unable to exercise 'supreme, comprehensive, unqualified and exclusive rule over its territorial domain', as compared to previous historical periods.[6] However, some commentators have pointed out that such transformations in governance did not take place in a vacuum, but in a period characterised by the ascendant material, institutional and discursive dominance of neoliberal policy frameworks that were prescribing liberalisation, deregulation and demand-side approaches to development and economic integration.

Not surprisingly this literature has placed a strong emphasis on efficient steering, management and control for the regaining of certainty and/or legitimacy. In particular, commentators point to trends of increasing interdependence and connectivity that generate problems—such as migration, epidemics, terrorism, etc—which are too big to be handled by individual nation-states. From this perspective bi-regional mechanisms of governance, such as the EU–LAC strategic partnership, seem to contribute to the solution of particular problems occurring within, between and across regions. In addition, observers have emphasised the rise of the 'privatisation of governance', unfolding parallel to the proliferation of regional, sub-regional and extra-regional forms of global governance, in which private forms of authority increasingly and substantially influence the formulation, implementation, monitoring and enforcement of control, consent and decision making regarding public and general concerns such as trade, development and macroeconomic policies.[7]

Global governance and resistance

Influential authors in IR and IPE have explained global governance either as a networked multi-sided polycentric construct, as governmentality, or as Empire.[8] Interestingly, and similarly to previous explanations of the system of states in the 'Westphalian order', the three perspectives share a common assumption regarding the nature of global governance: it has a somehow inescapable and all-encompassing nature that is able to touch or transform all forms of social life either through rules, laws or institutions; systems of knowledge and norms; or violence. Certain important implications for the explanation of social resistance follow from this assumption.

In the most pessimistic case social resistance to global governmentality, to a polycentric-networked construct or to Empire has actually been explained as a force supporting the reproduction of the logic and dynamics of global governance. This is the case of transnational networks of civil society organisations and NGOs, which are seen as 'de-politicising forces' domesticating and subjugating the incivil (sub-altern) and uncivil components of world politics.[9] In the most optimistic case social resistance is explained as the logical reaction to processes of exploitation and oppression, which aim to reform or dismantle dominant forms of governance. For example, so-called transnational advocacy networks (TANs) in networked polycentric global governance are seen as using opportunities to hold local and national authorities accountable. In this perspective some mechanisms, such as the Tribunals, are explained as promoters of citizens' participation and the public scrutiny of governing authorities.[10]

Some commentators have emphasised that, in the era of neoliberal dominance, global governance has invariably served capitalist interests, in our case those of European MNCs and Latin American oligarchies. Seen from this perspective, the Tribunals' objectives of laying bare the impacts of the bias in global governance and of addressing these impacts in legal terms, would contribute eventually to the reform of global economic governance.[11] The Tribunals would then represent one of several reformist reactions aiming to roll back the expansion of the 'self-regulating market', constituting a kind of double movement *à la* Polanyi.[12] Other scholars have pointed at the analytical problem of understanding social resistance as a logical outcome of the historical processes of exploitation that characterise neoliberal globalisation, and hence as a reaction or, at best, a dialectical response to globalisation and the depoliticisation involved with it. The problem with such explanations is that they conflate the understanding of the context where resistance emerges—that is, the history and the conditions of 'neoliberal globalisation'— with the understanding of the dynamics and the emergence of resistance.[13] To further understand these dynamics, the following sub-sections offer a brief introduction to recent ideas on cognitive justice as a necessary condition for global social justice, as developed by Boaventura de Sousa Santos, and on resistance as an act of questioning a supposedly 'unitary' system of oppression, as developed by María Lugonés.

On cognitive justice and resistance

Boaventura de Sosa Santos' project for reinventing social justice has been a rich source of debates on global justice and globalisation.[14] A crucial element of the project is Santos' acknowledgment of the historical power asymmetries produced by European cultural imperialism and capitalism, which have led to the imposition of epistemologies and ways of knowing at the expense of existing knowledges. The imposition has been so violent that, according to Santos, it has produced an 'epistemicide':

> The epistemological privilege granted to modern science ... was ... instrumental in suppressing other, non-scientific forms of knowledges and, at the same time, the subaltern social groups whose social practices were informed by such knowledges. In the case of the indigenous peoples of the Americas and of the African slaves, this suppression of knowledge, a form of epistemicide ... was the other side of genocide.[15]

In the same vein Coleman and Johnson have argued that a central goal of Santos' project on social justice is 'the breaking down of hierarchies and exclusions related to knowledges', expressed in his proposition that 'there is no global justice without global cognitive justice'.[16] Santos' acknowledgment of the epistemological diversity in the world as immense and commensurate with the existing degree of cultural diversity, has a key implication for the dynamics and emergence of resistance. The position implies that 'differences between worldviews become explicit and turn into sites of struggle'.[17]

Following Santos' ideas, Vázquez has argued that the struggles for social justice are struggles for 'political visibility'. This refers to 'bringing the claims for justice into the light of the public' and 'signal[ling] the close relation that there is between the material means of oppression and epistemic discrimination'.[18] Thus cognitive justice aims at increasing the political visibility of knowledges that otherwise remain ignored. Santos' and Vázquez' perspectives help us to understand the potential that the Tribunals have for promoting social justice by enhancing the political visibility of knowledges and cultures that have been 'erased' by neoliberal governance. The Tribunals have focused on a number of cases related to the violation of rights of communities, of indigenous nations and of African descendants. For example, the Tribunals' processes, discussions and rulings have paid much attention to Andean conceptions such as *el buen vivir* (the fullness of life).[19]

On resistance as questioning

The theoretical work of feminist philosopher and activist Maria Lugonés on the resistance to oppression provides the possibility of problematising both the supposedly unitary hegemony of the system and the one-dimensional view of the agents of social resistance that are prevalent in accounts of civil society and social movements against global capitalism. For example, in the case of neo-Gramscian and liberal IR/IPE approaches, commentators have focused on detecting 'progressive' forces among civil society actors, understanding these as 'totalities' of strategic (instrumental) action. A key assumption underlying such analyses is that agency and the actors—in our case civil society, the state or business—can be understood in one-dimensional terms: they are either hegemonic or not, restorationist or not, progressive or not, supportive of or against neoliberal regionalism, and so on.[20]

Lugonés' understanding of social resistance departs from questioning oppression as unitary and 'as inescapable through the subjects' joint or separate exercise of their own volition, power, or agency'.[21] In her view systems are characterised by the existence of fragmented self-identities and consciousness and this implies the possibility to 'pose questions to "unitary" hegemonic powers'.[22] For Lugonés the system of oppression determines agents' self-identity but, since there is more than one system, resistance to oppression is made possible. Lugones' ideas offer the opportunity to highlight the way that social resistance contributes to cognitive justice, because the very presence of existing and diverse knowledges unveils the fractures of 'all-encompassing' neoliberal governance. To be sure, this is not to say that neoliberal governance, as manifested in diverse mechanisms of control, consent and regulation, is not powerful, exploitative, gendered and racialised, as the cases presented to the Tribunals demonstrate, but there certainly is not a unified view on how social life should be and is actually being organised.

EU–LAC relationship: a tale in two acts

This section discusses recent developments in the ongoing 'making' of neoliberal governance frameworks that aim to regulate bi-regional relations involving European and LAC countries. Elsewhere it has been suggested that regional governance is 'made' by different types of actors, unfolding processes and narratives at different but interrelated policy levels. This perspective understands regionalism mainly as a contested political project driven by state and market actors and influenced by communities around the world. Moreover, some of the 'actors' are understood as powerful makers of regionalism and its governance, but they are far from monolithic and not free from internal disputes.[23] Accordingly, this section focuses on the 'official' views, as products of inter-bureaucratic arrangements, of those actors that have traditionally been understood in the IR and IPE literature as drivers of EU–LAC bi-regional governance: the European Union institutions, LAC governments and, increasingly, MNCs.

Act 1: The European Union, Latin America and the Caribbean Strategic Partnership

The 1999 Strategic Partnership was officially launched at the Rio de Janeiro Ministerial Summit as an initiative to institutionalise unfolding interactions among the EU and LAC countries. Its initial objective was the creation of a bi-regional association that would establish a Euro-LAC space before 2010 on the basis of three components: political dialogue, co-operation and free trade. According to the European Commission, the institutionalisation of high-level dialogue between heads of state and governments of the two regions has unfolded through the summitry process and the EU–Rio Group. This dialogue has also involved regular meetings between senior officials, parliaments, private corporate actors and civil societies at regional, sub-regional (Mercosur, Andean Community, Central America) and bilateral levels (Mexico, Brazil, Chile, Bolivia, etc).

Over the years the Commission's strategic policy objectives on Latin America—political dialogue, social cohesion, and regional integration through Association Agreements—have guided further adaptations of the strategic partnership frameworks (as presented in Table 1). Recently the Commission's recommendations for EU–Latin American relations have focused on four policy orientations for the future: stepping up and focusing bi-regional dialogue, strengthening regional integration and inter-connectivity,

TABLE 1. EU–LAC strategic partnership summits and outcomes

Summits	Thematic focus	Main outcomes
Rio de Janeiro, 1999		Launch of the strategic arnership between the EU and LAC; EU–Mercosur negotiations opened
Madrid, 2002		Announcement of the EU–Chile Association Agreement (AA); launch of the ALBAN programme; launch of EU–LAC Common Higher Education and Knowledge Area concept
Guadalajara, 2004	Social cohesion	Launch of EUROsocial programme
Vienna, 2006	Democracy and human rights	Opening of EU–Central America negotiations on an AA; launch of negotiations on an AA between the EU and the Andean Community of Nations (CAN); EuroLAT set up
Lima, 2008	Poverty, inequality, inclusion; sustainable development (climate change, environment, energy)	Launch of EUroCLIMA; first EU–LAC Investment Forum decision to start a 'structured and comprehensive dialogue on migration'
Madrid, 2010	Innovation and technology for sustainable development and social inclusion	Expected outcomes: the setting up of the Latin America Investment Facility (LAIF); marking of the creation of the EU–LAC Foundation

Source: Delegation of the European Commission to Chile, 'The Commission lays out a new vision for EU–Latin America Relations', 30 September 2009, at http://www.delchl.ec.europa.eu/en/whatsnew/NEWS_2009_30_09_UE_LATAM.htm, accessed 26 November 2009.

strengthening bilateral relations and taking greater account of diversity, and tailoring and adapting co-operation programmes.

The EU is the biggest donor of development assistance to Latin America and the Caribbean: recently the European Commission's budget for aid to the region has been on average around €600 million per year.[24] Since 2004 social cohesion, understood as the fight against poverty, inequality and exclusion, is the priority for development co-operation programmes, in line with the Millennium Development Goals and financed through the Development Cooperation Instrument (DCI). After 10 years 'more than 450 projects and programmes accounting for more than €3 billion' have been financed within the framework of the EU–LAC partnership, including: EuroSocial (2004) on the promotion of social cohesion; UrbAL on co-operation at the local level; AL-Invest supporting the internationalisation of Latin American small and medium-sized enterprises; Alpha III supporting the modernisation of higher education; Erasmus Mundus providing postgraduate scholarships; @LIS supporting the integration of Latin America into the global information society; and EurocLIMA dealing with global warming and sustainable sources of energy.[25] A central trade component of the strategic partnership has been the differentiated approach aimed at bi-regional co-operation with better-off countries in LAC through the promotion of activities of mutual interest and through freer reciprocal trade.[26] This component is in line with the Commission's 1995 strategy document *The Present Situation and Prospects for Closer Partnership 1996–2000*, which shifted EU co-operation with middle-income countries from preferential treatment to reciprocity.

Particular neoliberal views on development and regionalism, and the role that private actors should play in it, lie at the heart of the strategic partnership. In line with post-Washington Consensus-type reforms, the state is seen as the key supervisor of the governance of bi-regional interactions and hence becomes central to the constitution of state–businesses–civil society partnerships. Meanwhile, free trade is the main tool for turning national markets into economic units. Here, the full integration of markets between Europe and LAC countries would indicate that the latter have a greater potential to expand their exports to other countries, regions and sub-regions. This view is driven not only by demand-led economic integration, but also contains elements of so-called 'open regionalism'. This form of regionalism is not about responding to external competition, but about 'catching up' with processes of regional integration through liberalistion of trade and investment.[27] Market actors are assumed to be the key drivers of regionalism and development—most notably MNCs, which are the drivers of growth and jobs in Europe in the so-called Global Europe strategy.

According to the perspective sketched above, the EU–LAC strategic partnership is a comprehensive network of decision-making mechanisms and programmes for bi-regional governance, or what one of its supporters calls 'a tightly-woven net of diverse relationships, activities and cooperation mechanisms'.[28] One of the critics of the partnership asserts, on the other hand, that 'ambitious declarations left much to be desired with regard to their real impact'.[29] At the time of writing the 10th anniversary of the EU–LAC partnership had led to contrasting judgements among its supporters, reformists and radical opponents, in parallel to diverse explanations of current developments. The following section presents some of these analyses.

Act 2: explaining the shift

Earlier IR/IPE analyses of the strategic partnership have tended to emphasise, on the one hand, its reactive nature to US pressure for regionalism in the Americas, especially after the launch of the North American Free Trade Agreement (NAFTA) and the proposals for a Free Trade Area of the Americas (FTAA) in the 1990s. On the other hand, authors have noted the convergence of values and aspirations concerning bi-regionalism, free trade and good governance among economic and political elites in both regions.

Ten years later regionalist scenarios for Latin America and the Caribbean have changed dramatically and so have the explanations of the ongoing trends in EU-LAC bi-regional governance frameworks. The scenario of regionalism is now analysed against the background of the legitimacy crisis of neoliberal reforms in LAC countries, and especially of free trade as a driver of development. For some this crisis explains the rise of left-to-centre governments in South and Central America that are openly critical of free trade agreements (FTAs) with the USA and the EU and actively promote South–South inter-regionalism agendas, including the South American Community of Nations (SACN), the Bolivarian Alternative for the Americas (ALBA), the People's Commercial Agreements (PCAs), the Bank of the South, etc.

In addition to this, the collapse of the FTAA negotiations in Mar del Plata (2001) and of the World Trade Organization's (WTO) Doha Round in Cancun (2003) are seen as driving the USA's and EU's emphasis of liberalisation of trade and services on a bilateral basis. The European Commission strategy document of 2005 reveals a commitment to a 'stronger' partnership on the basis of a network of Association Agreements, in line with ongoing discussions on Europe's global competitiveness.[30] One year later the Global Europe strategy document established a direct link between securing open markets around the world for European companies and economic growth and job creation in Europe: 'To build a stronger EU economy at home, Europe has to be more competitive abroad'.[31] The highly controversial issues of deregulation of services, investment, public procurement and competition policy, and the enforcement of intellectual property rights (IPR) that derailed the WTO meeting in Cancun were presented as necessary conditions for achieving the strategic objectives set by the Lisbon Agenda: "stimulate growth and create more and better jobs, while making the economy greener and more innovative".[32] In sum, the European Commission presented private corporate interests as public interests in order to increase general welfare.

Just as with the case of NAFTA and the FTAA, the Global Europe strategy has been interpreted as an aggressive reaction to defend a share of the emerging markets of China, Brazil and India for European MNCs against their most important competitors: US MNCs.[33] Recent developments in the negotiations on the Association Agreements (AAs) between the EU and the Andean Community of Nations (CAN) and Mercosur seem to suggest that the European Commission's drive to conclude these AAs is detrimental to the (rhetorical) promotion of regional integration in Latin America and the Caribbean. This has been reflected in a more general trend that has affected bi-regional negotiations between the EU and the Gulf states, the ACP, ASEAN and the Mediterranean.[34]

Specific developments in the negotiations with CAN illustrate how the European Commission has contributed to the internal crisis of this regional mechanism. At the time of writing, negotiations with CAN are taking place on an *ad hoc* basis, where trade liberalisation is only being negotiated with the governments of Peru and Colombia, because Bolivia and Ecuador have rejected a deepening of their respective trade agreements with the EU. As expected, the European Commission explains the fracture of the CAN bloc, and also the stagnant negotiations with Mercosur, with reference to political disagreements between Latin American countries. The European Commission's drive to conclude AAs in line with the so-called Global Europe strategy could, however, be seen as part and parcel of the disagreements, with

Bolivia's and Ecuador's left-of-centre governments taking a position opposed to that of the Commission.

The difference in position between the governments of Bolivia and Ecuador and those of Colombia and Peru not only caused the failure of EU–CAN negotiations, but also displayed the contested nature of bi-regional integration through trade and services liberation that is at the core of the EU–LAC partnership. This became clear in a recent seminar to celebrate the 10th anniversary of the strategic partnership that was sponsored by the European Commission and organised by the Chilean think-tank CELARE. The conclusions of the seminar note that the 'Commission's proposal to negotiate with CAN has been based upon the acknowledgment of different speeds while what is being asked from the Commission is the acknowledgment of different models of society and development, especially of Andean conceptions such as "el buen vivir" (the plenitude of life)'.[35]

The Tribunals' contributions to epistemic justice

As mentioned above, the process of identification of supra-state duty and power bearers, including the European Commission and European MNCs, has proven to be central to the bi-regional efforts and strategies of civil society actors and social movements. Their efforts are aimed at promoting the realisation of rights through mobilisation, lobby campaigns and, as in the case analysed here, mechanisms of informal litigation. Litigation mechanisms are applied within society and across regions and often target public–private mechanisms of governance, international institutions, and bi-regional or transatlantic governance frameworks, including the decision-making mechanisms of the strategic partnership (involving the European Commission, Council and Parliament, *ad hoc* mechanisms, etc). The practices are seen to differ from 'market-based notions of access and entitlement to resources' as they seek to increase the capacity of rights-holders to claim their rights from authority, duty and power holders.[36] This has been the case in the European, Latin American and Caribbean network, Enlazando Alternativas, which was officially launched in 2004 as a bi-regional coalition of NGOs, think-tanks, and social movements. Its ultimate goal was to influence the decision-making process and content of the strategic partnership. As part of the so-called 'anti-globalisation movement', the network is opposed to 'the neoliberal policies and trade agenda of the European Union (EU) [that] is being led by powerful transnational corporations [with the] objective ... to ensure its countries unrestricted access to Latin American and Caribbean markets'.[37]

The Tribunals: events, spaces, processes, instruments

The public awareness campaigns of Enlazando Alternativas have included the organisation of 'people's tribunals' to expose human rights and environmental violations by EU-based MNCs or their subsidiaries. The literature considers the tribunals as innovative and informal vehicles of participation that not only have the potential to achieve direct change in corporate conduct, but also have symbolic value and the potential to mobilise new communities of activists. In our case communities are mobilised around the bi-regional governance framework of the EU–LAC partnership.[38] The Permanent People's Tribunals (PPTs) were set up in 1979 as the successor to the Russell Tribunals on Vietnam (1966–67) and on the Latin American Dictatorships (1974–76). The PPPs' *raison d'être* is to raise awareness about social grievances that 'receive no institutional recognition or response, whether at a national or an international level', and also 'to qualify such situations in legal terms'.[39] The Tribunals against European Multinationals and Neo-liberalism thus raise awareness of the impacts of a pro-corporate business economic system on human rights. The organisers, participants and supporters of the Tribunals also tend to understand them as events and spaces where social grievances are voiced, hence as a tool for promoting reforms in international law.

Since 2006, the Tribunals have had sessions in Peru (2006), Colombia (2007), Nicaragua (2007), Guatemala (2008) and Honduras (2009). The session in Lima has been described by one of its core organisers 'as the moment when everything started to make sense and when we had all the information carefully researched for the ruling'.[40] The Lima session identified some specific types of violations by European MNCs and the mechanisms that produced these violations. The MNCs put on trial included: Aguas de Barcelona, Bayer, BBVA, Botnia, Camposol, Cermac Mainstream, Marine Harvest, HSBC, Monterrico Metals, Proactiva, Repsol-YPF, Roche, Santander, Shell, Skanska, Suez, Syngenta, Telecom Italia, Thyssen Krupp, Unilever and Unión Fenosa. Norwegian Camposol was the only company to send a representative to testify before the Tribunal.

In total, 21 cases from 12 sectors were presented and discussed in relation to their negative impacts on labour relations, environmental standards, the use of transgenic seeds, health, corruption and the financial system. The impacts were described as ecological debt, the theft of common resources, the systematic violation of people's rights, violence, and the violation of national sovereignty. Three mechanisms were held responsible for these impacts: legislative mechanisms, which had led to changes to the rules of the game; financial mechanisms, resulting in the use of public money to finance investment projects; and techno-productive mechanisms related to transport, communications, water and energy use, and the implementation of technologies to promote the exploitation of goods and services.[41] On the basis of this identification, the Lima Tribunal ruled that two levels of responsibility were involved: 1) the responsibility of the state, which had failed to perform its duties; and 2) responsibility by commission. The following quote specifies these levels, together with some of the mechanisms that are held responsible for the violation of rights:

> In terms of the activities of transnational companies and human rights, the PPT identifies various levels of responsibility. On the one hand, there are the States who have a duty to prevent, protect and sanction violations of human rights by their own agents or private actors (above all the most powerful, such as

European transnationals). This creates liability by omission in the case of negligence in the duty to protect rights against the conduct of the European transnationals; liability by commission when they actively stimulate the presence of these European transnationals, granting operating licences, increasing flexibility of labour, environmental and tax laws to favour the interests of these companies.[42]

Further, the ruling concluded that the violations of rights by European MNCs or their subsidiaries in Latin America

> are no accidents. They are indications and fairly 'normal' expressions of how the overall policies and specific practices of European transnationals violating rights can be developed with absolute impunity and/or with the permissiveness of the responsible public authorities (in the countries of origin of the European transnationals and/or in the countries where the victims of the violations are).[43]

Accordingly, the Tribunal accused European MNCs as well as those actors who were held responsible for enabling, legitimating and supporting MNCs in their actions. The latter group of actors includes national and international governance mechanisms in the financial, media and legal sectors, and governments. In so doing and without denying the role of the state—as ultimately responsible to 'promote, respect, guarantee and enforce human rights'—the sessions contributed to the identification of an array of duty holders, besides local and national state authorities, to which social grievances and claim-making strategies are directed.[44]

At this point it could be argued that the Tribunals are symbolically contributing to the dismantling of the European Union's commercial policies. The contribution that this analysis aims to make, however, is a different one. By attributing responsibility to particular actors as duty holders, with faces or brand names, the Tribunals have contributed to what feminist political economists call a 'challenge [of] the dominant script of [neo-liberal] globalisation' that represents it as an abstract dominant and unified force or system.[45]

Who are the peoples?

The Tribunals have based their rulings on the Universal Declaration of the Rights of Peoples (Algiers, 1976) which, together with a set of international laws, recognises certain rights and the holders of these rights. For example, in the Guatemala sessions (October 2008), the Swiss Multinational Holcim and its subsidiary Cementos Progreso were denounced by communities of Maya Kaqchikeles from San Juan Sacatepéquez and condemned by the Tribunals for violating the right of indigenous communities to hold a consultation among the members of their community. This ruling was concluded in accordance with the communities' customary law, on the basis of the International Labour Organisation's (ILO) Convention concerning Indigenous and Tribal Peoples in Independent Countries (1989) and the Declaration on the Rights of Indigenous Peoples (2007).[46] On the same legal grounds

Spanish multinational Repsol was condemned by the Colombia Tribunal (2007) for environmental destruction and its attempts to secure access to oil reserves in Catleya without proper consultations with the u'was indigenous people who inhabit this area.[47]

The Honduras Tribunal of March 2009 condemned Italian multinational Green Power, SpA and its local subsidiary Geo, SA de CV for the contamination of water reserves with muriatic acid and caustic soda in the Alegria and Berlin municipalities of the Usulutan department. This ruling was made on the basis of the Declaration on the Right to Development (1986) and the Additional Protocol to the American Convention on Human Rights in the area of Economic, Social and Cultural Rights (1988).

Interestingly, the ruling of the Lima Tribunal (2008) presented the physical destruction of the natural environment by European MNCs (Repsol, Union Fenosa, MAJAZ) as moral aggression against *Pachamama*, the Andean conception of Mother Earth:

> In the indigenous people's cosmovision, human beings, children of the water and land, live in symbiosis with nature from where they can take the means to live. For that reason, the destruction of the Earth is a lack of respect for life itself. It is a work of death.[48]

Tensions

As mechanisms for bottom-up informal litigation to reclaim community rights and seek justice and restitution, the everyday practices and outcomes of the Tribunals are not without tensions. The most committed and critical activists tend to idealise Andean conceptions and understand these aspirations as *the* solution to the problems of the dominant development paradigm driven by capitalist accumulation and the commodification of all forms of life.[49] Yet such a view is contrary to Santos' understanding that all cultures are incomplete and problematic in their conceptions of human dignity—a position that is central to his project for a multicultural construction of human rights: 'The incompleteness derives from the very fact that there is a plurality of cultures ... [I]f each culture were as complete as it claims to be there would be just one single culture'.[50] A recent analysis by Otzoy, which indicates how Western and Maya customary laws have both failed to protect indigenous women from domestic violence, contributes to Santos' notions of incompleteness of cultures.[51]

Others have argued that the Tribunals have contributed to cognitive justice by making visible the fractures of neoliberal bi-regional governance. By their actions the Tribunals translate social grievances into legal terms through the application of international law. Nevertheless, this practice gives rise to one important tension. As this legal qualification results in the 'translation' of social grievances, the practice runs the risk of erasing and making invisible what doesn't fit or cannot easily be attached to a particular international law.[52] This is what has been termed 'translation as epistemic erasure'.[53] In practical terms this erasure might be subtle and not premeditated, but it has certainly resulted in the selection of 'model cases' that were felt to be relevant in terms of 'the implications and structural consequences, and in terms of their legal analysis'.[54]

An additional tension related to the Tribunals' contributions to cognitive justice concerns the reality of neoliberal bi-regional governance as an all-encompassing system of oppression; the cases presented at the Tribunals are qualified as 'merely specific manifestations of broader logics' that 'reflect the more general tendencies of global competitiveness that govern the world today'.[55] As was argued above, neoliberal bi-regional governance is powerful and erodes rights but the transformative possibilities of the notions of cognitive justice that the Tribunals promote are related to the fractures that their informal litigation made visible. This is a relevant issue for all those who aspire to realise the emancipatory potential of the Tribunals.

Conclusions

This article has offered an account of the role of social resistance in unveiling the nature of EU–LAC neoliberal bi-regional governance. The account was based on a closer examination of the practice of identifying power and authority holders as duty bearers, which has been promoted by the Permanent People's Tribunals. Most importantly, the analysis has highlighted the sort of questioning that results from this practice for neoliberal bi-regional governance. The article's argument was developed in three steps.

First, the article analysed the explanatory limitations of key IR/IPE perspectives on global governance and social resistance. The perspectives present the former as an inescapable unitary system of oppression and the latter as a reaction to it or simply as a force reproducing the system's dynamics. With the help of theories on cognitive justice and social resistance, developed by Santos and Lugonés, the article identified the Tribunals' capacity to challenge the one-dimensional notion of global governance and resistance.

Second, the article focused on the 'neoliberal' nature of the EU's governance approach to LAC and, in particular, the way this has been framed by the EU–LAC strategic partnership and the Global Europe strategy. Bi-regional governance was portrayed as a comprehensive network of decision-making mechanisms and programmes, following IR/IPE perspectives that consider EU institutions, LAC governments and MNCs as key and powerful 'makers' of regionalism.

Finally, this contribution discussed the Tribunals' attempts to identify power and authority holders, the mechanisms and tools used for this identification and the tensions deriving from their contributions to cognitive justice.

The analysis has sought to contribute to an emerging IR/IPE agenda of critical governance studies, by unveiling the mainstream narratives that inform EU–LAC bi-regional governance, especially those deriving from the Post-Washington Consensus and involving good governance principles. Furthermore, the article has presented a critique of IR/IPE views on resistance to neoliberal global governance. Alternative ways of theorising this resistance focus on the challenge of the unitary system of bi-regional control, steering and domination, posed by the knowledges and cultures that were 'erased' by neoliberal governance. As part of ongoing research on alternative regionalisms in Latin America, the article has explored the emerging principle of cognitive justice that has informed the process of the Permanent People's Tribunals and the formulation of an alternative agenda to neoliberal policies of open regionalism.

Notes

I would like to thank Karim Knio and Wil Hout for their comments on earlier drafts of this paper, and to Rolando Vazquez for his detailed suggestions for improvement. I am deeply grateful to Cecilia Olivet and Brid Brennan from the Transnational Institute (TNI) and to Claudia Torelli (former member of Friends of the Earth—Uruguay) for their trust and support.

1 R Icaza, *Civil Society in the Making of Regionalisms: Power and Resistance across Borders*, London: Routledge, 2010.
2 At www.enlazandoalternativas.org, accessed 26 November 2009.
3 I make use of Sawyer and Gomez's characterisation of transnational governmentality on resource extraction as ongoing and 'far from a *fait acommpli*'. I do so with the intention to highlight the fractures that practices of cognitive justice might help to unveil, as explained later in this article. See S Sawyer & ET Gomez, *Transnational Governmentality and Resource Extraction: Indigenous Peoples, Multinational Corporations, Multilateral Institutions and the State*, UNRIDS Identities, Conflict and Cohesion Program Paper 12, September 2009.
4 MI Saguier, *Global Governance and the HIV/AIDS Response: Limitations of Current Approaches and Policies*, Centre for the Study of Globalisation and Regionalisation Working Paper 225, 2007, p 5.
5 JA Camillieri & J Falk, *The End of Sovereignty? The Politics of a Shrinking and Fragmenting World*, Aldershot: Edward Elgar, 1992, p 97; and JA Scholte, *Globalization and Governance: From Statism to Polycentrism*, CSGR Working Paper 130, 2004, p 2.
6 *Ibid*, p 6.
7 *Ibid*.
8 On the networked polycentric view, see D Held & A McGrew (eds), *Governing Globalization: Power, Authority and Global Governance*, Cambridge: Polity, 2002; and JA Scholte, 'Global capitalism and the state', *International Affairs*, 73(3), 2007, p 428. On global governmentality, see RD Lipschutz, 'Global civil society and global govermentality: or, the search for politics and the state amidst the capillaries of social power', in M Barnett & R Duvall (eds), *Power in Global Governance*, Cambridge: Cambridge University Press, 2006. On the interpretation of Empire, see S Soederberg, *Global Governance in Question: Empire, Class, and the New Common Sense in Managing North–South Relations*, London: Pluto Press, 2006.
9 HM Jaeger, 'Global civil society and the political depoliticization of global governance', *International Political Sociology*, 1(3), 2007, pp 257–277; and J Sen, 'The power of civility', *Development Dialogue*, 49, 2007, pp 51–68.
10 JH Zubizarreta, 'El derecho comercial global frente al derecho internacional de los derechos humanos', *Observatorio de Multinacionales en America Latina*, 1998, at http://www.omal.info/www/article. php3?id_article=1577&var_recherche=Teitelbaum, accessed 26 November 2009.
11 The network Enlanzando Alternativas submitted the proposal 'Profit before People and Human Rights: European Transnational Corporations in Latin America and the Caribbean' to the UN Consultation on Business and Human Rights organised by the Office of the High Commission of the United Nation for Human Rights, held in Geneva, 5–6 October 2009. This was the first time since the Global Compact voluntary principles adopted by enterprises and sponsored by the UN that the question of an international tribunal to judge multinational corporations had been raised.
12 B Hettne, 'The double movement: global market versus regionalism', in RW Cox (ed), *The New Realism: Perspectives on Multilateralism and World Order*, London: Macmillan/UNU, p 224.
13 R Icaza & R Vazquez, 'Chiapas rebellion and the Battle of Seattle: understanding transborder resistances as political events', paper presented at the International Studies Association Annual Convention, Chicago, 2007.
14 B de Sousa Santos, *The Rise of the Global Left: The World Social Forum and Beyond*, London: Verso, 2006, p 14.

15 B de Sousa Santos, JA Nunes & MP Meneses, 'Opening up the canon of knowledge and recognition of difference', in B de Sousa Santos (ed), *Another Knowledge is Possible: Beyond Northern Epistemologies*, London: Verso, 2007.
16 WD Coleman & NA Johnson, 'Building dialogue on globalization research: what are the obstacles and how might these be addressed', paper presented at the workshop on 'Building South–North Dialogue on Globalization Research: Phase II', Centre for International Governance Innovation, Waterloo, Ontario, 22–23 August 2008, p 4.
17 Santos *et al*, 'Opening up the canon of knowledge', p xx.
18 R Vázquez, 'Modernity coloniality and visibility: the politics of time, *Sociological Research Online*, 14(4), 31 August 2009.
19 *El buen vivir* is an aspiration to a full life, not a better one or a life detrimental to others (including people and nature), and prescribes a harmonic relationship between individuals in communities and of these with Pachamama (Mother Earth). This is the author's translation from a letter sent by Bolivan President Evo Morales to South American presidents, inviting them to the South American Summit of Nations in Cochabamba, Bolivia, in December 2006. The letter is quoted in R Fernandez Duran, *America Latina en una Encrucijada Historica*, at http://www.tni.org//archives/act/16214, accessed 26 November 2009. The right to *buen vivir* has been recently included in the Bolivian and Ecuadorian constitutions of 2008. See http://pdba.georgetown.edu/constitutions/bolivia/bolivia.html and http://pdba.georgetown.edu/Constitutions/Ecuador/ecuador.html, accessed 26 November 2009. See, further, Enlazando Alternativas, *Documento Marco Tribunal: Nucleos Conceptuales—Apuntes estrategicos para la presentacion de casos y la organizacion del Tribunal de Lima*, 2008, at http://www.enlazandoalternativas.org/IMG/pdf/DOCUMENTO_MARCO_TRIBUNAL-2.pdf, accessed 26 November 2009.
20 R Icaza, 'Alternative regionalisms and civil society: setting a research agenda', *Pensamiento Propio*, 29(4), 2009, pp 235–244.
21 M Lugonés, *Pilgrimages/Peregrinajes: Theorizing Coalition against Multiple Oppressions*, Boulder, CO: Rowman and Littlefield, 2003, pp 53–64.
22 M Lugonés, 'Methodological notes towards a decolonial feminism', paper presented at the 53rd International Conference of Americanists, Mexico, July 2009.
23 R Icaza, 'NAFTA parity in real time and the "making" of the EU–Mexico transatlantic partnership', in P De Lombaerde & M Schulz (eds), *The EU and World Regionalism: The Makeability of Regions in the 21st Century*, London: Ashgate, 2009; and R Icaza, 'Regionalism in the Americas', in R Munck (ed), *Globalization and Security: An Encyclopaedia*, New York: Praeger, 2009.
24 See European Commission, *Latin America Regional Programming Document 2007–2013*, E/2007/1417, 12 July 2007, at http://ec.europa.eu/external_relations/la/rsp/07_13_en.pdf, accessed 26 November 2009; Europa Press Release, *EU–Latin America: 10 years of Strategic Partnership*, Memo/09/426, Brussels, 30 September 2009, at http://europa.eu/rapid/pressReleasesAction.do?reference=MEMO/09/426&format=HTML&aged=0&language=EN&guiLanguage=en, accessed 26 November 2009; and Independent European Development Portal, at www.developmentportal.eu/wcm, accessed 26 November 2009.
25 Europa Press Release, *EU–Latin America*.
26 European Commission, *The European Union and Latin America: The Present Situation and Prospects for Closer Partnership 1996–2000*, Communication from the Commission to the Council and the European Parliament, COM(95)495 final, 23 October 1995.
27 Icaza, 'NAFTA parity in real time and the "making" of the EU–Mexico transatlantic partnership'.
28 German Federal Foreign Office, Press Release, 21 August 2009, at http://www.auswaertiges-amt.de/diplo/en/Europa/Aussenpolitik/Regionalabkommen/LateinAmerika.html, accessed 26 November 2009.
29 K Dykmann, 'The Common Foreign and Security Policy of the European Union towards Latin America', *Nord–Süd Aktuell*, 18(4), 2004, p 674.
30 European Commission, *A Stronger Partnership between the European Union and Latin America*, Communication from the Commission to the Council and the European Parliament, COM(2005)636 final.
31 European Commission, *European Competitiveness*, at http://ec.europa.eu/trade/creating-opportunities/trade-topics/european-competitiveness/index_en.htm, accessed 26 November 2009.
32 European Commission, *Lisbon Strategy for Growth and Jobs: Towards a Green and Innovative Economy*, at http://ec.europa.eu/growthandjobs/index_en.htm, accessed 26 November 2009.
33 European Commission, *Global Europe Competing in the World: A Contribution to the EU's Growth and Jobs Strategy*, at http://trade.ec.europa.eu/doclib/docs/2006/october/tradoc_130376.pdf, accessed 26 November 2009.
34 M Maes, 'The EU's Global Europe strategy: where is that strategy goday?, introductory presentation made at the informal meeting 'Building of a Common Platform between Developing Countries'

organised by the South Centre, Brussels, 4–5 December 2008, at http://www.enlazandoalternativas.org/IMG/pdf/Global_Europe_Today_MM_081204.pdf, accessed 26 November 2009.
35 CELARE–Union Europea, *Conclusiones del Seminario '10 Anos de la Asociacion Estrategica America Latina y El Caribe–Union Europea: Evaluacion y Analisis Prospectivo'*, 5–6 October 2009, Santiago: CEPAL, at http://www.celare.org/index.php?option=com_content&task=view&id=5096&Itemid=81, accessed 26 November 2009. These and further quotes have been translated from Spanish by the author.
36 P Newell & J Wheeler, 'Rights, resources and the politics of accountability: an introduction', in Newell & Wheller (eds), *Rights, Resources and the Politics of Accountability*, London: Zed Books, 2006, p 1.
37 At http://www.enlazandoalternativas.org/IMG/pdf/ea-en.pdf, accessed 26 November 2009.
38 R Icaza, P Newell & M Saguier, *Democratizing Trade Politics in the Americas: Insights from the Feminist, Environmental and Labour Movements*, IDS Working Paper 328, Brighton: Institute of Development Studies, June 2009.
39 Permanent People's Tribunal, *Session on Neoliberal Policies and European Transnationals in Latin America and the Caribbean*, Lima, 13–16 May 2008, at http://www.tni.org/article/permanent-peoples-tribunal-session-neoliberal-policies-and-european-transnationals-latin-ame, accessed 26 November 2009.
40 Conversation with Ms Claudia Torelli, Friends of the Earth Uruguay, Guatemala, 10 October 2008.
41 *Ibid*.
42 Permanent People's Tribunal, *Session on Neoliberal Policies*, pp 11–12.
43 *Ibid*, p 5.
44 *Ibid*, p 11.
45 S Bergeron, *Fragments of Development: Nation, Gender and the Space of Modernity*, Ann Arbor, MI: University of Michigan Press, 2006, pp 156–157.
46 Tribunal Permanente de los Pueblos, Audiencia CentroAmericana, *Politicas Neoliberales, Transnacionales y Grupos Economicos*, Jury Indictment, Guatemala, 10–11 October 2008, at http://www.enlazandoalternativas.org/spip.php?article298, accessed 26 November 2009.
47 Tribunal Permanente de los Pueblos, Sesion Colombia, *Audiencia sobre Empresas del Petroleo: Indictment on the Multinational Corporations BP, Oxy and Repsol*, 5 September 2007, at http://www.omal.info/www/article.php3?id_article=986, accessed 26 November 2009.
48 Permanent People's Tribunal, *Session on Neoliberal Policies*, p 8.
49 For example, Duran, *America Latina en una Encrucijada Historica*.
50 B de Sousa Santos, 'Towards a multicultural conception of human rights', in B Hernandez-Truyol (ed), *Moral Imperialism: A Critical Anthology*, New York: New York University, 2002, p 46.
51 I Otzoy, 'Indigenous law and gender dialogues', in P Pitarch, S Speed & X Leyva Solano (eds), *Human Rights in the Maya Region: Global Politics, Cultural Contentions and Moral Engagements*, Durham, NC: Duke University Press, 2008, pp 171–186.
52 Santos *et al*, 'Opening up the canon of knowledge', p xxvi.
53 R Vazquez, 'Translation as Erasure, exploring modernity's epistemic violence', Economic and Social Research Council (UK) *Working Papers, Research Program Connected Histories/Connected Sociologies: Rethinking the Global*, forthcoming.
54 Permanent People's Tribunal, *Session on Neoliberal Policies*, p 5.
55 *Ibid*, p 8.

Between Development and Security: the European Union, governance and fragile states

WIL HOUT

ABSTRACT *This article focuses on the recent attention in the European Union on fragile states, as expressed, among others, in the European Security Strategy of 2003 and the European Consensus on Development of 2006. Most understandings of the notion of state fragility concern limited state capacity, the inability of institutions to deal with social and political tensions or problems of state legitimacy. The EU is no exception to this general trend of seeing state fragility in terms of governance deficits. Its approach to preventing and responding to state fragility, which was adopted by the European Council in 2007, is being tested in six pilot countries. The article analyses the governance-oriented measures that have been adopted in the Country Strategy Papers (CSPs) agreed between the European Commission and five of the six pilot countries, concluding that there is a profound gap between the political-economic analyses of the CSPs and the support policies implemented by the EU. The approach of the European Commission revolves around attempts to reconstruct state capacities in fragile states through technocratic measures. Fundamental problems of state capture, ethnic relations, human rights violations and extreme inequalities are beyond the purview of policy makers in the European Union.*

Over the past five to seven years most international aid donors have started to pay attention to so-called 'fragile states'. Generally the interest in state fragility has been spurred by security considerations in the wake of the terrorist attacks of '9/11'. Fragile states came to be seen as a potential incubator of state collapse, which would result in the creation of 'ungoverned spaces', where crime and terrorism could develop.[1]

Overall the focus on fragility is part of a more general trend of 'securitisation of development', which is preoccupied with creating conditions for stability in the developing world. As Duffield has argued, 'stability is achieved by activities designed to reduce poverty, satisfy basic needs, strengthen economic sustainability, create representative civil institutions, protect the vulnerable and promote human rights'.[2] The reconstruction of 'fragile states' is the latest witness to the securitisation of development.

The European Union has been no exception to the general trend of addressing fragile states, although it took the Union roughly four years to translate the concerns about 'state failure' voiced in the European Security Strategy of 2003 into a policy on fragile states.[3] The linkage of the EU's policy on fragile states to security concerns has led to an emphasis of a wide set of policy instruments that make an explicit connection between development, humanitarian, military and security aspects—sometimes referred to as a 'whole-of-EU approach'.[4] Within this framework the governance dimension is emphasised—indeed, as will be argued in the third section of this article, the EU defines fragile states largely in terms of weak governance structures—but the way in which the agenda regarding those fragile states is implemented has strong security overtones.[5]

Having emphasised more formal and technical aspects of governance since the mid-1990s (the era of the so-called post-Washington Consensus), various international aid agencies have recently started to emphasise the need for more profoundly political or political-economic analyses of the governance situation in aid-receiving countries.[6] In a report on the 'lessons learnt' of its involvement in 'low income countries under stress' (LICUS), the World Bank was already emphasising in 2005 the desirability of performing 'political economy and conflict analysis' when selecting and sequencing priorities for the rebuilding of fragile states. This position was reinforced by the Bank's Independent Evaluation Group, which emphasised the need for 'commissioning and consuming' good political analysis regarding countries where the Bank is actively involved.[7]

In those instances where the European Union has incorporated governance issues into its strategies for fragile states, its approach to governance has a highly technocratic character, with a strong emphasis on public sector reform and public finance. This approach, it will be argued here, is in stark contrast to the increasing awareness in the donor community of the political-economic dimensions of governance reforms. In particular, the EU's failure to take cognisance of the lessons formulated by the World Bank on the application of political-economy and conflict analysis is highly surprising.

This article presents an analysis of recently adopted EU policies on fragile states. The next section gives an overview of diverging interpretations of fragile states, and discusses some general observations on policies towards fragile states. The subsequent section discusses the concept of fragile states as applied in the EU context. The fourth section provides an analysis of several Country Strategy Papers that were drawn up for fragile states in the context of the 10th European Development Fund (2008–13), and specifically the way in which concerns regarding governance rehabilitation have been entered into these documents. The final section presents some general conclusions.

Fragile states: definitions and approaches

Many authors have noted that the literature on fragile states has produced a wealth of definitions of state fragility. As observed by the World Bank, the term fragile states has gradually replaced concepts that were applied earlier—such as difficult partnerships, countries at risk, difficult environments, failing states and low income countries under stress—since the adoption of the Paris Declaration on Aid Effectiveness in March 2005.[8]

Despite the widespread use of the concept, a recent review of 'thinking and practice' concerning fragile states has noted that there is no single, 'unambiguous' definition. The survey argues that definitions can be grouped on the basis of a limited number of characteristics. The three types of definitions distinguished by Cammack *et al* focus on, respectively:

- *state functions*: definitions of this type understand fragile states in terms of the lack of capacity or will to perform certain functions that contribute to the security and well-being of a country's citizens;[9]
- *state outputs*: this type of definition sees fragile states as bringing about a host of problems, including poverty, violent conflict, terrorism, global security threats, refugees, organised crime, epidemic diseases and environmental degradation; such problems may cause difficulties in neighbouring countries or across a whole region;[10]
- *relationships with donors*: this category of definition understands fragile states in terms of the difficult relationship they have with a particular donor or group of donors. It implies that fragility is seen to result from 'factors that have more to do with the relationship (eg a particular shared history) than with the nature of the state itself'.[11]

The main elements of the fragile state agenda implemented by international aid donors, according to Cammack *et al*, revolve around three key objectives: the promotion of human security, basic needs and peace by providing humanitarian aid and peace building; the furthering of development and improvement of governance; and the provision of global security.[12] Underlying this variety of objectives, some commentators have argued, is a focus on the inadequate functioning of the state; most remedies consequently revolve around the strengthening of government institutions.[13]

Most policy-related definitions of fragile states can be classified in terms of one of the three categories mentioned above, as their focus is, understandably, on specific instances of state fragility that agencies wish to address. For instance, the definition applied by the OECD's Development Assistance Committee (DAC) falls squarely within the first of Cammack *et al*'s categories. According to the DAC, 'states are fragile when state structures lack political will and/or capacity to provide the basic functions needed for poverty reduction, development and to safeguard the security and human rights of their populations'.[14] The World Bank's understanding of state fragility, which is laid out in two aspects, straddles the first and second categories of Cammack *et al*'s classification. The first aspect mentioned by the World Bank focuses on the weakness of state policies and institutions; this is felt to seriously reduce the state's capacity to deliver services, control corruption and provide sufficient voice and accountability. The second aspect concerns the increased risk that such countries will experience conflict and political instability.[15]

Despite the desire in policy-making circles to develop clear-cut models of state fragility and differentiate fragile from stable developing countries, several important caveats have been formulated with regard to the implementation of policies on fragile states. The DAC has pointed out that state fragility in not an either/or issue, but rather a 'spectrum ... found in all but the most developed and institutionalised states'. This notion links to a wider set of factors, most or all of which highlight the need for a political response to fragility. According to the DAC, the understanding of fragility as a range instead of a single condition leads to a focus on resilience ('the ability to cope with changes in capacity, effectiveness, or legitimacy') rather than stability as the opposite of fragility: 'Resilience, we argue, therefore derives from a combination of capacity and resources, effective institutions and legitimacy, all of which are underpinned by political processes that mediate state–society relations and expectations'.[16]

The emphasis on the political nature of the response to fragile states has brought both the DAC and the World Bank to call for context-specific action. The first of the 'Principles for good international engagement in fragile states and situations', drafted in early 2005 and adopted by development ministers and heads of agencies in the OECD's Development Assistance Committee in April 2007, emphasises the need to distinguish whether problems derive from a lack of capacity, political will or legitimacy. Moreover, the principles point out that policies on fragile states need to be tailored to the dynamics of the countries concerned. In line with similar conclusions reached earlier by the World Bank, the OECD argued that it is crucially important to recognise whether countries are going through a phase of political transition, are in a situation of deteriorating or improving governance, or have become locked into a political impasse.[17]

In a discussion of its experience with the LICUS framework the World Bank argued that the implementation of institutional reform in fragile states should recognise local dynamics instead of adopting a one-size-fits-all approach:

> In most fragile state contexts, developing technical suggestions for institutional reform is easy; managing the political process of reform is much more difficult. It is therefore important that institution-building initiatives avoid purely technocratic approaches, devoting considerable attention to the process of decision-making and implementation, and to well-designed participation and widespread communication of reform initiatives. The 'fit' of institutional structures with local realities has also frequently been problematic in fragile states, due to ill-adapted colonial legacies or the imposition of inappropriate external models: remaining open to new ideas for locally-driven institutional reforms and supporting local debate and discussion on options is critical.[18]

Among a host of other observations the 2006 review of the LICUS framework by the Bank's Independent Evaluation Group produced a set of conclusions about the need for analysis of the political situation and the causes of conflict in fragile states. An incisive comment regarding one of the fragile states targeted by the Bank illustrates the need for internalisation of political analysis:

For example, the Interim Strategy in Papua New Guinea has a good discussion of the political system. It recognizes the problems of clan loyalties, political patronage, corruption, lack of capacity, and other factors, but the Strategy then goes on to disregard some of this vital knowledge and treat these issues as technical problems.[19]

In particular, four types of political analysis seem relevant to policy making on fragile states. Political risk analysis would produce an assessment of the likelihood of future instability in a fragile state, while structural analysis would enhance understanding of the weakness of the state as a result of structural (for instance, ethnically or religiously based) sources of conflict. Analysis of day-to-day politics would lead to more insight into the distribution of power at the national, regional and local level, and would provide a clue as to whether decentralisation policies are likely to succeed or not. Analysis of the history of reform in the country and in neighbouring countries would contribute to an understanding of which reform policies are likely to be accepted by the population and which stand more chance of being resisted.[20]

This section has highlighted different understandings of the nature of fragile states and agendas to address the problems associated with such states and has summarised some of the lessons drawn with regard to the political aspects of the response to fragile states. On the basis of the above it seems safe to conclude that most understandings of fragile states revolve around the (mal)functioning of the state in developing countries as a result of limited capacity, the inability of institutions to deal with social and/or political tensions or the lack of state legitimacy. Analyses of the implementation of the policies on fragile states (by, for instance, the World Bank and OECD) indicate the centrality of adopting political analyses of processes and events in developing countries in order to understand local specificities that are causing fragility.

The EU and fragile states

The European Union has begun to place increasing emphasis on so-called 'fragile states' with the adoption of its 'security strategy', drafted by CFSP High Representative Javier Solana, in 2003. The key threats to Europe outlined in the strategy included 'state failure', which was perceived both as a threat in itself and as a possible contributing factor to other types of threat. The European security strategy defined state failure as a 'key threat', because:

> bad governance—corruption, abuse of power, weak institutions and lack of accountability—and civil conflict corrode States from within ... Collapse of the State can be associated with obvious threats, such as organised crime or terrorism. State failure is an alarming phenomenon, that undermines global governance, and adds to regional instability.[21]

The strategy argued that various instruments should be applied by the EU, ranging from military force to diplomatic engagement, trade relations, development aid and humanitarian assistance. In relation to developing countries the strategy argued that 'security is the first condition for development'.[22] Further to this, the 'European Consensus on Development', agreed by the Council, Commission and European Parliament in December 2005, called for a 'comprehensive prevention approach to state fragility, conflict, natural disasters and other types of crises'.[23]

In 2003 the European Commission presented a framework on governance and development that distinguished several types of relations that would later be subsumed under the label of 'fragile states': 'difficult' and 'extremely difficult' partnership and 'post-conflict' situations.[24] Each of these relations, the Commission argued, would require different approaches. In the case of difficult partnerships, which are 'characterised by a lack of commitment to good governance', alternative approaches to co-operation would have to be found, including the provision of humanitarian aid, collaboration with NGOs and civil society organisations, and political initiatives at the international and regional level. In 'extremely difficult partnerships' the only option would be to suspend co-operation entirely. Post-conflict situations, where state institutions are either non-functioning or non-existent, would call for attempts at reconciliation between parties involved in the conflict, a process of relief, rehabilitation and development, and the provision of humanitarian aid. The aim of the approach would be to have the authorities address governance issues, which were seen to lie at the root of the conflict in many cases.[25]

The Conclusions formulated by the General Affairs and External Relations Council (GAERC) in November 2007 on the basis of the Commission's Communication understood state fragility in reference to:

> weak or failing structures and to situations where the social contract is broken due to the State's incapacity or unwillingness to deal with its basic functions, meet its obligations and responsibilities regarding the rule of law, protection of human rights and fundamental freedoms, security and safety of its population, poverty reduction, service delivery, the transparent and equitable management of resources and access to power.[26]

The Commission's Communication referred to fragility as a feature mainly of low and middle income countries that are faced with structural weaknesses in their economy, and are vulnerable to crises, external shocks, epidemics, drug trafficking, natural disasters, environmental degradation, and endangered cultural diversity. Governance deficits, however, were seen as the main cause of state fragility: 'Fragility is often triggered by governance shortcomings and failures, in form of lack of political legitimacy compounded by very limited institutional capacities linked to poverty'.[27]

The Council Conclusions of November 2007 contained a long list of 'issues' that should be addressed in the EU's approach to preventing and responding to state fragility. Apart from general issues such as attention to democratic governance, support of state capabilities and gender equality, the list included:

- improvement of existing governance assessment tools;
- development of early warning mechanisms on democratic governance issues, rule of law, human rights, poverty levels and conflict;

- strengthening of the role of Country Strategy Papers (CSPs) as the preferred framework to prevent and address fragility;
- strengthening of allocation criteria in the various aid schemes applied by the European Community for both African Caribbean and Pacific (ACP) and non-ACP countries;
- integration of democratic governance and institutional development into the so-called Linking Relief, Rehabilitation and Development (LRRD) framework; and
- use of the EU Code of Conduct on Complementarity and Division of Labour in order to channel more funds to developing countries which display signs of state fragility and which would run the risk of being excluded from development assistance (so-called 'aid orphans').[28]

In order to start addressing the issue of state fragility at the level of European Community development policy, the Council requested the Commission to 'test' the EU response in pilot cases. Burundi, Sierra Leone, Guinea Bissau, Haiti, Timor-Leste and Yemen were selected as pilot countries for this purpose.[29]

Governance-oriented responses to state fragility: analysis of Country Strategy Papers

This section contains an analysis of governance-oriented responses in several of the 'pilot' countries selected by the European Commission: Burundi, Guinea-Bissau, Sierra Leone, Timor-Leste and Yemen.[30] The analysis is performed on the basis of the CSPs concluded by European Community and the countries concerned in the context of either the Development Cooperation Instrument (for non-ACP countries) or the 10th European Development Fund (EDF) for the period between 2008 and 2013 (for ACP countries).

Burundi

In the framework of the 10th EDF, Burundi has been allocated €188 million as so-called A allocation under the ACP–EC Partnership Agreement for macroeconomic support, sectoral policies and for programmes and projects in support of focal and non-focal areas of Community assistance. The country will be receiving another €24.1 million as B allocation for unforeseen needs, such as emergency aid, debt relief and support to mitigate instability of export earnings.[31]

The analysis of the political and institutional situation in Burundi in the CSP highlights the continuing violation of human rights and the rule of law, despite the 'political will' to make improvements in both respects. The failure to bring an end to the armed struggle between the government and the rebel Hutu party is ascribed to the lack of experience and capacity of the armed forces and the police. The constitutional guarantees for ethnic and religious diversity, adopted in 2005, and power-sharing arrangements in state institutions and state-owned enterprises are judged to have improved the relations between the rival ethnic groups (Hutus and Tutsis).[32] The democratic process is still felt to be fragile; further democratic consolidation is seen to require better co-operation between the majority party, the other political parties and civil society.[33]

Burundi's Strategic Growth and Poverty Reduction Framework (Cadre stratégique de croissance et de lutte contre la pauvreté, CSLP), adopted in 2006, contains four central 'axes', among which improvement of governance and security was considered a *sine qua non* for national reconciliation and economic development. The main activities relate to the security sector, and include general and permanent ceasefire; disarmament, demobilisation and reintegration (DDR) of former combatants; professionalisation of the security forces; and disarmament of the population. In addition, strengthening of the rule of law and the fight against impunity are mentioned as central to the strengthening of governance.[34]

The CSP for 2008–13 notes that various measures on good governance which had formed part of the previous CSP (for 2003–07) concluded between Burundi and the European Community were not implemented until February 2007. The €19.75 million involved will be allocated to strengthening the central and local legal system, public sector management, and decentralisation of public administration.[35]

In the CSP 2008–13 rural development and health are chosen as the concentration areas for EC support. Good governance issues, most notably public finance management, are mentioned as a component of the programmes to be implemented in each of these areas, as well as for budget support.[36] Governance-oriented projects and programmes, which are included in the non-focal areas of the CSP, will receive an allocation of €10 million during the 10th EDF. These funds are intended for:

- state reform with an eye to issues of justice, decentralisation, civil service, security, and land and infrastructure;
- reinforcement of control mechanisms such as the national auditor's office, anti-corruption services and inspection services;
- bringing national legislation in line with international human rights norms; and
- support for decentralisation policies;
- co-financing of the next elections.[37]

Guinea-Bissau

The CSP agreed between the European Community and Guinea-Bissau for the 2008–13 period resulted in an allocation of almost €103 million to the country. The A allocation of €100 million contains an allocation of €27 million for programmes aimed at strengthening the rule of law and democracy.[38]

A political and institutional analysis of Guinea-Bissau emphasises the country's history of political violence and *coups d'état*. The causes of the political problems, according to the CSP, are diverse, and include the country's weak economic basis, its lack of social cohesion produced by ethnic cleavages, and the recent military conflict.[39] The CSP considers the national elections of 2004 and 2005 as steps on the way to a normal constitutional and political situation, despite the fact that political stability has remained fragile as a result of tensions between the president and the parliamentary majority. Moreover, the CSP notes that civilian control over the armed forces and the presence of arms among the population remain problematic, and necessitate reform of the security sector.[40]

The CSP argues that Guinea-Bissau's public administration structures, in particular public control institutions, are weak. The low degrees of transparency in resource management and public finance are seen as serious issues, as weaknesses in these areas lead to corruption, fraud, money laundering and tax evasion. As the legal framework is weak, the population has insufficient access to justice and the business environment is unfavourable.[41]

Guinea-Bissau's poverty reduction strategy for 2006–08 (Documento de Estratégia Nacional para a Redução de Pobreza, DENARP) contains a focus on strengthening governance, modernising public administration and improving macroeconomic stability, along with promoting economic growth, improving access to social services and basic infrastructure, and improving the living conditions of vulnerable groups.[42] The CSP 2008–13 emphasises, in particular, measures to support the rule of law and democracy, aimed at the consolidation of central state organs, public sector reform and reform of the security sector, including reintegration of former soldiers. These activities receive 90% of the €27 available for this domain. Next to this, support for the National Authorising Officer and electoral support involve another €3 million. A further amount of €32 million in budget support is intended for economic stabilisation, and should assist Guinea-Bissau on the way to establishing 'good economic governance' and public finance management.[43]

Sierra Leone

Under the 10th EDF, Sierra Leone received an allocation of €242 million in the A envelope and an additional €26.4 in the B envelope. Roughly 15% of the A envelope will be spent on good governance and institutional support.[44]

The CSP's analysis of the political situation focuses on the impact of the civil war, which lasted from 1991 until 2002, destroyed the country's infrastructure and political institutions, and led to a massive outflow of refugees to neighbouring countries. The roots of the civil war are traced to the centralisation of power, the absence of accountability in the co-opted civil service, and widespread corruption. The EU's assessment is that the country 'remains an extremely "fragile state", with a poorly resourced civil service that lacks capacity, operated inefficiently and lacks even the basic facilities to deliver adequate services'.[45]

Although national and local elections have been held since 2002, the CSP concludes that Sierra Leone is lacking democratic and effective governance, as well as effective oversight mechanisms (such as parliament and the judiciary). Regionalism and locality are important in the country, and political allegiance, according to the CSP, is based in social networks that are tied to particular places. The danger of internal instability is assessed to be real.[46]

The Joint Response Strategy, set up by the EC and the UK, is aimed at governance, peace and security; the promotion of pro-poor growth; and basic service delivery and human development. Measures suggested as supporting good governance and institutional reform are:

- the strengthening of democratic institutions by improving the country's capacity for holding free and fair elections and by giving assistance to the electoral process, including voter and civic education, political registration and awareness-raising;
- support for the decentralisation process (a first phase focusing on finalisation of the legal framework and capacity building in financial management, procurement and human resources, and a second phase of capacity building aimed at the management structures of decentralised sectors and services);
- support for civil service reform, aimed at restructuring and 'right-sizing', and capacity building within the civil service for the implementation of the country's Poverty Reduction Strategy; and
- support for a variety of actors in the public sector and for civil society.[47]

Timor-Leste

In 2007 Timor-Leste received an allocation of about €64 million as part of the 10th EDF multi-annual agreements, €63 million of which is assigned in the country's A envelope.[48]

Timor-Leste's CSP emphasises that the country's road to independence was rather violent, with Indonesian military forces attempting to maintain that country's grip on East Timor. After independence in 1999 there were several periods of violent unrest, most recently in 2006. Causes of the 2006 crisis included the resurfacing of divisions that predated 1999—in particular the failure to mete out justice for the crimes preceding independence—and poverty among youth and urban populations, resulting in a legitimacy crisis of the government. Although peaceful elections were held in 2007, several sources of instability persist, such as the presence of many weapons among the civilian population, the vast number of displaced persons and the widespread discontent among members of the security forces.[49]

Under the ninth EDF, a CSP was agreed in 2006 to provide support for rural development and institutional capacity building. The latter priority led to a focus on the development of a trade policy, support for electoral processes and the electoral system, and institutional capacity building in the area of public finance management.[50]

The EC's assistance under the 10th EDF aims to support the government's National Development Plan in three areas: rural development, health, and institutional capacity building. Institutional capacity building, which is supported with €13 million, or 21% of the means provided in the CSP, focused on five main activities:

- support for the judiciary, such as the training of judges and lawyers and capacity building of various courts;
- improvement of the capacity and performance of the civil service and support for decentralisation processes;
- strengthening of the institutional capacities of the national parliament;
- support for communication media, with the aim of enhancing understanding and providing information within institutions and to the population; and
- support for the National Authorising Officer to improve implementation of EC programmes in Timor-Leste.

Apart from assistance for these activities, the CSP contains support for non-state actors and for governance-related joint initiatives with Portuguese-speaking African countries.[51]

Yemen

Being a developing country outside the group of ACP countries (in the Commission's parlance it is part of its relationships with 'East of Jordan developing countries'), Yemen was allocated €60 million in the 2007–10 Multiannual Indicative Programme to promote good governance and fight poverty and hunger. This allocation draws on various Commission instruments, notably the Development Cooperation Instrument, the so-called Instrument for Stability, the European Instrument for Democracy and Human Rights, and certain thematic programmes.[52]

Yemen's CSP emphasises the lack of reform of the country's political system, despite the continued existence of serious political problems. Notably, the CSP highlights the weak role of the legislative and judiciary institutions *vis-à-vis* the executive, the existence of widespread corruption in the country (referred to as a 'deal-killer' of many initiatives), continued human rights issues and discrimination against women, and security issues springing from the presence of terrorist groups in the country and its use as a transit point for militants and weapons.[53] Despite its analysis, the CSP argues that 'by regional standards, democracy is reasonably well-developed in Yemen'.[54]

The four priority areas of Yemen's CSP for the 2002–06 period (food security; poverty reduction; good governance, democracy and human rights; and business development and the strengthening of economic institutions) were reduced to two in the current CSP. Two-thirds of the Commission's funds reserved for Yemen in 2007–10 have been allocated to strengthening 'the Yemeni government's capacities to fight poverty'. The €19.5 million allocated to strengthen governance quality is divided over a programme aimed at strengthening the electoral framework and institutions, groups of parliamentarians and political parties, and a programme targeting the judicial system in order to strengthen the rule of law and human rights. The components of the programmes targeting governance quality in Yemen are the following:

- support for the Supreme Election Committee to deliver credible free and fair elections, in particular through voter education and the raising of citizens' awareness;
- assistance to a selected group of members of parliament belonging to political parties across the political spectrum, in order to develop their capacity to represent citizens' interests and to link with civil society;
- support for six commercial courts and certain courts of the civil and penal judiciary to train judges and implement court rules in a transparent manner; and
- attention to the mainstreaming of human rights in penal courts and the security forces, with an emphasis on dealing with suspects and interrogating them according to international standards.[55]

CSPs and the EC response to fragile states

The discussion of the Country Strategy Papers agreed by the European Commission with various fragile states has illustrated some of the challenges inherent in the formulating of a strategy to deal with state fragility. As all CSPs follow the same format, it has been possible to compare the political(-economic) analyses that underlie the EC's approach to the different fragile states, as well as the main components of the EC's response strategy for these countries.

The analyses of the political-economic situation in the five cases described above illustrate the resolve of the European Commission to ground its response strategy in an understanding of the local dynamics of the countries concerned. From a methodological point of view one could question the transparency and reliability of the analyses, which do not provide an insight into the sources on the basis of which judgements are made, and have apparently not involved independent analysts from outside the Commission. The Commission's account of political-economic problems in the countries concerned do, however, demonstrate a wish to present a substantively sound and policy-relevant comprehension of the main causes of state fragility. In a majority of cases (Burundi, Guinea-Bissau, Sierra Leone and Yemen), it was argued, with reference to some independent accounts, that the Commission's analyses did not seem to dig deep enough to uncover the structural or root causes of the problems experienced by the countries concerned. Yet, despite this criticism, it is clear that the Commission's analyses reflect a general agreement about the manifestation of the problems in the five fragile states.

The content of the response strategies for the fragile states shows a profound gap between the political-economic analyses and the measures adopted in the EC's support packages, however. The various measures are

TABLE 1. EC support strategies in five fragile states

	Burundi	Guinea-Bissau	Sierra Leone	Timor-Leste	Yemen
Public sector reform	x	x	x	x	
Decentralisation	x		x	x	
Public finance management	x	x		x	
Electoral support	x	x	x		x
Security sector reform	x	x			x
Support/reform of justice sector				x	x
Support of parliament and central state organs		x		x	x
Anti-corruption	x				
Civil society support			x		

Sources: République de Burundi–Communauté européenne, *Document de stratégie pays*, 2007, pp 20–22; République de Guinée-Bissau–Communauté européenne, *Document de stratégie pays*, 2007, pp 31–38; Sierra Leone–European Community, *Country Strategy Paper*, 2007, Part 2, pp 3–4; Timor-Leste–European Community, *Country Strategy Paper*, 2007, pp 70–77; and Yemen–European Community, Strategy Paper for the Period 2007–2010, pp 6–8.

compared in Table 1. The table illustrates the dominance of certain types of responses to the problems in fragile states: public sector reform, decentralisation and public finance management are key to the EC's approach in all the cases analysed above. Also, support for electoral processes at the national or local level shows up as a measure in a majority of the fragile states studied. Security sector reform, support for the justice sector and support for central state organs are each mentioned in the case of two of the five fragile states. Finally, anti-corruption and civil society support show up in one case.

The listing of priority areas in Table 1 makes it clear that the general approach of the European Commission is to assist in *reconstructing* state capacities in fragile states through essentially technical and managerial measures. In a good number of the cases analysed in this article such technocratic measures do not seem to square with the analysis of the problems made either in the CSPs or by independent analysts. Issues raised in the analyses of state fragility relate to problems of state capture, including patronage and clientelism, violent resistance of groups against central government, ethnic divisions, human rights violations, weak socioeconomic bases, and extreme inequalities and social exclusion or marginalisation of particular groups. The failure to address the fundamental problems underlying state fragility raises serious questions about the effectiveness of the EC's policy on fragile states (cf Taylor's contribution to this special issue).

Conclusions

This article has tried to make sense of the current focus, within the European Union, on the issue of state fragility. It has argued that the EU's concern with the issue has had strong security overtones, and that the EU response fits in with the overall trend of securitisation of development. The choice of countries for inclusion in the fragile state framework seems to reflect the central role played by security considerations, but the paucity of data at this moment does not permit more than a provisional answer. In this context, Briscoe has made an important observation that may serve as a hypothesis for further research. He argued that the choices made in Europe and North America on fragile states have been informed by 'the significant role played by many of the world's most fragile states in supplying to the developed world energy and raw materials, producing and trafficking drugs, purchasing arms, generating off-shore capital, or serving as significant outposts in the "war on terror"'.[56]

The EU's approach to fragile states has tended to concentrate on the governance dimensions of the problems in the countries concerned: the definition of state fragility that was adopted by the General Affairs and External Relations Council in November 2007 reflects this focus. The EU's understanding, discussed above, is that state fragility implies a breakdown of the social contract as a result of a state's failure to perform its major functions, including the provision of the rule of law, security, poverty reduction, service delivery and resource management.

As was argued, the recent discussion on governance and fragile states in policy-making circles has produced several lessons for external actors. In particular, assessments of earlier interventions have led organisations such as the World Bank and the OECD to emphasise context-specific action, based on thorough knowledge of the local situation, and the need for a political analysis of processes and events spurring state fragility. The EU's approach to governance and state fragility does not seem to pay sufficient attention to these insights. The EU's methodology on assessing governance, as reflected in the recently adopted 'governance profile' (see the Introduction to this special issue), emphasises formal indicators of governance quality and pays insufficient attention to salient political or political-economic issues, such as social exclusion, inequality and state capture. Moreover, the analysis of various Country Strategy Papers has illustrated that the European Commission's 'response strategies' for the pilot fragile states show quite some disparity between the understanding of local political-economic dynamics and the measures adopted to support the fragile states. In particular, the CSPs focus on the reconstruction of state capacities predominantly by technical and managerial means that overlook more fundamental political-economic problems in the countries concerned.

It seems safe to conclude that the EC's approach to reconstructing fragile states reflects the view, discussed above, that the real problem of these countries lies in the inadequate functioning of the state, inadequate, that is, when looked at from prevalent Western conceptions of the 'modern' state. This approach overlooks the fact that the state is essentially an institution that is embedded in local social, political and economic realities, and that the way in which the state functions (or not) needs to be understood in terms of specific social, political or economic interests. In this respect Chabal and Daloz's analysis of the African state is very pertinent. These authors have argued that judgements on the 'failure' of the state in Africa are essentially a function of the Weberian approach to the state. The dominance of the 'fundamentally instrumental concept of power' has given rise to the 'informalisation of politics' and the 'instrumentalisation' of the state.[57] The question, therefore, is not so much whether the fragile state 'works', but rather *for whom* it works. Attempts to reconstruct fragile states need to be grounded in an understanding of the political-economic realities of the countries concerned, in particular of the incentives, challenges and opportunities faced by various actors.[58] Policies that do not take account of the local political economy of fragile states are bound to fail.

Notes

This article was first presented as a paper at the Conference on 'New Modes of Governance and Security Challenges in the Asia-Pacific', Murdoch University, Perth, 12–13 February 2009.

1 M François & I Sud, 'Promoting stability and development in fragile and failed states', *Development Policy Review*, 24(2), 2006, p 145.
2 M Duffield, 'Governing the borderlands: decoding the power of aid', *Disasters*, 25(4), 2001, p 310.
3 Council of the European Union, *A Secure Europe in A Better World: European Security Strategy*, Brussels, 12 December 2003, at http://www.consilium.europa.eu/uedocs/cmsUpload/78367.pdf, accessed 4 September 2009; and Council of the European Union, *An EU Response to Situations of Fragility: Conclusions of the Council and the Representatives of the Governments of the Member States meeting within the Council*, Note 15118/07, Brussels, 19 November 2007.
4 European Commission, *EU Response to Situations of Fragility in Developing Countries: Engaging in Difficult Environments for Long-term Development*, Report of the External Debate, 2007, at http://ec.europa.eu/development/icenter/repository/Consultation2_Fragile_states_report_EN.pdf, accessed 4 September 2009.
5 Cf R Youngs, 'Fusing security and development: just another Euro-platitude?', *Journal of European Integration*, 30(3), 2008, p 435.
6 See W Hout, 'Development and governance: an uneasy relationship', in W Hout & R Robison (eds), *Governance and the Depoliticisation of Development*, London: Routledge, 2009; and G Hydén, 'Beyond governance: bringing power into policy analysis', *Forum for Development Studies*, 33(2), 2006, pp 215–236.
7 World Bank Operations Policy and Country Services, *Fragile States: Good Practice in Country Assistance Strategies*, Washington, DC: World Bank, 2005, p 8; and World Bank Independent Evaluation Group, *Engaging with Fragile States: An IEG Review of Work Bank Support to Low-Income Countries under Stress*, Washington, DC: World Bank, 2006, p 21.
8 World Bank Operations Policy and Country Services, *Fragile States*, p 1.
9 Milliken and Krause have pointed out that many of the states that gained independence after the Second World War were conceptualised as 'pseudo-states' rather than real states and that 'the puzzle is not how and why they may fail, but how and why they exist or persist at all'. Their perceptive analysis leads to the conclusion that such states may never have been very effective in the performance of central state functions. Although very relevant for a thorough political understanding of the dynamics of fragile states, this line of analysis is not taken up in the current paper as its focus is on donor policies rather than political processes in recipient states. See J Milliken & K Krause, 'State failure, state collapse, and state reconstruction: concepts, lessons and strategies', *Development and Change*, 33(5), 2002, p 763.
10 The World Bank has estimated that countries bordering fragile states face a reduction of their gross domestic product of 1.6% per year on average as a result of the spillover of such problems. See World Bank Operations Policy and Country Services, *Fragile States*, p 27.
11 D Cammack, D McLeod, A Rocha Menocal & K Christiansen, *Donors and the 'Fragile States' Agenda: A Survey of Current Thinking and Practice*, Report Submitted to the Japan International Cooperation Agency, London: Overseas Development Institute, 2006, pp 16–18.
12 *Ibid*, pp 25–26.
13 For instance, C van der Borgh, 'A fragile concept: donors and the fragile states agenda', *The Broker Online*, 9 July 2008, at http://www.thebrokeronline.eu/en/layout/set/print/articles/A-fragile-concept, accessed 4 September 2009.
14 Organisation for Economic Co-operation and Development (OECD), *Fragile States: Policy Commitment and Principles for Good International Engagement in Fragile States and Situations*,

DCD/DAC(2007)29, 2007, at http://www.aideffectiveness.org/web/images/pdf/38293448.pdf, accessed 4 September 2009.
15 World Bank Operations Policy and Country Services, *Fragile States*, p 1.
16 OECD, *Concepts and Dilemmas of State Building in Fragile Situations: From Fragility to Resilience*, OECD/DAC Discussion Paper, Paris: OECD, 2008, p 12.
17 World Bank Operations Policy and Country Services, *Fragile States*, p 13; and OECD, *Fragile States*, p 6.
18 World Bank Operations Policy and Country Services, *Fragile States*, p 5.
19 World Bank Independent Evaluation Group, *Engaging with Fragile States*, p 21.
20 *Ibid*, p 97.
21 Council of the European Union, *A Secure Europe in a Better World*.
22 *Ibid*, p 13.
23 European Parliament, Council and Commission, 'The European Consensus on Development', *Official Journal of the European Union*, 24 February 2006, C46, p 14.
24 European Commission, *Staff Working Document Accompanying the Communication 'Governance in the European Consensus on Development: Towards a Harmonized Approach within the European Union'*, SEC(2006)1020, 30 August 2006, p 8.
25 European Commission, *Governance and Development*, Communication from the European Commission to the European Council, the European Parliament and the European Economic and Social Committee, COM(2003)615 final, 20 October 2003, pp 20–24.
26 Council of the European Union, *An EU Response to Situations of Fragility*, p 2.
27 European Commission, *Towards an EU Response to Situations of Fragility: Engaging in Difficult Environments for Sustainable Development, Stability and Peace*, Communication from the Commission to the Council, the European Parliament, the European Economic and Social Committee and the Committee of the Regions, COM(2007)643 final, 25 October 2007, p 8.
28 Council of the European Union, *An EU Response to Situations of Fragility*, pp 4–6.
29 See European Commission, *Fragile States*, 2007, at http://ec.europa.eu/development/policies/9interventionareas/governance/fragile_states_en.cfm, accessed 4 September 2009. Apparently these pilot countries were chosen under the Portuguese presidency of the European Council, which may explain why countries like Guinea-Bissau and Timor-Leste were included. Yet no formal statements on the selection process have been uncovered.
30 No CSP was available for Haiti.
31 République de Burundi–Communauté européenne, *Document de stratégie pays et programme indicatif national pour la période 2008–2013*, Lisbon, 9 December 2007, p 23, at http://ec.europa.eu/development/icenter/repository/scanned_bi_csp10_fr.pdf, accessed 4 September 2009.
32 The CSP does not refer to other than ethnic and religious causes for the tensions between the Hutus and Tutsis. This is in contrast to analyses of deeper structural political-economic causes of the conflict, related to the unequal distribution of and access to resources, which have been discussed in the literature on Burundi. For instance, MB Jooma, '*We Can't Eat the Constitution*': *Transformation and the Socio-economic Reconstruction of Burundi*, ISS Paper 106, Pretoria: Institute for Security Studies, 2005.
33 République de Burundi–Communauté européenne, *Document de stratégie pays*, pp 3–4.
34 *Ibid*, pp 10–11.
35 *Ibid*, p 14.
36 *Ibid*, pp 20–21.
37 *Ibid*, p 22.
38 République de Guinée-Bissau–Communauté européenne, *Document de stratégie pays et programme indicatif national pour la période 2008–2013*, Lisbon, 9 December 2007, p 36, at http://ec.europa.eu/development/icenter/repository/scanned_gw_csp10_fr.pdf, accessed 4 September 2009.
39 *Ibid*, p 29. Magalhães Ferreira adds several 'structural conditions' to these causes brought about by the country's unequal distribution of wealth and the grip on resources by the political group in power, which rules by maintaining profound clientelist networks. The structural conditions mentioned by Magalhães Ferreira include poor and inefficient governance, profound divisions within the political elite and the military, incapacity of public institutions to provide basic social services, corruption, poverty and dependence on foreign aid. P Magalhães Ferreira, 'Guinea-Bissau: between conflict and democracy', *African Security Review*, 13(4), 2004, p 54.
40 République de Guinée-Bissau–Communauté européenne, *Document de stratégie pays*, pp 5–6
41 *Ibid*, pp 6–7.
42 *Ibid*, p 19.
43 *Ibid*, pp 31, 37–38.
44 Sierra Leone–European Community, *Country Strategy Paper and National Indicative Programme for the Period 2008–2013*, Lisbon, 9 December 2007, Part 2, p 1, at http://ec.europa.eu/development/icenter/repository/scanned_sl_csp10_en.pdf, accessed 4 September 2009.

45 *Ibid*, p 6. Keen discusses the deep-rooted causes of the conflict in Sierra Leone, which are related to the underdevelopment of the country's economy and the pervasiveness of social exclusion. In his view the lack of education, unemployment and failure of local justice produced grievances among all participants in the Sierra Leone conflict, and the violence that swept the country in the 1990s can be explained largely in terms of group efforts to draw attention to these grievances. See D Keen, *Conflict and Collusion in Sierra Leone*, Oxford: James Currey, 2004, pp 289–296.
46 Sierra Leone–European Community, *Country Strategy Paper*, pp 6–7.
47 *Ibid*, Part 2, pp 3–4.
48 Timor-Leste–European Community, *Country Strategy Paper and National Indicative Programme for the Period 2008–2013*, Lisbon, 9 December 2007, p 2, at http://ec.europa.eu/development/icenter/repository/scanned_tl_csp10_en.pdf, accessed 4 September 2009.
49 *Ibid*, pp 9–12.
50 *Ibid*, p 23.
51 *Ibid*, pp 70–77.
52 European Commission, *Multiannual Indicative Programme (2007–2010)*, pp 3–4, at http://ec.europa.eu/external_relations/yemen/csp/mip_07_13_en.pdf, accessed 4 September 2009.
53 Yemen–European Community, *Strategy Paper for the Period 2007–2010*, pp 12–14, at http://ec.europa.eu/external_relations/yemen/csp/07_13_en.pdf, accessed 4 September 2009.
54 *Ibid*, p 12. Hill has pointed out that the government of Yemen, which faces the risk of civil war in the north of the country, a separatist movement in the south, as well as the activity of terrorist groups, has gradually been losing control over the country as the oil revenues that support it have started to fall. As a result of this, Hill argues, the government is less able to maintain its tribal power base, which had been supported by the 'web of personal loyalty through the distribution of oil rents'. See G Hill, *Yemen: Fear of Failure*, Chatham House Briefing Paper MEP BP 08/03, London: Royal Institute of International Affairs, 2008, p 6.
55 European Commission, *Multiannual Indicative Programme*, pp 6–8.
56 I Briscoe, 'The EU response to fragile states', *European Security Review*, 42, 2008, p 9.
57 P Chabal & J-P Daloz, *Africa Works: Disorder as Political Instrument*, Oxford: James Currey, 1999, p 4.
58 V Fritz & A Rocha Menocal, *Understanding State-Building from a Political Economy Perspective: An Analytical and Conceptual Paper on Processes, Embedded Tensions and Lessons for International Engagement*, London: Overseas Development Institute, 2007, p 44.

Understanding EU Development Policy: history, global context and self-interest?

STEPHEN R HURT

Policy Coherence and EU Development Policy
Maurizio Carbone (ed)
London: Routledge, 2009

Beyond Market Access for Economic Development: EU–Africa Relations in Transition
Gerrit Faber & Jan Orbie (eds)
London: Routledge, 2009

Trade, Poverty and the Environment: The EU, Cotonou and the African–Caribbean–Pacific Bloc
Adrian Flint
Basingstoke: Palgrave Macmillan, 2008

In Search of Structural Power: EU Aid Policy as a Global Political Instrument
Patrick Holden
Farnham: Ashgate, 2009

EU Development Policy in a Changing World: Challenges for the 21st Century
Andrew Mold (ed)
Amsterdam: Amsterdam University Press, 2007

EU development policy appears to have gone through substantial change during recent years.[1] In line with a wider reconsideration of the 'Washington Consensus' during the late 1990s, the EU declared it was to follow the approach of other multilateral actors and focus on poverty reduction as the main objective of its development policy.[2] This was followed in December

2005 with agreement on the 'European Consensus on Development', which sought to set out a common vision for the development policy of both the EU and the individual member states.[3] The Post-Washington Consensus concerns of poverty reduction, democracy and good governance, and developing country ownership were reaffirmed in this document. In this review, with reference to the five books under consideration, I outline some of the key issues that are pertinent when we consider how to understand these developments

The edited book by Mold provides a critical overview of the increasingly complex interactions between the EU and developing countries. The diverse chapters in *EU Development Policy in a Changing World: Challenges for the 21st Century* focus in the main on the impacts of the enlargement of the EU on development policy. The book then goes on to analyse specific developments related to the various different regions that the EU engages with. Read as a whole, this broadly critical book highlights how both internal and external pressures make it difficult for the EU to achieve the kind of effective and coherent approach outlined in the European Consensus of 2005. In his concluding chapter Mold suggests that perhaps the goal of coherence is an impossible dream. He says that 'it is useless, for instance, to constantly exhort policy co-ordination and coherence in aid delivery if structural constraints and bureaucratic procedures do not allow this to take place'.[4]

It is this goal of policy coherence that is addressed by Carbone's edited collection. The Lisbon Treaty, which was recently ratified by the last outstanding member state, makes it clear that EU development policy will remain focused on poverty eradication, but that it should be conducted within the broader framework of the EU's external relations.[5] Hence, coherence in this context means the impact that other EU policy areas can potentially have on international development. In *Policy Coherence and EU Development Policy* the authors look at the developmental impacts of a number of related policy areas. In particular, they focus on trade, agriculture, fisheries, security, migration and the social dimensions of globalisation. The various chapters come to a similar conclusion about the limited impact that policy coherence for development has had on other policy areas. Instead, the EU's economic and/or security interests continue to dominate.

Flint's contribution to the literature is to consider the coherence of the EU's development policy in relation to concerns over environmental degradation. In *Trade, Poverty and the Environment: The EU, Cotonou and the African–Caribbean–Pacific Bloc*, he focuses his critique on the Cotonou Agreement and the EU's attempts to promote sustainable development in its relations with the African, Caribbean and Pacific (ACP) group of states. He concludes that the continued dominance of neoliberal thinking in EU policy towards the ACP states results in neither a genuine focus on poverty alleviation nor a convincing case for sustainability.

Faber and Orbie's comprehensive edited collection also looks at recent developments in EU–ACP relations. They direct their attention to the negotiation of Economic Partnership Agreements (EPAs), which result from the decision taken in the Cotonou Agreement to replace the preferential trade agreements that defined the relationship in the past with reciprocal free trade agreements (FTAs) between the EU and seven sub-regions of the ACP group. In *Beyond Market Access for Economic Development: EU–Africa Relations in Transition*, the contributors seek to interrogate the claim made by the EU that EPAs are in fact comprehensive development partnerships. They focus on Africa and the trade-related aspects of EPAs rather than on the more familiar debates over market access. Particular attention is paid to the new trade issues (services, investment, intellectual property rights, etc), aid for trade measures, the impact on African regionalisation, and the wider foreign policy implications of EPAs.

It is these implications for EU foreign policy that are the focus of Holden's book. *In Search of Structural Power: EU Aid Policy as a Global Political Instrument* focuses on how development aid should be considered as part of the EU's attempts to increase its structural power in international relations. Holden draws on the work of Susan Strange and understands structural power as the attempt to 'mould the formal institutions and deeper material and ideational structures of the international system'.[6] The book then focuses on an analysis of country case studies from each of the main regions that the EU engages with, to assess how effective the EU has been in achieving structural change in these 'partner' countries. Holden concludes that in general the EU has been more effective in shaping change in the legal realm and in economic policy making than in encouraging political change and democratisation. In addition, he notes that there remains significant variation in the impact of EU structural power across the various regions.

In this review of these five recent publications, which as a whole add significantly to the literature on EU development policy, I focus on four main themes. First, the historical legacies, from colonialism to the enlargement of the EU, that have shaped the approach witnessed today. Second, the global context, whether it be links between the security agenda and development thinking, or the ongoing difficulties in reaching agreement in the Doha Development Round of the World Trade Organization (WTO). Third, a discussion of the increasing uniformity in approach adopted by the EU to different regions of the world, based on the three pillars of aid, free trade and political dialogue. Fourth, the extent to which EU self-interest is driving policy and how this may be linked to moves towards realising an effective Common Foreign and Security Policy (CFSP) at the European level.

Historical legacies

Contemporary relations between the EU and the developing world continue to be shaped by three interrelated historical circumstances: European colonialism, the Cold War, and the creation and various waves of enlargement of the EU.[7] The EU's relationship with Africa can be traced back to the Treaty of Rome. Although the Cotonou Agreement has been described by many as something of a watershed, we should not forget that, to a degree, we have simply come full circle. As van Reisen usefully reminds, us the Treaty of Rome's provision for an association between Europe and the original member states' colonies created what in essence was a free trade area between the two.[8] So, when considering the negotiation of EPAs with the ACP group of states, we should appreciate that in effect what we are actually witnessing is a normalisation of relations. The limited concessions made to ACP states in the first Lomé Convention of 1975 have been progressively removed ever since. This view stands in contrast to attempts made by the EU to dismiss the significance of the legacies of colonialism. The Green Paper of 1996 that set the path for the Cotonou Agreement claimed that the EU's relationship with ACP states had already moved beyond both the colonial and post-colonial phase.[9]

The history of EU development co-operation is also directly related to the process of enlargement. The first enlargement in 1973, which saw the UK, Ireland and Denmark join the EU, was significant in expanding the focus of European policy beyond the associated countries. A number of former British colonies, particularly those in Asia (eg India), were seen as too developed to join what became the Lomé Convention and therefore it was clear that additional development co-operation instruments would be necessary. In 1976 a European budget line for aid to countries from Asia and Latin America was created.[10] The accession of Greece, Portugal and in particular Spain, to the EU during the 1980s increased the focus towards Latin America. Freres notes that during the past decade relations between the two regions have stagnated and he suggests that the most recent EU enlargements from 15 to 27 member states, together with a number of leftist governments coming to power in Latin America, are the main reasons for this.[11]

More recent enlargements of the EU do present an opportunity to shift development policy away from just being a continuation of Europe's colonial past. However, the problem is that the new member states appear less interested in development policy.[12] There are also the negative economic impacts that European enlargement can have on developing countries. For example, the accession of Greece, Spain and Portugal in the 1980s meant that many of the key agricultural exports of North Africa were now being produced within Europe itself.[13]

Global context

EU development policy exists within a broader framework of international development initiatives. While I outline below how self-interest is part of the explanation for understanding the direction of EU development policy, there is also an ideological component. The EU has consciously aligned the objectives of its development policy with the wider consensus that has formed around the UN's Millennium Development Goals.[14] The emphasis on reciprocity in EU trade relations is underpinned by the international consensus on the benefits of free trade for development, while the focus on promoting regional integration between developing countries is based on a distinctly European view of the benefits of economic integration.[15]

One of the most significant global contexts in recent years has been the continued failure to reach agreement in the Doha Development Round of the

WTO. This impasse in multilateral negotiations has increased the importance of the trade dimension of the EU's relations with developing countries.[16] In its bilateral trade negotiations towards both Euro-Mediterranean Agreements (EMAs) and EPAs with the ACP states it appears that the EU is trying to advance the inclusion of services and the 'Singapore issues' that were rejected during WTO negotiations. The EU has been an enthusiastic advocate of the inclusion of investment, competition policy, government procurement, and trade facilitation (the so-called 'Singapore issues') within the WTO. However, developing countries have consistently argued against their inclusion in the multilateral trade system, most notably during the WTO Ministerial Conference in Cancún in 2003.

A number of the authors in the books under review are critical of these attempts by the EU to include them in bilateral agreements. In discussing EMAs, Mold concludes that there is a danger that they will become 'bereft of all social and developmental content'.[17] Similarly their inclusion is one of the most controversial aspects of the EPAs being negotiated with ACP states. Although they have not been included in the interim EPAs signed with Africa and the Pacific, the only full EPA that has been agreed so far with the Caribbean group of ACP countries (Cariforum) does include rules on investment, competition policy and government procurement.[18]

The global development agenda in the era after 9/11 has seen Western donors increasing links to security concerns, with a focus on 'fragile' states in particular. The EU is no different in this regard. The European Consensus on Development suggests there is a two-way relationship between security and development. It is stated that 'without peace and security, development and poverty eradication are not possible, and without development and poverty eradication no sustainable peace will occur'.[19] Youngs claims that this attempt at coherence is liable to result in the different parts of the EU policy-making machinery trying to obtain greater resources and influence. Certainly the fear that resources for development aid might be diverted towards what are arguably security matters has some grounds, given recent examples of development spending on immigration controls, technical assistance for anti-terrorism, and security patrols of the Mediterranean border.[20] However, in other areas, such as the negotiations towards EPAs, there has been no attempt to make links to their security implications. Olsen suggests that the main reason for this is the departmentalisation of EU policy making, which has resulted in the Directorate General (DG) for Trade being solely responsible for these negotiations with ACP states.[21]

Uniformity of approach

The EU's development policy has in recent years become explicitly more uniform in approach. Relations with the Mediterranean region, ACP states, Latin America and Asia are all built on three main pillars: development assistance (aimed at poverty alleviation and democracy promotion), bilateral trade agreements, and political dialogue. This approach fails to take sufficient account of the particular circumstances that exist in different parts of the world. Although the EU may have moved in recent years to a development policy closely resembling the Post-Washington Consensus this does not overcome the weaknesses of adopting a 'one-size-fits-all' approach.

The Euro-Mediterranean Partnership, recently re-launched in 2008 as the 'Union for the Mediterranean', focuses on three main areas: political/security issues, economic and financial co-operation, and social, cultural and civil society matters. As in its relations with other regions, the EU has made limited progress in all areas except that of economic co-operation. Bilateral trade agreements have been agreed with all the Mediterranean partners, except Libya.[22] The aim is to eventually create a Euro-Med FTA by 2010. To achieve this, the EU is also encouraging regional trade liberalisation among the Mediterranean countries. So far the Agadir FTA between Tunisia, Morocco, Jordan and Egypt has been agreed and is open to the inclusion of new members.

The EU's relationship with the ACP states has historically been more explicitly developmental in focus. However, the Cotonou Agreement has to a significant extent normalised the approach adopted so that it is in line with that for other regions. The negotiation of EPAs is driven by a desire for greater economic integration with the EU and the promotion of regional trade liberalisation within the various sub-regions. The EU has portrayed the need to conform to WTO rules as an 'outside' force in its justification of EPAs.[23] This fails to acknowledge that WTO rules are a political construct and that the EU has a significant say in these rules.[24] Aid continues to be provided through the European Development Fund and, although conditionalities exist, they are not tied directly to the signing of FTAs, as they are with aid to the near abroad.[25] Political dialogue now takes place through the Africa–EU Strategic Partnership.

In relations with Latin America only limited progress has been made in the realm of trade agreements. Bilateral agreements with Mexico and Chile have been concluded and talks continue with Central America and the Andean Community. However, negotiations on an FTA with the Common Market of the South (Mercosur) have been suspended pending progress on the Doha Development Round in the WTO. Political dialogue includes biennial EU–Latin American and Caribbean summits, inter-parliamentary conferences and limited dialogue among civil society organisations. Freres argues that, while in the past it may have been possible to argue that the EU offered an alternative to the hegemonic approach of the USA, it is questionable now whether the European approach to Latin America is any different.[26]

EU relations with East Asia have been focused on the Association of South East Asian Nations (ASEAN). Asia is arguably the region that has witnessed the least progress in the three-fold approach adopted by the EU elsewhere. Negotiations towards the creation of an EU–ASEAN FTA were launched in 2007 but appear a long way from any resolution. In recent years the vast majority of development aid to ASEAN has gone to Vietnam and Indonesia, but unlike in areas of more strategic interest for the EU, there is little evidence of the inclusion of democratic conditionality.[27] Political dialogue is conducted via the Asia–Europe Meeting, which also includes China, Japan and South Korea.

In emphasising the broadly similar policy measures adopted by the EU towards the different regions in its development policy, we should not discount the variations in strategic importance observed by European policy makers. Since the end of the Cold War there has been a much greater emphasis on the 'near abroad' in EU development co-operation; the more recent inclusion of security and migration issues (discussed below) have only served to accentuate this trend.[28] This is demonstrated by the fact that pre-accession aid is the biggest single area of expenditure within external aid spending.[29] The creation of the Neighbourhood Policy in 2004, although not an official arm of development co-operation, does include relations with the Mediterranean. It is this increasing self-interest, related to a desire to increase the significance of the EU as a global actor, which is also central to our understanding of contemporary development policy.

EU self-interest?

When we consider the external relations of the EU more broadly, it is clear that a concern for the needs of developing countries is often of secondary importance. It has been suggested that a more mercantilist approach, in line with that of the USA, has been adopted.[30] Van Reisen concludes that 'EU development co-operation has ... been continuously under the pressure of subordination to the EU's Common Foreign and Security Policy and of being linked to other external priorities'.[31]

The Common Agricultural Policy (CAP) has had a deleterious impact upon many developing countries. It accounts for a greater share of the EU budget than any other single expenditure. EU subsidies have often led to over-production, with the excess being 'dumped' on developing countries. It has become commonplace for the removal of the CAP to be seen as a panacea for the whole of the developing world. However, as Flint explains, it is only certain developing countries (chiefly those that comprise the Cairns Group) that would benefit from the dismantling of the CAP.[32] The CAP results in very high domestic prices and those developing countries that do get preferential access to the European market are able to benefit from these high prices.[33] Moreover, CAP protection is not the only barrier to the export of agricultural produce from developing countries. The ever more stringent sanitary, phyto-sanitary and environmental standards imposed by the EU present an additional obstacle.[34]

The EU has also been criticised for its plans to pressure developing countries to introduce measures to control migration. Historically the EU's approach to migration has centred on limiting migration and creating a 'fortress Europe'. Article 13 of the Cotonou Agreement was one of the first attempts by the EU to incorporate migration into its development policy. In 2002 the European Council agreed that any 'future EU association or cooperation agreement should include a clause on joint management of migration flows and compulsory readmission in the event of illegal immigration'.[35] In 2005 the EU outlined what it claimed was a more 'global approach' to its migration policy.[36] This document outlined the importance of remittances, the role of members of the various diasporas in development, and measures to limit the impact of the 'brain drain'. Despite these recent attempts by the EU to adopt a more development-focused approach, Lavenex and Kunz conclude that an approach based on the control of immigration persists.[37]

Crawford's work on Ghana reveals the interaction between the strategic interests of the EU and the type of development assistance pursued. He argues that the reality of democracy promotion is far less impressive than the rhetorical claims made by the EU suggest. Ghana receives limited support for democracy promotion because European interests are marginal. Moreover, the form that democracy promotion takes is centred on decentralisation, public sector reform, and targeted support for certain civil society actors. This approach, according to Crawford, is more about limiting the power of the state than increasing popular participation. This is an approach that is theoretically consistent with neoliberalism and the promotion of trade liberalisation in particular.[38] Holden provides a similar view of European policy to Ghana and argues that the proposed EPA may harm the economic development that will be necessary to consolidate the type of political reforms pursued by the EU.[39]

Institutional changes within the European Commission have also played a role in the relegation of development to the foreign policy interests of the EU. During the same period that the EU has claimed to have a greater focus on poverty alleviation, organisational changes within the Commission appear to contradict this claim. The DG for External Relations (DG RELEX) is in charge of programming and policy to the Mediterranean, Latin American and Asian regions. Trade negotiations with ACP states were moved from DG Development to DG Trade. Although on paper the Commissioner for Development has the portfolio for all developing countries, in practice DG Development has become an 'empty shell'.[40] Holden suggests there are evident tensions here, with DG RELEX thinking that DG Development is not focused enough on the wider foreign policy goals of the EU.[41]

Conclusions

In conclusion, the books under review highlight the comprehensive nature of contemporary EU development policy. Drawing on the thoughts of many of the authors, it is important to put current policy into historical and global context. The increasing uniformity of approach should be understood as part of an attempt to lock in liberal capitalism to regional projects in different parts of the developing world. Holden understands this as the EU's drive to increase its structural power in the global political economy.[42] What his book fails to address is whether this is in the interests of the poor majority in the developing world or not. The failure to achieve much more than a rhetorical commitment to policy coherence for development highlights how European self-interest is becoming more apparent given the desire for a CFSP. Here

I would be less optimistic than Carbone, who argues that 'achieving better policy coherence for development is no longer a "mission impossible"'.[43]

Notes

1 Throughout this article I use EU to represent the European Union and the organisation, pre-Maastricht Treaty, officially referred to as the European Community.
2 European Commission, *The European Community's Development Policy: Statement by the Council and the Commission*, Brussels: European Commission, 2000.
3 European Parliament, Council, Commission, 'The European Consensus on Development', *Official Journal of the European Union*, 24 February 2006, C46, pp 1–19.
4 A Mold, 'Between a rock and a hard place—whither EU development policy?', in Mold (ed), *EU Development Policy in a Changing World: Challenges for the 21st Century*, Amsterdam: Amsterdam University Press, 2007, p 241.
5 S Dearden, 'Introduction: European Union development aid policy—the challenge of implementation', *Journal of International Development*, 20(2), 2008, p 191.
6 P Holden, *In Search of Structural Power: EU Aid Policy as a Global Political Instrument*, Farnham: Ashgate, 2009, p 13.
7 M van Reisen, 'The enlarged European Union and the developing world: what future?', in Mold, *EU Development Policy in a Changing World*, p 59.
8 van Reisen, 'The enlarged European Union', p 33.
9 European Commission, *Green Paper on Relations between the European Union and the ACP Countries on the Eve of the 21st Century: Challenges and Options for a New Partnership*, COM (1996) 570, 1996, p iv.
10 van Reisen, 'The enlarged European Union', p 42.
11 C Freres, 'Challenges of forging a partnership between the European Union and Latin America', in Mold, *EU Development Policy in a Changing World*, p 157.
12 van Reisen, 'The enlarged European Union', p 60.
13 A Mold & S Page, 'The evolution of EU development policy—enlargement and a changing world', in Mold, *EU Development Policy in a Changing World*, pp 17–18.
14 M Holland, 'The EU and the global development agenda', in M Carbone (ed), *Policy Coherence and EU Development Policy*, London: Routledge, 2009, p 26.
15 G Faber & J Orbie, 'EPAs between the EU and Africa: beyond free trade?', in Faber & Orbie (eds), *Beyond Market Access for Economic Development: EU–Africa Relations in Transition*, London: Routledge, 2009, p 7.
16 Mold & Page, 'The evolution of EU development policy', p 12.
17 A Mold, 'To reciprocate or not to reciprocate? Is that the question? A CGE simulation of the Euro-Mediterranean agreements', in Mold, *EU Development Policy in a Changing World*, p 133.
18 O Elgström, 'From Cotonou to EPA light: a troubled negotiating process', in Faber & Orbie, *Beyond Market Access for Economic Development*, p 33.
19 European Parliament, Council, Commission, 'The European Consensus on Development', p 7.
20 R Youngs, 'Fusing security and development: just another Euro-platitude?', in Carbone, *Policy Coherence and EU Development Policy*, p 107.
21 GR Olsen, 'The missing link: EPAs, security and development interventions in Africa', in Faber & Orbie, *Beyond Market Access for Economic Development*, p 343.
22 R Pace, 'Clash of civilisations or intercultural dialogue? Challenges for EU Mediterranean policies', in Mold, *EU Development Policy in a Changing World*, p 89.
23 A Flint, *Trade, Poverty and the Environment: The EU, Cotonou and the African–Caribbean–Pacific Bloc*, Basingstoke: Palgrave Macmillan, 2008, p 18.
24 S Hurt, 'Co-operation and coercion? The Cotonou Agreement between the European Union and EPA states and the end of the Lomé Convention', *Third World Quarterly*, 24(1), 2003, p 174.
25 Holden, *In Search of Structural Power*, p 148.
26 C Freres, 'Challenges of forging a partnership between the EU and Latin America', p 159.
27 Holden, *In Search of Structural Power*, p 156.
28 van Reisen, 'The enlarged European Union', p 51.
29 Holden, *In Search of Structural Power*, p 33.
30 Mold & Page, 'The evolution of EU development policy', p 19.
31 van Reisen, 'The enlarged European Union', p 60.
32 A Flint, *Trade, Poverty and the Environment*, p 82.
33 *Ibid*, p 106.
34 A Matthews, 'The European Union's Common Agricultural Policy and developing countries: the struggle for coherence', in Carbone, *Policy Coherence and EU Development Policy*, p 75.

35 S Lavenex & R Kunz, 'The migration–development nexus in EU external relations', in Carbone, *Policy Coherence and EU Development Policy*, p 120.
36 European Commission, *Migration and Development: Some Concrete Orientations*, Communication to the Council, the European Parliament, the European Economic and Social Committee and the Committee of the Regions, COM (2005) 390, 2005.
37 Lavenex & Kunz, 'The migration–development nexus in EU external relations', pp 127–128.
38 G Crawford, 'The EU and democracy promotion in Africa: high on rhetoric, low on delivery?', in Mold, *EU Development Policy in a Changing World*, pp 183–189.
39 Holden, *In Search of Structural Power*, p 142.
40 van Reisen, 'The enlarged European Union', pp 52–56.
41 Holden, *In Search of Structural Power*, p 41.
42 Holden, *In Search of Structural Power*.
43 M Carbone 'Mission impossible: the European Union and policy coherence for development', in Carbone, *Policy Coherence and EU Development Policy*, p 18.

Index

Page numbers in *Italics* represent tables

absolutism 57
Pre-Accession Assistance Programme 75
accession states 77
Action Plans 111
Africa 51–65; agricultural exporters 65; China 62; development challenges 61; regeneration 56; rulers 57; unity 60
Africa, the Caribbean and the Pacific (ACP) 4, 21, 32; ACP-EC Partnership Agreement 145; Council of Ministers 40; development agendas 45; EU relations 44; Governance Initiative for ACP states 38
Africa Summit (2007) 35
African Union (AU) 54
aid 6; allocation 24; co-ordination 13–27; foreign aid 17–18; Paris Declaration on Aid Effectiveness 17
Ake, C. 56, 59
Andean Community of Nations (CAN) 129
Annan, K. 33
Assessing Aid (World Bank) 16
Association of South East Asian Nations (ASEAN) 162

The Balkans in Europe's Future (International Commission on the Balkans) 71
Barcelona Initiative (2005) 112–13
Barcelona Process 113
Beijing 62
Berdimukhamedov, G. 91
Bickerton, C. 77
Bilal, S.: and Stevens, C. 40
Birdsall, N. 35, 45
Bishkek conference 98
Blair Commission 60–1
BOND (UK NGOs international development): governance profiles 39
Bosnia 81
Bradley, A.: and Slocum-Bradley, N. 9, 31–46
Bretton Woods 15
Briscoe, I. 152
Burundi 145–6

Cammack, D.: *et al* 141
Campbell, B. 37
Carbone, M. 8–9, 13–27
Caribbean Strategic Partnership 126–8
Central Asia 87–102; political regimes 90–3
Chandler, D. 9, 69–83
China 61–3; global economy 62
China-Africa Cooperation 62
CIDSE (Catholic network) 39
civil service reform and good governance (Tajikistan) 97
civil society 73–4, 80
Clapham, C. 58
co-ownership 113
Code of Conduct on Complementarily and Division of Labour 20, 24
cognitive justice 124–5
Commission Communication 39
Common Agricultural Policy (CAP) 163
Communication on Governance and Development 35–6; democracy 38
Communication on 'Governance in the European Consensus' 7
Community Assistance for Reconstruction, Development and Stabilisation (CARDS) 75
Comprehensive Development Framework (CDF) 16
conditionality 15–17, 79
post-conflict situations 144
constructivist institutionalism 110
corruption 15
Cotonou Agreement 21, 32, 35; Article (9.3) 33–4; Article (96) 36; revision 43
country 'ownership' 75
Country Policy and Institutional Assessment (CPIA) 16
Country Strategy Paper (CSP) 6, 145–51
Crawford, G. 164

de Sosa Santos, B. 124
democracy 20–3; discourse 80; promotion 101
development policy 18–20

INDEX

Development of the Policy Dialogue Advice Programme (PDAP) 98
Duffield, M. 139

e-silk-highway 96
East African (newspaper) 55
Eastern enlargement 111
Ecofin meeting 114
Economic Partnership Agreement (EPA) 40–2
economic sociology 109
education initiative 96
Enlazando Alternativas (Caribbean network) 130
epistemic justice 130–4
EU Development Policy in a Changing World (Mold) 158
Euro-Mediterranean Development Bank (EMDB) 105–18
Euro-Mediterranean free trade area 111
Euro-Mediterranean Partnership 162
Europe 3–8
European Commission (EC) 7, 18, 32, 72, 118, 164; aid budgets 127; aid commitments 5; fragile state support *151*; governance 33; *Governance in the European Consensus on Development* 14, 52; governance profile *8*; *The Present Situation and Prospects for Closer Partnership (1996–2000)* 128; strategy document (2005) 129
European Consensus on Development 5, 13–14, 144, 158
European Council: development policy 19; negative conditionality 23
European Council Conclusions 144–5
European Development Fund (EDF) 18, 42–3
European Mediterranean Partnership (EMP) 110–11
European Neighbourhood Policy (ENP) 4, 111–12
European Security Strategy (2003) 140
European Stability Initiative 72
European Union Delegation to the African Union 53
European Union (EU) 2, 13, 13–27; Africa relations 51–65; Central Asia relations 94; Central Asia Strategy 88; democracy 18–25; development assistance 6–8; donor co-ordination 23; five-year strategy 112; fragile states 139–53; LAC neoliberal bi-regional governance 134; LAC relationship 126–30; LAC strategic partnership 123, 128; LAC strategic partnership summits *127*; power 44; Security Strategy 93; self-interest 163–4; Special Representative (EUSR) 78;

Strategy for a New Partnership 88, 93; *Strategy Paper for Central Asia (2002–2006)* 95
Extended Impact Assessment tool 114

Faber, G.: and Orbie, J. 158–9
Falkenberg, K. 41
Fatton, R. 57; policy advice 58–9
Financing for Development conference 19
Fisheries Partnership Agreements 43–4
Flint, A. 158
foreign aid 17–18, *see also* aid
fragile states 7, 139–53
Franco-Africa Summit 59
free trade 128
Freedom House democracy index 90
French regulation school 110

G-8 59
General Affairs and External Relations Council (GAERC) 25, 144, 152
Georgetown Agreement 32
Ghana 164
Ghani, A.: and Lockhart, C. 70
global context 160–1
Global Europe 129
global governance 124
good governance 2, 13–27, 52; international development 15–18
governance 1–11, 78–81, 105–18; mechanisms 37–44
Governance Action Plans (GAPs) 38
Governance in the European Consensus on Development (European Commission) 14, 52
Guatemala sessions 132
Guinea-Bissau 146–7; poverty reduction 147

Hale, H. 89
High-Level meeting (1993) 17
highly indebted poor countries (HIPC) 65
historical institutionalism 109
Hoffmann, K. 9–10, 87–102
Honduras Tribunal (2009) 133
Hout, W. 1–11, 10–11, 139–53; and Robison, R. 106
human rights dialogue 97
Hurt, S.R. 11, 157–65

Icaza, R. 10, 121–35
Independent Evaluation Group 140
institutionalism 116
institutionalist paradigm 71–4
interest-based institutionalism 109–10
International Commission on the Balkans: *The Balkans in Europe's Future* 71

INDEX

Interstate Oil and Gas Transport to Europe (INOGATE) 100
Inzko, V. 73

Joint Parliamentary Assembly 43, 44
Joint Programming Framework (JPF) 19
Joint Response Strategy 148

Kazakhstan 91–2, 101
Keohane, R. 83
Kiffer, C. 73–4
Knio, K. 10, 105–18
Kortmann, K. 61
Kyrgyzstan 90, 92

Latin American and Caribbean (LAC) countries 121–35
law initiative 96, 97, 98
liberal agenda 72
post-liberal governance 69–83
post-liberal state 81
liberalisation 92
Lima Tribunal (2008) 133
Lisbon Treaty 158
litigation mechanisms 130
Lockhart, C.: and Ghani, A. 70
Lomé Convention (1975–2000) 21, 160
London 60
low income countries under stress (LICUS) 140, 142
Lugonés, M. 125

Maastricht Treaty 18
Mandelson, P. 41
Manservisi, S. 41
Mayaki, I.A. 65
Mediterranean entrepreneurs 115
Michel, L. 22, 42
Millennium Africa Recovery Plan (MAP) 59
Millennium Challenge Account 14
Moesby, O. 52–3
Mold, A. 158
Montagner, M. 34
Müller-Jentsch, D. 117

Nabucco Pipeline project 100
National Development Plan 148–9
neo-patrimonialism 57, 90
neoliberalism 123–6
new institutional economics (NIE) 106
New Partnership for Africa's Development (NEPAD) 51–65; Coordinating Unit 64; prescriptions 53–6
Nielson, P. 35
North American Free Trade Agreement (NAFTA) 128
North, D. 107, 108

Obiorah, N. 61–2
OECD: Development and Assistance Committee (DAC) 17, 141
Omega Plan 59–60
Operation Enduring Freedom 94–5
Orbie, J.: and Faber, G. 158–9
Organisation for Security and Co-operation in Europe (OSCE) 74, 92
Oxfam International 41, 44

Paris Declaration on Aid Effectiveness 17
partner preferences 42
Partnership Agreement 35
Partnership and Cooperation Agreements (PCAs) 93
partnership principle 35
partnerships discourse 55
Permanent People's Tribunals (PPTs) 131
Policy Coherence and EU Development Policy (Carbone) 158
policy processes 115
political management 79
political reform 88–90
political risk analysis 143
political subjects 81
poverty eradication 19
Poverty Reduction Strategy Papers (PRSPS) 6, 16
power 34–6; insularity 109–10
power-relations perspective 106
The Present Situation and Prospects for Closer Partnership (1996–2000) (European Commission) 128
Pridham, G. 89
property rights 108

rational-choice institutionalism (RCI) 107
Rio de Janeiro Ministerial Summit 126
Robison, R.: and Hout, W. 106
Rustow, D. 89

selectivity 15–17
Sierra Leone 147–8
Sino-African activity 61
Skinner, D. 74
Slocum-Bradley, N.: and Bradley, A. 9, 31–46
social cohesion 127
social power dynamics 45
social resistance 125
Solana, J. 143
South African Department of Foreign Affairs 60
Southeast Europe 69–83
sovereignty 74–8
Stabilisation and Association Agreements (SAAS) 75–6
state fragility 139

state institutions 72–3
Stevens, C.: and Bilal, S. 40
Stiglitz, J. 1–2
Strategic Growth and Poverty Reduction Framework 146
Strategic Partnership 121
strategy implementation 97–100
Strategy for a New Partnership (EU) 88, 93
Strategy Paper for Central Asia (2002–2006) (EU) 95

Tajikistan 92; civil service reform and good governance 97
Taylor, I. 9
Technical Aid to the Commonwealth of Independent States (TACIS) 94
techno-managerialism 107–10
Timor-Leste 148–9
transnational advocacy networks (TANs) 124
Transport Corridor between Europe and Asia (TRACEA) 100
Turkmenistan 91, 92, 101

uniformity 161–3
United Nations Commission on Human Rights 33

United Nations Security Council: Resolution (1244) 75; Resolution (2000/64) 33
Universal Declaration of the Rights of Peoples 132
Uzbek-EU media conference 99
Uzbekistan 99, 101

Vázquez, R. 125

Wade, A. 59, 60, 64
Post-Washington Consensus 2, 54, 134, 158
Weaver, C. 58
West Europe 71
Western Balkan society 80
post-Westphalian governance 123
Westphalian order 123
World Bank 2; *Assessing Aid* 16; *Worldwide Governance Indicators* 7

Yanakopoulos, H. 35
Yemen 149–50; governance quality 150
Youngs, R. 117, 161

Zagreb Summit 75

www.routledge.com/9780415688802

Related titles from Routledge

Accountability and European Governance

Edited by Deirdre Curtin, Peter Mair and Yannis Papadopoulos

In recent years there has been a considerable effort in some transnational organizations and institutions to confront a crisis of legitimacy by promising more accountability and openness. This volume takes as its central focus the role of accountability in democratic governance, and attempts to position a broad understanding of the notion of accountability within the overall context of the evolving political system of governance in Europe and in particular of the European Union. Bringing together new work by some of the leading scholars in the field, this volume considers the relationship between accountability and a wide range of other themes in European governance such as problems of representation, transparency, bureaucracy, and transnational relations. The volume also deals with the role of accountability in multi-level governance, and its relationship to both direct democracy and civil society.

This book was published as a special issue of *West European Politics*.

October 2011: 234 x 156: 264pp
Hb: 978-0-415-69633
£85 / $145

For more information and to order a copy visit
www.routledge.com/9780415688802

Available from all good bookshops

www.routledge.com/9780415695671

Related titles from Routledge

European 'Security' Governance

Edited by George Christou and Stuart Croft

This book argues that we can understand and explain the EU as a security and peace actor through a framework of an updated and deepened concept of security governance. It elaborates and develops on the current literature on security governance in order to provide a more theoretically driven analysis of the EU in security. A theoretical framework is constructed with the objective of creating a conversation between these two literatures and the utility of such a framework is demonstrated through its application to the geospatial dimensions of EU security as well as specific cases studies in varied fields of EU security.

This book was originally published as a special issue of *European Security*.

George Christou is Associate Professor in European Politics, Department of Politics and International Studies, University of Warwick, Coventry, UK.

Stuart Croft is Professor of International Security, Department of Politics and International Studies, University of Warwick, Coventry, UK.

December 2011: 246 x 174: 208pp
Hb: 978-0-415-69567-1
£80 / $125

For more information and to order a copy visit
www.routledge.com/9780415695671

Available from all good bookshops